Charles Mollet and his World
Daily Life in Georgian Guernsey

Charles Mollet and his World
Daily Life in Georgian Guernsey
Rose-Marie Crossan

MÒR MEDIA LIMITED

© Rose-Marie Anne Crossan 2024

All rights reserved. Except as permitted under current legislation, no part of this work may be photocopied, stored in a retrieval system, published, performed in public, adapted, broadcast, transmitted, recorded or reproduced in any form or by any means, without the prior permission of the author.

Rose-Marie Anne Crossan has asserted her right to be identified as the author of this work in accordance with sections 77 and 78 of the Copyright, Designs and Patents Act 1988.

First published 2024

Mòr Media Limited, Benderloch, Argyll, Scotland

www.mormedia.co.uk

ISBN 978-1-9196371-7-4

A catalogue record for this book is available from the British Library.

The publisher has no responsibility for the continued existence or accuracy of URLs for external or third-party internet websites referred to in this book, and does not guarantee that any content on such websites is, or will remain, accurate or appropriate.

Contents

List of Illustrations	vii
Acknowledgements	xi
Notes on the text	xiii
Introduction	xx

1	Georgian Guernsey – General Background	27
2.	Charles Mollet – Personal Background	43
3.	Economic Life, Part 1: Farming	51
4.	Economic Life, Part 2: Investments and Enterprises	81
5.	Civic and Communal Life	117
6.	Domestic Life	139
7.	Social Life	155
8.	Private Life, Part 1: Health, Interests, Opinions	181
9.	Private Life, Part 2: Relationships	203

Conclusion	225

Appendices

1.	Marjorie Barnes' ancestry	229
2.	Mollet family tree, ascending	230
3.	Mollet family tree, descending	231
4.	Composition of principal families associated with Mollet	232
5.	Frequently mentioned employees of Mollet's	237
6.	Relatedness of Mollet's employees	238
7.	Mollet's symbols and codes	239
8.	Mollet's language	242
9.	Apple and pear varieties grown by Charles Mollet	248
10.	French *émigrés* mentioned by Mollet	250
11.	Books owned by Charles Mollet	254
12.	Spring bird arrivals	256

Bibliography	257
Index	265

Illustrations

Maps and plans

1. Channel Islands and adjacent French and English coasts   xiv
2. Parishes of Guernsey   xv
3. Eighteenth-century Guernsey   xvi
4. Detail from 1787 map of Guernsey showing Charles Mollet's farm and neighbouring properties   xvii
5. Early nineteenth-century Guernsey   xviii
6. Detail from 1816 map of Guernsey showing Castel parish   xix
7. Eighteenth-century St Peter Port   xx
8. Eighteenth-century Alderney   xxi

Plates

1. Mary Brock, *née* Mourant (1767–1852), Mollet's niece   103
2. Anne Brock, *née* Mourant (1769–1838), Mollet's niece   103
3. Peter De Havilland (1747–1821)   104
4. Jean Carey of 'Choisi' (1748–1821)   104
5. Thomas De Sausmarez (1756–1837)   105
6. Jean Guille, jun. (1733–1820)   105
7. Sir Thomas Saumarez (1760–1845)   106
8. John Savery Brock (1772–1844)   106
9. Rev. Etienne Gibert (1736–1817)   107
10. Peter Le Mesurier (1750–1803), Alderney Governor   107
11. Sir Hew Dalrymple (1750–1830)   108
12. Mary Bruce (1740–96), Duchess of Richmond   108
13. Józef Boruwlaski (1739–1837), musician and writer   109
14. Jean-Pierre Blanchard (1753–1809), pioneer balloonist and showman   109
15. Candie in Victorian times   110
16. Garden at Candie, 1830s   110
17. Woodlands, 1840s   111

18. La Domaillerie, 1840s   111
19. Woodlands, 1950s   112
20. Woodlands apple-crusher, 1950s   112
21. Typical Guernsey kitchen hearth   113
22. Cart with horses and oxen, late 18th century (Joshua Gosselin)   114
23. Château des Marais, late 18th century (Joshua Gosselin)   114
24. Ships in Guernsey roads, 1777 and 1778 (Elisha Dobrée)   115
25. Louis XVI at Cherbourg, 1786   116
26. Mouriaux House, Alderney   116

In memory of a dear uncle and friend
Rev. Father Charles Louis Chauvel
1920–2013

Acknowledgements

This book, which is based on original documents held by Guernsey's Priaulx Library, would not have been possible without the co-operation and assistance of the Library's management and staff, to whom I would like to express my most particular gratitude. I would also like to thank the staff of Guernsey's Greffe and Island Archives Service for their kind help with background research. Among others to whom my thanks are due are Richard Hocart, who has contributed much to my understanding of Georgian Guernsey through his published work and personal communications, and Yan Marquis, who has provided linguistic advice. Last but certainly not least, I am most grateful to Helen Crossan for her help in preparing my text for publication, and to my husband Jonathan for patiently supporting me through yet another all-consuming three-year project.

Rose-Marie Crossan, MA (Oxon), PhD
Guernsey, February 2024

Notes on the text

1. Charles Mollet always used the French names of Guernsey's parishes in his diary.[1] I use the English versions throughout this text, and render those prefixed 'St' with a terminal 's' unpreceded by an apostrophe to reflect present usage, where the final 's' has effectively become accreted to the names (as in the British towns of St Albans, St Helens, St Andrews, etc.).

2. Throughout Mollet's life, Guernsey's currency was the French *livre tournois* (divided into 20 *sous* of 12 *deniers* each). Fourteen *livres tournois* were worth £1 sterling by the official London exchange rate, and where sterling equivalents are given here, they are calculated on this basis. Various French coins were in local circulation, the most common of which were gold six-*livre* pieces, silver *écus* and *livres*, copper *sous* and *deniers*.[2] Coins of other nations were also used, including Spanish dollars and British guineas, sovereigns, shillings and pennies. In the 1770s and 1780s, Mollet chiefly used *tournois* coins but increasingly turned to British coins as the French Revolutionary and Napoleonic Wars led to local shortages of French specie. His journals juxtapose sums in *tournois* with sums in sterling seemingly haphazardly.

3. Many Guernsey surnames are preceded by particles (*De* Sausmarez, *De* Carteret, *Le* Cheminant, *De La* Mare, etc.). According to the historian and linguist Marie De Garis, 'the property-owning classes always used capital letters for the prefixes [but] the artisan classes used the more humble small letters.'[3] Mollet, following local practice, only felt it *de rigueur* to insert a particle where surnames were of less than two syllables.[4] However, this did not mean he totally eschewed particles in longer names, and his diaries contain many examples of polysyllabic surnames preceded by particles. Mollet was equally inconsistent in his capitalisation of initial letters, sometimes writing *De* or *Le* and sometimes *de* or *le*. In this study, capitals are used for the first letters of all particles, irrespective of the social class of the individual referred to.

---

[1] The names Mollet used were *St Sauveur, St André, le Valle, la Forêt, Torteval, St Martin, le Castel, St Samson* and *St Pierre*. By *St Pierre* Mollet meant the country parish sometimes referred to as *St Pierre du Bois*, but he never added the '*du Bois*'. Similarly, Mollet never used the name *St Pierre Port*, and instead always referred to the town parish simply as *la ville*.

[2] A French law of 1795 replaced the *livre tournois* with the *franc*, but as the *franc* had by law to have the same metal content as the *livre*, the two were interchangeable. Old *tournois* coins remained in circulation, locally and in France, until well into the nineteenth century. One *écu* was nominally worth six *livres*.

[3] M. De Garis, *Dictiounnaire Angllais–Guernesiais* (1967; Chichester, 1982), p. 114.

[4] *Ibid.*, p. 114.

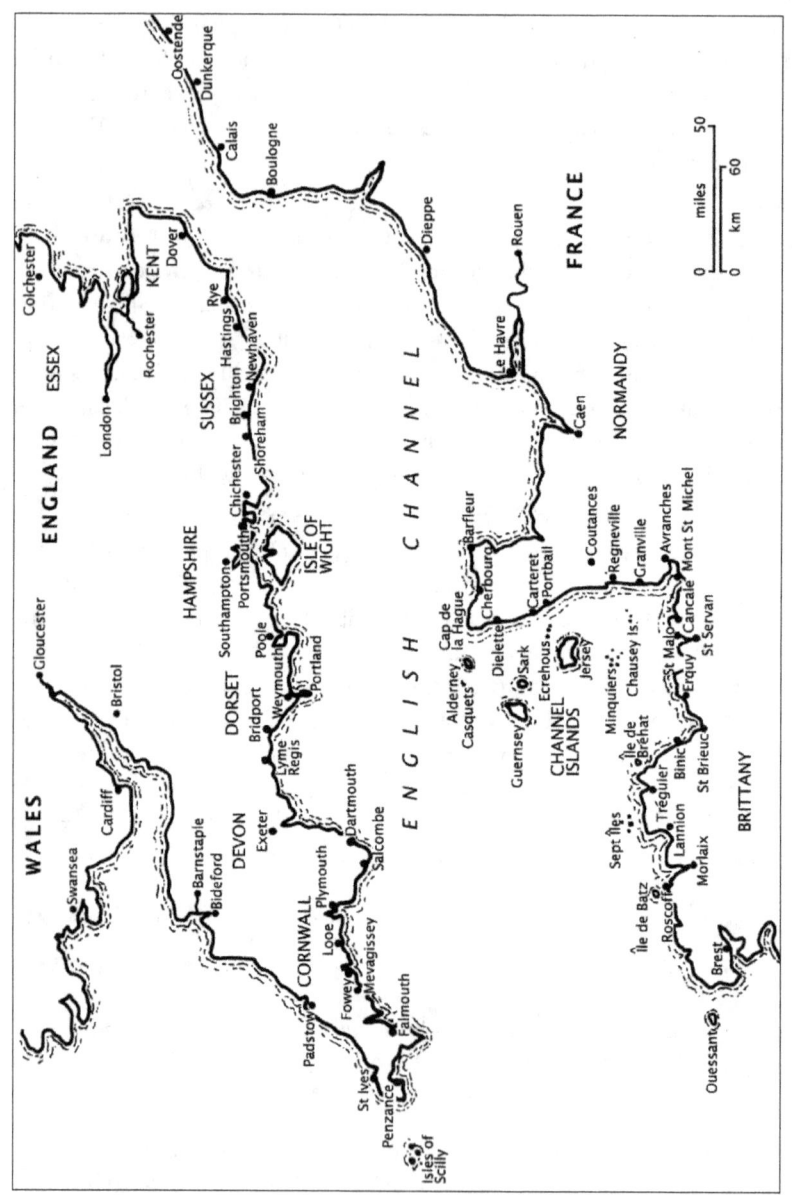

Map 1. Channel Islands and adjacent French and English coasts

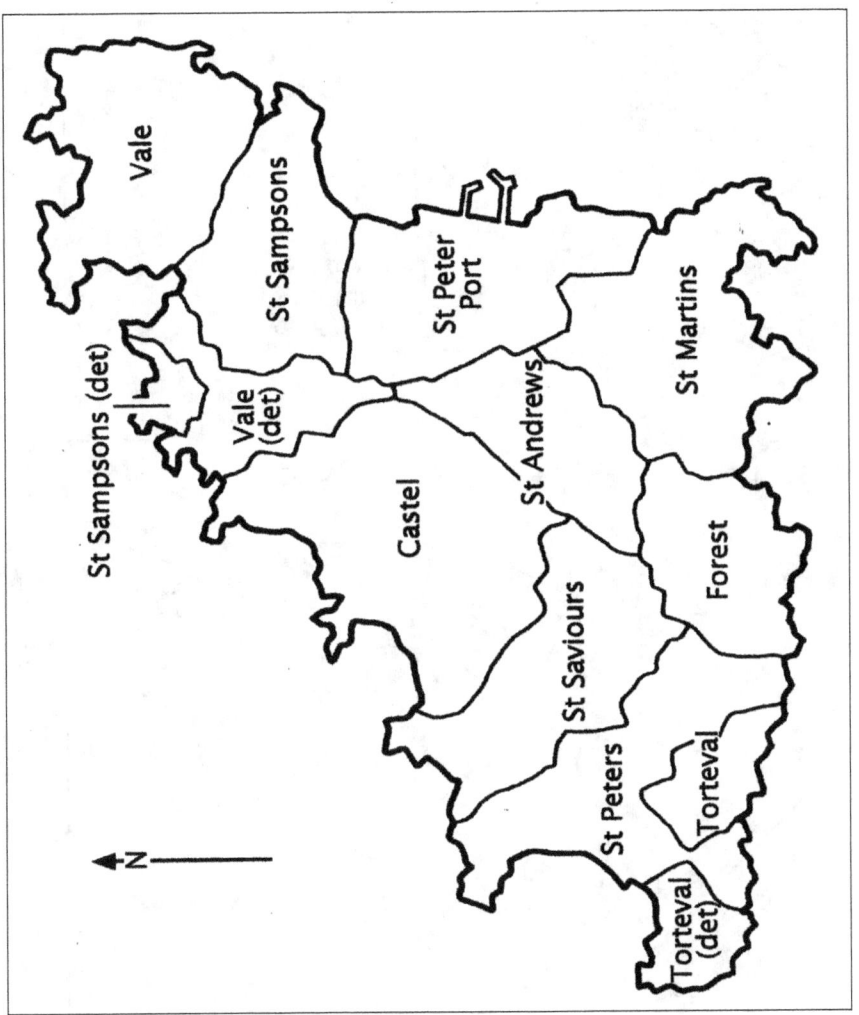

Map 2. Parishes of Guernsey

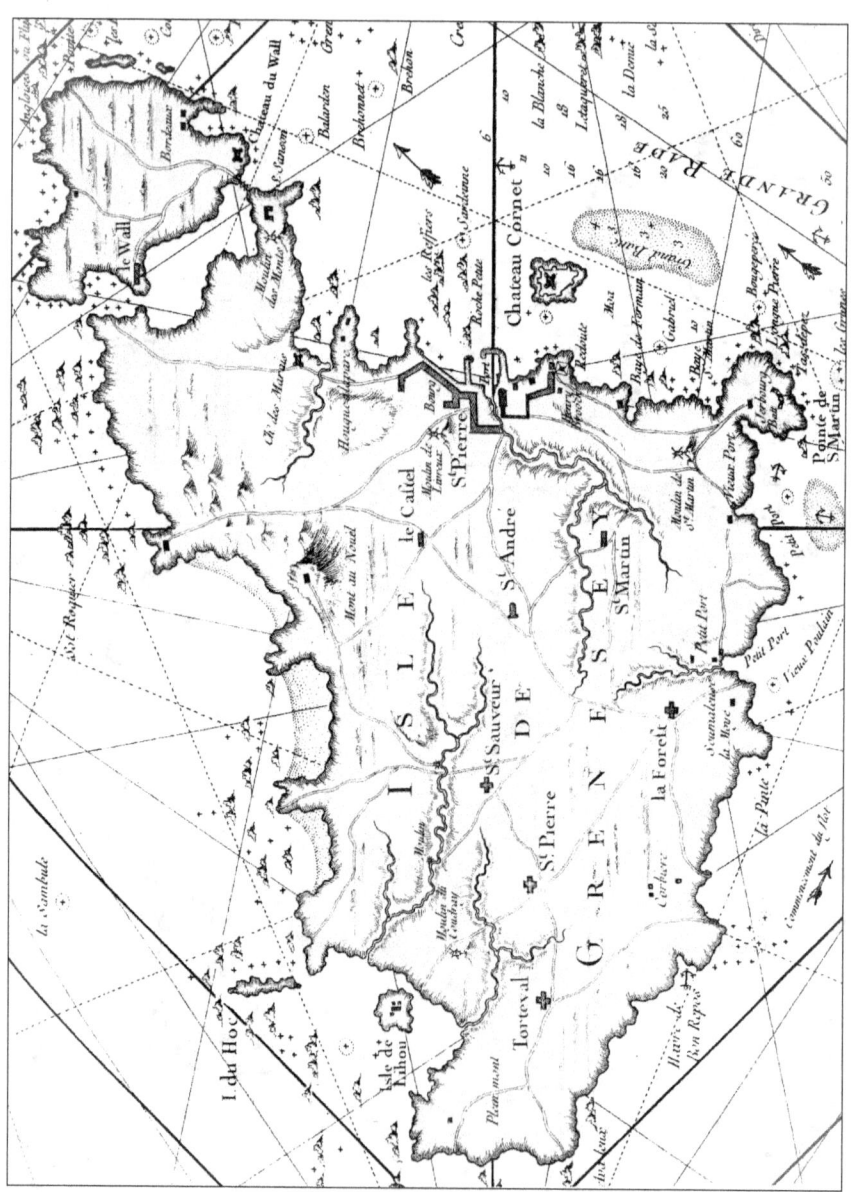

Map 3. Eighteenth-century Guernsey
(Jacques Nicolas Bellin, 1757; public domain)

Key to principal properties mentioned in Mollet's journal:

486 – Le Moulin de Haut
515 – Le Moulin du Milieu
517 – Le Groignet
520 – Les Grands Moulins
526 – La Porte
528 – La Houguette
533 – Mollet's farm
534 – the 'upper' house
535 – Les Vallées
536 – Les Roussiaux
537 – Les Pelleys
541 – Le Ponchez
544 – La Fontaine
552 – Les Effards
554 – Les Queux
556 – Castel Rectory
558 – Les Covins
1038 – Les Beaucamps de Haut

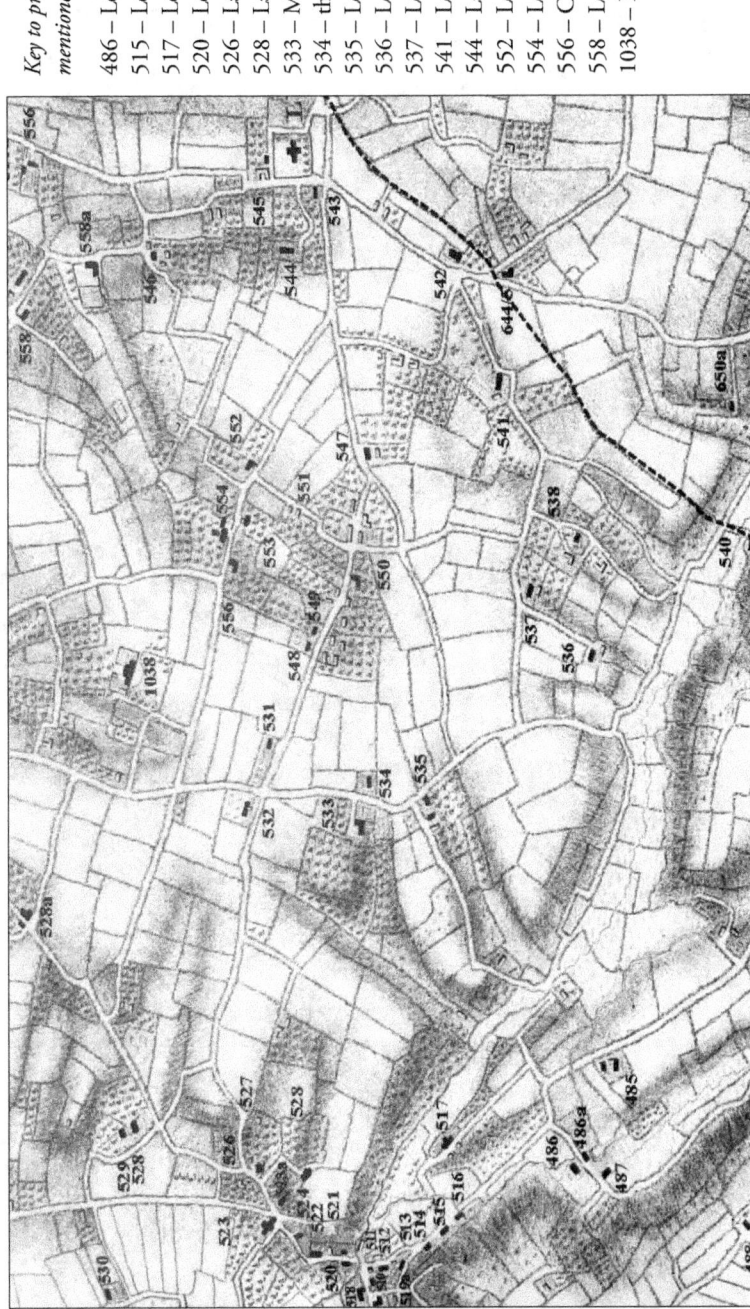

Map 4. *Detail from 1787 map of Guernsey showing Charles Mollet's farm and neighbouring properties* (Reproduced from J. McCormack, *Channel Island Houses* (Guernsey, 2015) by kind permission of the author)

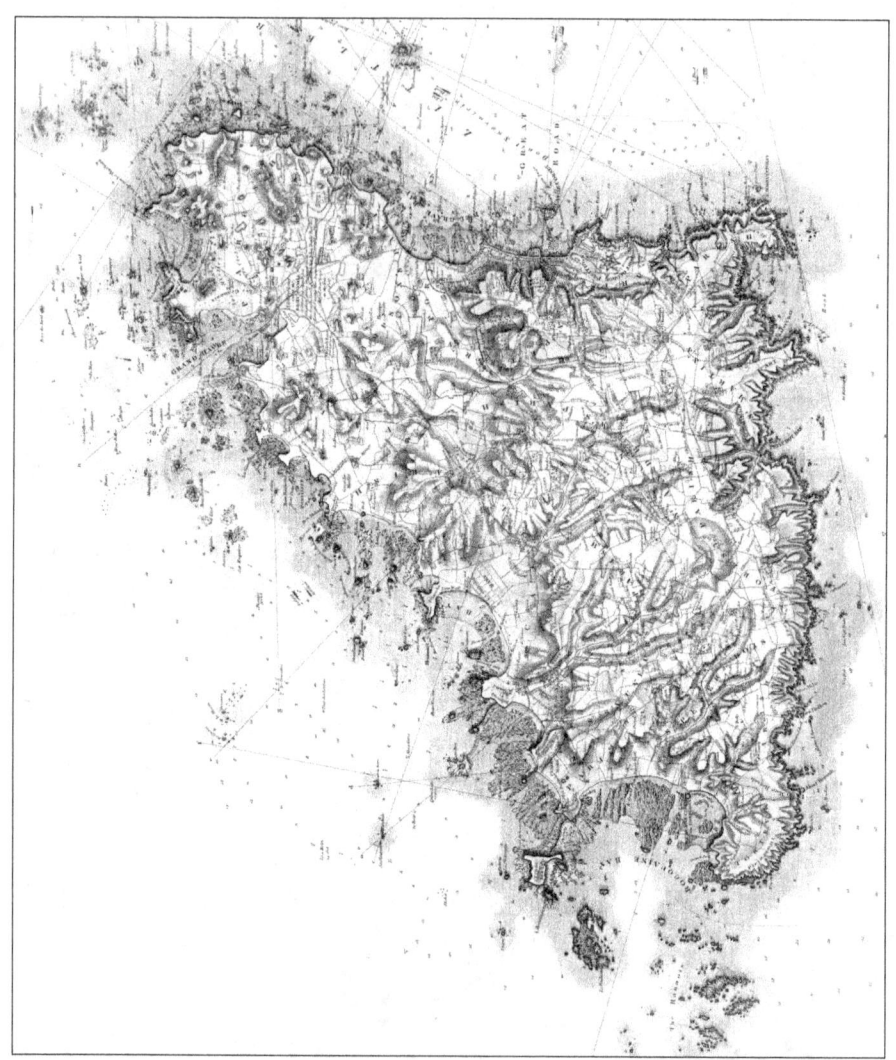

Map 5. Early nineteenth-century Guernsey

xix

Map 6. Detail from 1816 map of Guernsey showing Castel parish

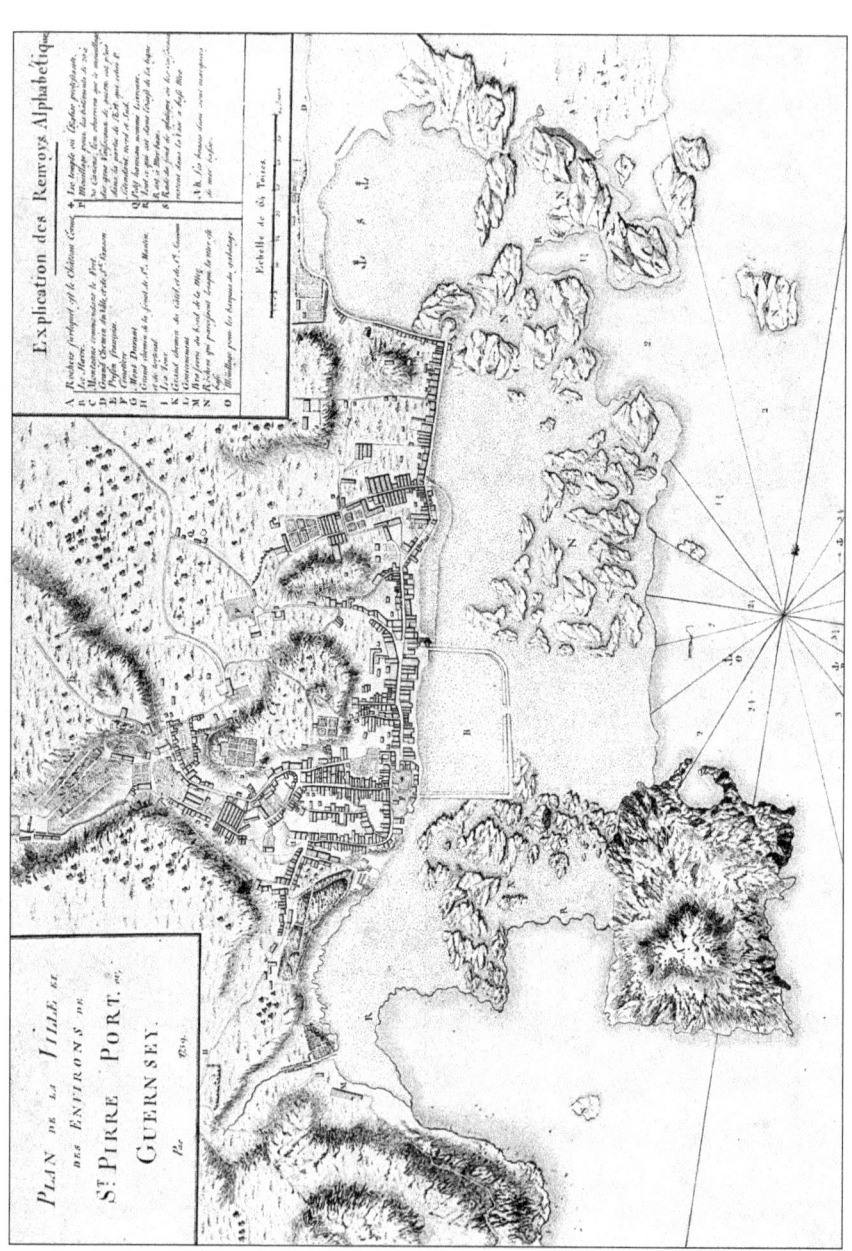

Map 7. *Eighteenth-century St Peter Port*
(unknown cartographer, 1759, Island Archives Service, Guernsey)

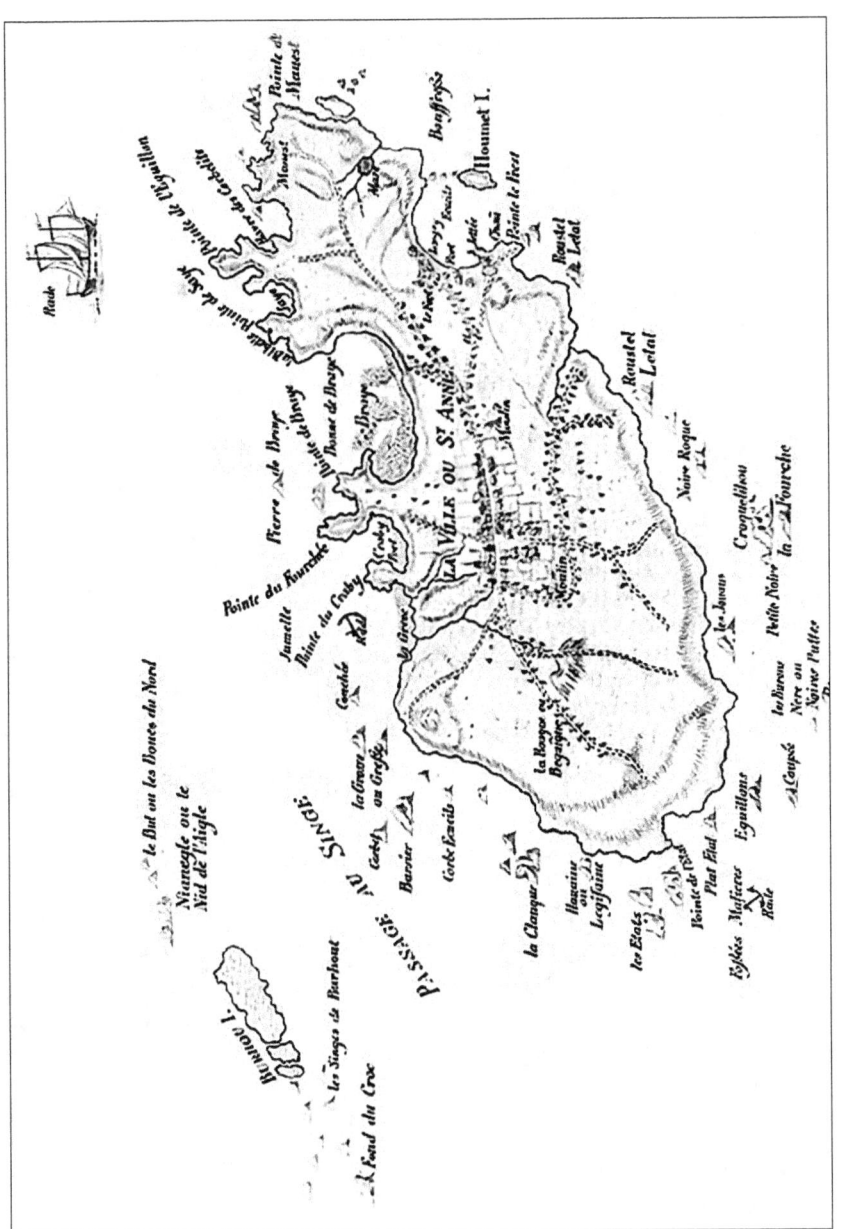

Map 8. *Eighteenth-century Alderney*
(after Jean de Beaurain, 1757; public domain)

Introduction

This book is based on the journal kept by the Guernseyman Charles Mollet between 1771 and 1818, which is held by Guernsey's Priaulx Library. Other local journals from this period have survived (notably that of Mollet's contemporary Elisha Dobrée),[1] but Mollet's is by far the longest and most detailed. The six extant volumes of Mollet's journal fill more than 1,500 pages and contain over half a million words. They document an extraordinary five decades at the junction of the eighteenth and nineteenth centuries, characterised both by warfare on an unprecedented scale and rapid and unparalleled change.

Charles Mollet was a farmer, and the primary purpose of his journal was to keep track of his agricultural activities. The journal is however infinitely more than a farming diary, as Mollet also used it to record his other commercial activities, his public life, his domestic arrangements, his social life, his travels, matters relating to his family, and his observations on external events. For all of these reasons, Mollet's journal affords us a unique insight into late eighteenth-century processes of transformation as they unfolded. It is also unique in a Guernsey context in that it provides singular detail on a hitherto obscure portion of the local community. For although Mollet belonged to Guernsey's upper class, he recorded his dealings with all social strata, thus yielding detail on the characters, lifestyles and behaviours of individuals which does not normally emerge from other historical sources.

I personally first read Charles Mollet's diaries in 2019 while carrying out research for a previous book. Quite unexpectedly, I discovered that we were near neighbours, albeit three centuries apart. I grew up about 300 metres from Mollet's house, the sight of which was a permanent daily fixture. In reading his diary, I readily recognised the landscape in which it was located – the land contours, the field patterns, even some of the houses. In many ways, the topographical environment in which Mollet was formed was also the environment which formed me. This engendered a very human feeling of connection with the diarist and inspired a curiosity to know him better.

---

[1] Guernsey's Island Archives hold three volumes of Dobrée's journal: AQ 1572/03 (1771–85); AQ 1572/04 (1786–99); AQ 1572/05 (1800–17). Dobrée was fourteen years Mollet's junior but well-known to him.

Previous to this encounter, I had only been dimly aware of the existence of Mollet's journals. Extensive though they are, they have been under-exploited as a historical source.[2] One explanation lies in the language in which the journals were written. In the eighteenth century, Guernsey was still a francophone island, and Mollet's first language was *guernésiais*, a variant of Norman French. *Guernésiais* had no written form, so that by the eighteenth century, islanders normally used standard Parisian French for writing. Mollet, too, used standard French in his journals, but they are nevertheless thoroughly peppered with *guernésiais* vocabulary and heavily influenced by *guernésiais* grammar and syntax. The very fact that the diaries are in French – let alone the peculiarities of that French – erects a formidable barrier to twenty-first-century islanders, most of whom are monoglot anglophones.[3] In a bid to make the diaries more accessible, I therefore set about translating them into English.[4] Initially, my translation was to be followed only by publication of a volume of excerpts, but, despite liberal footnoting, I found it difficult to provide all the necessary context for a proper understanding. The idea for the present volume then arose. Its aim is to integrate material from the diaries with interpretation and contextualisation, so that a rounded impression of Mollet's life and times is conveyed.

The first of Charles Mollet's six surviving journal volumes began in 1771 when he was aged twenty-eight and the last ended seven months before his death at the age of seventy-six in 1819. The volumes are uneven in length. Mollet became more home-focused in his declining years and his diaries grew correspondingly richer in domestic detail. His last volume (1815–18) is almost twice the length of his first (1771–6).

For all their 1,500 pages, the six extant volumes do not represent the entirety of the journal Mollet wrote over the course of his lifetime. There is internal evidence (in the form of references to past entries) that earlier, pre-1771, volumes existed. Two volumes covering intermediate periods are missing (January 1781 to December 1784, and August 1812 to August 1815). There are gaps within the diaries left by Mollet himself (notably in 1804 and 1805, when he only wrote entries for six out of twenty-four months). More seriously, parts of pages or ranges of pages have been

---

[2] To date, the only historian to have made significant use of them is Richard Hocart, notably in his *The Country People of Guernsey and their Agriculture, 1640–1840* (Guernsey, 2016).
[3] For more detail on Mollet's language use, see Appendix 8.
[4] The completed translation and accompanying index are now available at the Priaulx Library.

deliberately excised, the most egregious example falling at the end of Mollet's life, when the final eleven pages (twenty-two sides) have been cut out, leaving only the stubs, with fragments of his writing upon them. At this period, twenty-two sides would typically have contained six months of Mollet's journal. The intact entries finish on 1 August 1818, so the excised twenty-two sides would have brought the diary up to January 1819, about a month before Charles Mollet's death. It seems improbable that Mollet personally made these excisions. A more plausible scenario is that custodians of the diaries after his death found certain passages problematic and wished to expunge them.

There is also much that Mollet himself left inexplicit. Throughout the six surviving volumes, his written text is complemented with a range of symbols and codes inserted into adjacent margins. These symbols and codes are so lacking in pattern that it has been impossible to ascertain what they signified, and they almost certainly meant different things at different periods.[5] Whatever the case, they form at some points almost a parallel narrative to the diary entries.

So how did Mollet's journals make their way to the present day? In 1951, the six volumes and a small collection of Mollet's papers were gifted to the Priaulx Library by a Mrs Marjorie Sophia Barnes of Maiden Newton in Dorset. Though settled in England, Mrs Barnes, who lived from 1889 to 1961, had a quintessentially Guernsey pedigree. Born Marjorie Le Cocq, her mother was a Guille and her family tree featured an impressive array of Huberts, Androses, Le Marchants, Le Mesuriers, De Carterets and Dobrées.[6] As the tree shows, Marjorie Barnes was related to Charles Mollet through both the Guille and Le Cocq sides of her family. Mrs Barnes' maternal grandfather, John Guille (1788–1845), was the brother of the Reverend William Guille, who married Mollet's great-niece Judith Brock. Mrs Barnes' paternal grandfather, Hellier Dobrée (1761–1846), was the brother of Bonamy Dobrée, who married Mollet's niece Martha Mourant.[7] Charles Mollet was a lifelong bachelor and had no descendants of his own. Although the diaries' first steps after his death remain obscure, they could have descended to Marjorie Barnes through either branch of her family.

---

[5] A selection of these are reproduced in Appendix 7.
[6] Mrs Barnes' family tree is set out in Appendix 1.
[7] For Mollet's nieces and nephews, see Appendix 3.

It is clear from the slim file of Mollet papers accompanying the diaries that Charles Mollet was a prolific record-keeper. Among the heterogeneous assemblage are many fragments of accounts and correspondence. Unfortunately, these fragments are too scant and disconnected to be greatly informative.

A handful of Mollet papers also survive in other public repositories, notably five letters in the National Archives at Kew.[8] Guernsey's own Island Archives also hold a single isolated letter from Thomas De Sausmarez to Charles Mollet himself.[9] This letter, which came from a private collection, concerns a mundane matter and is uninteresting in itself. However, it is densely covered on the reverse with Mollet's handwritten notes about dahlias – which, if nothing else, proves that the letter once formed part of Mollet's own personal belongings. Given this intriguing circumstance, it is not inconceivable that yet more Mollet papers lie undiscovered in other private collections. Access to the full range of records generated by Mollet would certainly be valuable. A proper series of accounts would provide a clearer grasp of Mollet's finances, and *une correspondance suivie* would afford sharper insights into his character and relationships. There is however no point in hankering after the unavailable. We should rather be grateful for the 1,500 pages which we do have. Half a million words are after all no trifle and – as will be shown below – they afford ample material for analysis.

The first two chapters of this book will supply some basic background. Chapter 1 will provide a general introduction to Guernsey in the Georgian period, and Chapter 2 an introduction to Charles Mollet himself. Discussion of the diaries proper will begin in Chapters 3 and 4 with a consideration of Mollet's economic life. Chapter 5 will then examine Mollet's civic life; Chapters 6 and 7 will look at his domestic arrangements and social life; and Chapters 8 and 9 will delve into his personal and private life. Wherever appropriate, reference will be made to sources external to the journal in order to elucidate points of interest.

---

[8] These letters were written by Mollet between 1796 and 1800 to Philippe D'Auvergne (the Jersey-based administrator of relief to French *émigrés*). They relate chiefly to the supply of trees and shrubs. For references, see Bibliography.

[9] De Sausmarez to Mollet, 28.2.1817 (AQ 1085/33).

1

Georgian Guernsey – General Background

Demography and economy

Guernsey lies about 30 miles off the Normandy coast and 80 miles from the nearest English landfall. Together with the smaller islands of Alderney, Sark, Herm and Jethou, it forms a single semi-autonomous Bailiwick.[1] Jersey, some 27 miles to the south-east, forms a separate Bailiwick of its own. Both of the main Channel Islands are surprisingly small. Jersey's total area is just over 116 square kilometres, and Guernsey's 63.5 square kilometres.[2] This may be contrasted with the Isle of Wight's 380 square kilometres and the Isle of Man's 572 square kilometres. Guernsey's ten parishes are commensurately small, varying in size between 10 and 3 square kilometres.[3] Charles Mollet's home parish, Castel, is the largest in terms of area. Torteval, forming the island's south-west corner, is the smallest. Guernsey's small size notwithstanding, it has for many centuries supported a comparatively large population. This was partly because the island was endowed with the triple advantages of a fertile soil, a benign climate and abundant fish stocks. But it was also in no small measure due to the fact that its only town, St Peter Port, enjoyed a vigorous and substantial maritime trade.

Charles Mollet's lifetime spanned a particularly dynamic phase in Guernsey's demographic history. The population grew from around 12,000 in 1728 to around 21,500 in the second decade of the nineteenth century.[4]

---

[1] Note, however, that in the rest of this chapter, the term 'Guernsey' will refer only to the island of Guernsey, and not the whole Bailiwick.
[2] About 1.3 square kilometres were added to Guernsey's land area after 1806, when the Braye du Valle (a tidal channel separating the northern tip of the island from the rest) was reclaimed from the sea. Maps 3 and 5, above, show the island before and after reclamation.
[3] See Map 2.
[4] These are approximations based on figures reproduced in J.P. Warren, 'Extracts from the diary of Elisha Dobrée', *Transactions of la Société Guernesiaise*, 10 (1929) p. 495, and W. Berry, *History of the Island of Guernsey* (London, 1815), pp. 23–4.

At the latter date, St Peter Port alone accommodated at least 13,000 souls, or 61 per cent of the island's population. The majority of these 13,000 were packed into the built-up area around the harbour.[5] The belt of farmland which made up the rest of the parish was considerably less densely populated. St Peter Port's urban area – 'town', as Charles Mollet called it – was always run as an integral part of the parish of St Peter Port and never developed any municipal institutions of its own. However, the size of its late eighteenth- and early nineteenth-century population put it firmly on a par with many English provincial towns.[6]

The town of St Peter Port had grown up around a sheltered haven on Guernsey's east coast which was conveniently situated on the main sea route from Biscay into the Channel. It had long been a centre of international trade, the Channel Islands having since the fifteenth century enjoyed the privilege of neutrality during wartime, which permitted Islanders to engage in trade with France while that country was at war with England.[7] This neutrality was brought to an end at the beginning of England's Nine Years War against France in 1689, when an Order in Council confirmed that a prohibition on the import of goods from France should also be observed in the Channel Islands.[8] Although the Order abolished Guernsey's neutrality, it was not resisted by the island's ship-owning elite, some of whom saw it as an opportunity to engage in privateering.[9] The ship-owners who went on to engage in this new enterprise met with a degree of success, and this stimulated

---

[5] Map 7 depicts the extent of this area in the mid-eighteenth century.
[6] In 1801, Canterbury had a population of 9,000; Salisbury 9,114; Reading 9,770; Colchester 11,520; Preston 11,867; and Oxford 12,107 (J. Marshall, *An Analysis and Compendium of All the Returns made to Parliament Relating to the Increase of Population* (London, 1835), pp. 107, 166, 163, 112, 148, 158).
[7] For the historical origin of this privilege, see D.M. Ogier, *The Government and Law of Guernsey* (2005; Guernsey, 2012 edn), p. 181.
[8] For the Channel Islands' political relationship with England (and later the United Kingdom), see section on Politics and administration, below.
[9] Privateering was the practice whereby civilian-owned vessels were permitted to participate in maritime warfare under a commission of war known as a letter of marque. This empowered them to attack enemy vessels and take them and their cargoes as prizes, with the proceeds shared between sponsors, ship-owners, captains, crew, and the issuer of the commission.

local ship-owners and merchants to continue fitting out privateers in all ensuing Franco-British wars until 1815.[10]

Although privateering in itself did not provide a secure foundation for the economy, it did encourage the establishment of St Peter Port as an entrepôt in the Atlantic trade, and thus led to further economic expansion. St Peter Port became an entrepôt almost by default as prize cargoes were brought back to Guernsey by the privateers and stored in the town. Demand for space for the wines, spirits, tobacco, tea, etc., was such that, between 1719 and 1747, between twenty and thirty new warehouses were built in St Peter Port.[11] Some of these commodities were re-exported legitimately, but since most were luxury goods subject to high duties in England, they attracted the interest of English smugglers, who started visiting St Peter Port in their small sailing vessels to buy up supplies. In consequence, Guernsey rapidly became one of the main suppliers of contraband to smugglers from southern England.[12] This in turn stimulated local entrepreneurs to set up factories for processing raw tobacco into pipe tobacco and snuff; operations for decanting wine and spirits into portable barrels; and coopers' workshops for manufacturing these small containers.

The smugglers' demand for luxury commodities was by no means limited to periods when the privateers were active, so Guernsey's ship-owners responded by expanding their peacetime fleets to fetch these goods from their places of origin. By the time of Charles Mollet's birth, local ship-owners and merchants were significant participants in the Atlantic trade, bringing in wine, brandy and textiles from France and Iberia; tobacco from Maryland and Virginia; and rum from the West Indies.[13] At around this time, St Peter Port also acquired a parallel role as a depository and bulk-breaker for dutiable commodities destined for legal entry into Britain before the introduction of

---

[10] Between the Nine Years War and 1815, there were five further major Franco-British conflicts: the War of the Spanish Succession (1701–13), the War of the Austrian Succession (1740–8), the Seven Years War (1756–63), the War of American Independence (1776–83) and the French Revolutionary and Napoleonic Wars (1793–1815).
[11] G. Stevens Cox, *St Peter Port, 1630–1830: The History of an International Entrepôt* (Woodbridge, 1999), p. 21.
[12] A.G. Jamieson, 'The Channel Islands and smuggling, 1680-1850', in A.G. Jamieson (ed.), *A People of the Sea: The Maritime History of the Channel Islands* (London, 1986), p. 204.
[13] The Acts of Trade and Navigation, by which the shipment of colonial goods direct from the colonies to the Channel Islands was nominally prohibited, were not observed in Guernsey, largely owing to the entrenched opposition of the insular authorities and the fact that no eighteenth-century British administration chose to override this opposition.

the bonding system. The historian F.B. Tupper described St Peter Port harbour in the 1790s as 'often crammed to the very mouth', with 'twenty or thirty vessels in the roadstead waiting to enter.'[14]

The success of the entrepôt considerably enriched the mercantile class which formed the top tier of the insular community. This class was predominantly composed of long-established families who could trace their Guernsey pedigrees back to medieval times.[15] As well as dominating ship-owning and commerce, their members also occupied the highest ranks in Guernsey's militia, and monopolised leading roles in Guernsey's judiciary and administration. The majority of these families were town-based. This privileged class however formed only a tiny fraction of St Peter Port's population. Beneath them were the professional men (doctors, clergymen, etc.) and the large wholesalers and manufactory owners. These in their turn were followed by a stratum of smaller retailers and tradesmen. These three groups comprised between them most of St Peter Port's ratepayers. By the first decade of the nineteenth century, the combined value of their real and personal property as assessed for parish rates stood at around £1,834,400.[16]

At the base of the urban social pyramid, and below the threshold for paying rates, was a large residual class of journeymen artisans, labourers and domestic servants. To begin with, most of these workers were drawn from indigenous town families. However, as economic expansion increased demand for labour, there was a wave of in-migration from the town's rural hinterland. Growing numbers also came from across the sea – some from south-west England, and others (notably Huguenots) from France.[17] The British garrison further swelled the urban population: already comprising about 2,000 officers and men during the American War of Independence, their numbers doubled to around 4,000 at the height of the Napoleonic War, by which time St Peter Port also hosted a Royal Naval squadron.[18] The burgeoning population gave a further boost to the town's economy, increasing demand for housing, food, drink, and services of all kinds.

---

[14] F.B. Tupper, *The History of Guernsey and its Bailiwick* (Guernsey, 1854), p. 439. See also Plate 24.
[15] Charles Mollet knew most of these families. Their names – Bonamy, Carey, De Havilland, De Jersey, De Lisle, De Sausmarez, Gosselin, Le Marchant, Le Mesurier, Maingy, Priaulx – feature frequently in his diaries.
[16] Berry, *Island of Guernsey*, p. 161.
[17] Stevens Cox, *St Peter Port*, pp. 82–5.
[18] Tupper, *History of Guernsey*, pp. 373, 391.

St Peter Port's rising prosperity brought many improvements to the town during Charles Mollet's lifetime. In the mid-1770s, the two piers of St Peter Port harbour, formerly abutting directly on to the beach, were linked with a solid stone quay. In the mid-1780s, the town acquired a new paved marketplace, furnished on one side by covered *halles* surmounted with a set of elegant Assembly Rooms. In the mid-1790s, a new theatre was added to St Peter Port's amenities.[19] All of these projects were privately financed. In due course, however, increasing rate revenues and growing civic pride led to public funding of improvements. Many of St Peter Port's public thoroughfares were paved and provided with lamps around the turn of the nineteenth century. A new courthouse was built in 1799, a new prison in 1811. Finally, during Mollet's last three decades, a wave of private house-building extended the town's built-up area to the west, north and south, as the well-to-do sought modern townhouses and villas away from the overcrowded centre.[20]

St Peter Port operated successfully as an entrepôt for much – but not all – of Charles Mollet's life. In Mollet's penultimate and final decades, the positive trend which had marked his earlier years underwent a series of checks. The first setback, and perhaps the most serious, was the demise of the entrepôt. The initial blow came in 1803, when the introduction of the bonding system in the United Kingdom deprived St Peter Port of its role as a depository for dutiable goods destined for legal re-export.[21] Subsequent blows came in 1805 and 1807 after mounting revenue losses pushed Westminster to extend two stringent anti-smuggling Acts to the Channel Islands, which deprived St Peter Port of its less respectable role as a smugglers' supply-base.[22] These Acts effectively barred St Peter Port's merchants and ship-owners from their most lucrative activity. With the destruction of their

---

[19] G. Stevens Cox, *Social Life in Georgian Guernsey* (Guernsey, 2014), pp. 3, 31.

[20] The most extensive residential development was the 'New Town', on the hill to the west of St Peter Port, which was begun in 1792 as a speculative venture and eventually comprised six streets (R. Hocart, 'The building of the New Town', *Transactions of la Société Guernesiaise*, 23 (1992), pp. 342–77).

[21] The bonding system was introduced to the United Kingdom by Westminster's 1803 Warehousing of Goods Act.

[22] The 1805 Smuggling Act banned the import into or export from the Islands of spirits, wines and tobacco in vessels of under 100 tons or in casks of less than 60 gallons or packages of under 450 lb. The 1807 Smuggling Act ordered that all vessels leaving the Islands were to obtain a customs clearance, and forbade vessels coming from the Islands to break bulk or alter cargo during their voyage (Jamieson, 'The Channel Islands and smuggling', p. 209).

trading model, many of them retired, sold their vessels and warehouses, and invested the proceeds in government securities and real estate. The minority who chose not to do so continued to participate in privateering until the end of the Napoleonic War, and some also became active in the 'licence trade', whereby, from 1807, St Peter Port was permitted to become a trading post for the exchange of essential commodities between Britain and France.[23]

Privateering and the licence trade were, however, insufficient in themselves to provide employment to all of St Peter Port's redundant entrepôt workers. The town's workhouse saw a steep rise in admissions.[24] Some families decided that their fortunes would best be served by leaving the island. In 1806, 1807 and 1810, parties of Guernseymen departed for North America, where they founded Guernsey County in Ohio and Guernsey Cove on Prince Edward Island.

The advent of peace after Waterloo, though welcomed by many, exerted yet further negative effects on St Peter Port's economy. Privateering came to a definitive end. Even more seriously, the garrison was reduced to some 200–300 soldiers. This was a hard blow to St Peter Port's remaining retailers and tradesmen. Problems were then compounded in 1816/17 when Europe-wide harvest failure pushed up food prices to intolerable levels. As Charles Mollet's life came to a close in 1819, a second wave of emigration to North America was well under way.[25]

Although the economy of Guernsey's countryside was very different to that of the town, it too felt the impact of St Peter Port's changing fortunes, not least through the ebb and flow of demand for its produce. The country parishes, almost exclusively agricultural, were covered by hundreds of farms

---

[23] The King in Council issued an Order dated 18.12.1807 authorising licences to be issued for trade between Jersey and Guernsey and certain French ports. Imports and exports were held in St Peter Port and then re-shipped.

[24] St Peter Port had had a workhouse – the Town Hospital – since 1743. The country parishes had collectively maintained their own workhouse – the Country Hospital – since 1751. For early nineteenth-century admissions, see R.-M. Crossan, *Poverty and Welfare in Guernsey, 1560–2015* (Woodbridge, 2015), pp. 125–6.

[25] A late nineteenth-century newspaper article gave the number of those leaving Guernsey on emigrant ships between 1817 and 1819 as 1,310 (*Comet*, 21.9.1889). We should note that the economy largely recovered in the decade following Mollet's death, stimulated mainly by the advent of new industries, but also partly by the settlement of British half-pay officers and other genteel immigrants.

and smallholdings dispersed across a patchwork of enclosed fields.[26] Virtually all of these farms and smallholdings were owned by the families who worked them, since the island had lost the greater part of its large landowners in the thirteenth century.[27] Given the island's modest size and the large number of landowners, holdings were necessarily compact. A census of Guernsey's landholdings was taken in 1817 (in which Mollet himself participated). Only the returns of the Castel have survived, but this is quite fortunate, given that it was Charles Mollet's home parish.[28] The census counted 240 individual holdings in a parish just over 10 square kilometres in area. Nearly all of them consisted of a dwelling and attached land.[29] The size of each individual holding was recorded, including any land outside the parish boundary which also belonged to the owner. Only 12 per cent of holdings were over 20 acres in size; 70 per cent were under 12 acres; 38 per cent measured just 3 acres or less. In this, the Castel can be considered fairly typical of all the country parishes. Charles Mollet, with his 26⅓ acres, was among the top tenth of insular landowners.[30]

Estimates suggest that an average family needed at least 8 to 14 acres to live entirely off the land,[31] so that only a minority of rural holdings were large enough in themselves to sustain the families which owned them. Country parishioners nevertheless made the utmost use of the land they had. As a commentator observed, 'if it be only a garden, they cultivate fruit and vegetables [...] if they have also a field, they keep a cow and rear poultry,' adding that they consumed their own produce 'most sparingly', saving the bulk of it for market.[32] Like Scottish crofters, Guernsey's country parishioners

---

[26] There was some clustering of habitation, particularly around parish churches, but no villages as such. The island's original open fields had been gradually enclosed from the fifteenth century, as generations of landowners consolidated their strips by purchase and exchange to form parcels suited to enclosure.
[27] The reason for this will be explained below.
[28] The returns survive at the Island Archives in the form of a copy taken several years later (SG 23/43).
[29] Only eight dwellings in the parish did not have land attached.
[30] By way of comparison, a report for the United Kingdom Board of Agriculture in 1796 deemed 150–200 acres to be typical of 'good middle-sized farms' in Great Britain, and 30–40 acres 'the average of small farms' (T. Robertson, *General Outline of the Report upon the Size of Farms* (Edinburgh, 1796), p. 42).
[31] R. Hocart, *The Country People of Guernsey and their Agriculture, 1640-1840* (Guernsey, 2016), p. 216.
[32] *The Guernsey and Jersey Magazine*, 1 (1836), p. 311.

supplemented the yield from their land with other avocations. Some coastal families clubbed together to buy small boats and fished part-time. Male family members might practise a hereditary trade or craft – tailoring, basket-making, carpentry, thatching, stonemasonry – or they might hire themselves out as day labourers. Female family members invariably worked as servants in better-off neighbours' houses. St Peter Port – and seafaring – also provided important outlets for surplus rural offspring.

In the countryside, the social structure was somewhat flatter than in town. The top tier, to which Mollet himself belonged, was composed of the largest landowners and parish Rectors. Then there were the slightly smaller landowners who nevertheless lived off their land. Next came the smallholding master tradesmen, and beneath them the smallholding journeymen, fishermen and labourers. Very few non-natives settled permanently in the country parishes owing to the difficulty of acquiring land, which was jealously guarded by its local owners and kept within the same families for generations. The handful who did make their homes in the countryside usually did so by marrying into an established family.

Language and culture

The everyday spoken language of all country parishioners and most lower- and middle-ranking town parishioners was *guernésiais*. As noted in the Introduction, it was also that of Charles Mollet himself. *Guernésiais* supported a lively oral culture with its own distinctive legends, proverbs and sayings. Aside from *guernésiais*, however, nearly all country-dwellers and most lower- and middle-ranking town parishioners would also have had some knowledge of 'standard' French, in which church services were conducted, which was used in Court records and other official documents, and in which reading and writing were taught in schools. The linguistic situation of urban patricians was slightly different. These were educated to a higher level than the majority of their compatriots and sometimes spent time in France, so that while able to converse fluently in *guernésiais* with servants and tradesmen, they could also speak and write French with greater facility.

The linguistic situation as regarded the upper ranks began perceptibly to change during Mollet's lifetime. Many among this class were merchants who did business with England via the entrepôt. For commercial reasons, therefore, they were obliged to develop a reasonable command of English. In addition to this, almost constant Franco-British warfare from 1778 onwards disrupted longstanding cultural and trading links with France, which re-orientated the urban upper ranks very squarely towards Britain. Both of these factors motivated increasing numbers of wealthy families to send their children to English boarding schools, or to settle, temporarily or permanently, in England themselves. Such practices ultimately resulted in a language shift among the elite. Charles Mollet's own relatives followed these trends, and his diaries show that his great-nieces and great-nephews were all essentially anglophone.

Mollet also recorded the beginnings of a language shift in urban non-elite ranks. The large cohort of British soldiers and increasing number of economic migrants from south-west England in St Peter Port ensured that English was heard alongside *guernésiais* in every urban shop, street and tavern, with predictable effects. The linguistic position of country-dwellers was, however, more stable – for the time being, at least. This was largely owing to the continuing sparsity of non-natives in the rural parishes, which ensured that it was they who adapted to the prevailing francophone culture, rather than that culture to them. The Mesquêne family, neighbours of Mollet's who descended from a British soldier named McKane, are a case in point.[33]

The francophone heritage of islanders also conditioned the nature of their religious practice and belief. The Protestant Reformation had originally come to Guernsey not from England but from French-speaking Normandy and Geneva. Thus, between the mid-1500s and mid-1600s Guernsey's 'established' religion followed characteristically Continental Calvinistic and Presbyterian norms.[34] The island's Presbyterian regime was however brought to an end in 1662 when Charles II appointed an Anglican Dean with an order to introduce the Anglican liturgy to Guernsey. Although this met with a certain amount of resistance, by 1700 Anglicanism (with its own local characteristics) had by and large replaced Presbyterianism.[35] For several decades thereafter, neither Dissent nor Catholicism had a presence in the island. The first Nonconformists to establish themselves in Guernsey were Quakers, who founded a local congregation in 1782. Next to arrive was Methodism, brought to the island in 1785 by missionaries from England and

---

[33] The name appears as Mesquesne in both parish registers and Mollet's journal (see, for instance, 13.9.1780, 5.3.1785, 3.5.1793, 10.7.1793, 13.1.1817).

[34] See D.M. Ogier, *Reformation and Society in Guernsey* (Woodbridge, 1996).

[35] R. Hocart, *Guernsey in the Reign of Charles II* (Guernsey, 2020), pp. 58, 59, 67–8, 174.

Jersey. Roman Catholicism came last, reintroduced by *émigrés* fleeing the French Revolution in 1793.[36] As we shall see in subsequent chapters, Charles Mollet had many first-hand contacts with the last two of these denominations.

Guernsey society was strongly hierarchical. This was no exception to the general eighteenth-century norm, but it was perhaps accentuated owing to islanders' physical proximity to one another. Charles Mollet had dealings with members of all ranks, but they occupied quite separate compartments in his life, and he was careful never to mix members of one with members of the others. The way he referred to fellow islanders in his journal reflected the gradations into which both he and wider society divided them. Large landowners he often identified by the name of their property, as in Monsieur de St George (Jean Guille) or Monsieur des Touillets (Pierre De Jersey). Other gentlemen he usually referred to as 'Mr', as in Mr Robert Le Marchant or Mr Pierre De Havilland. Smaller farmers he designated *Sieur* ('Sr') and master tradesmen either *Sieur* or *Maître*. His own labourers he normally identified by their forenames only, and other parishioners of humble status by their forename and surname, usually also appending the forename of their father and sometimes the name of their holding.[37]

The naming of fathers was crucial to correct identification of parishioners owing to the high degree of homonymy in the local community. Not only was there a small stock of forenames, the number of surnames in any given parish was also limited. This arose largely from the expediency of marrying cousins in order to preserve and consolidate property. Mollet's journal is thus confusingly full of characteristically *câtelain* names: Nicolle, Girard, Ozanne, Lihou, Collenette, Le Page, often paired with identical forenames.[38] Cousin marriages were equally prevalent among islanders of Mollet's own rank, and indeed one of his great-nephews married one of his great-nieces, and another great-nephew married a first cousin from the paternal side of the family. A

---

[36] J. Jacob, *Annals of some of the British Norman Isles constituting the Bailiwick of Guernsey* (Paris, 1830), pp. 468–74.

[37] Similarly, Mollet referred to women of the non-elite class by their forename and maiden surname, and appended the name of their husband or father. However, references to the wives of large landowners might take the 'Madame des Touillets' form, and other elite women might appear as 'Mrs Robert Le Marchant' or 'Mrs Pierre De Havilland'.

[38] The commonest names for males (in Mollet's diaries, at least) were Pierre, Jean, Nicolas, Etienne and Daniel. For females, they were Marie, Judith, Rachel, Marthe and Anne.

local historian once observed that such inbreeding was highly undesirable because of the significant number of 'handicapped children' produced.[39]

Politics and administration

Geographically, the Channel Islands are offshore islands of France, not of Britain. From the tenth until the early thirteenth century, they belonged to the Duchy of Normandy and were governed as part of it. After Duke John of Normandy, who was also King John of England, lost the Duchy to King Philippe of France in 1204, the Islands were persuaded by various means to throw in their lot with the English monarchy. Norman tenants-in-chief of insular fiefs were presented with the choice of either subjecting themselves to the English Crown or forfeiting their lands. Since most of these were nobles who also held large estates in France, many opted to abandon their local holdings in order to retain their French domains. This left their numerous humbler sub-tenants in the unusual position of holding their little 'estates' directly of the Crown – which doubtless went some way towards winning their sympathies, especially when complemented by the assurance that they would be allowed to maintain local laws and administrative structures.[40]

Although the Islands' politico-diplomatic status was initially somewhat vague, it was substantially settled in the 1250s, when they were recognised as a personal possession of the English Crown. Whoever thenceforth was king of England was by that fact also lawful sovereign of the Channel Islands.[41] Sovereignty over the Islands gave the English monarch personal authority over them, but they were never politically subsumed into the realm of England, nor, later into the United Kingdom. This meant that they were outside the jurisdiction of the Westminster parliament and unrepresented within it. Over the thirteenth and fourteenth centuries, Jersey and Guernsey evolved into two distinct Bailiwicks. These Bailiwicks grew increasingly apart, and by at least the late fifteenth century, they were politically, legally and administratively quite separate.

---

[39] P.J. Girard, 'Country life and some insular enterprises of the late 19th century', *Transactions of la Société Guernesiaise*, 19 (1972), pp. 88-9.
[40] J.A. Everard and J.C. Holt, *Jersey 1204: The Forging of an Island Community* (London, 2004), pp. 79, 94–8, 121–2, 138–9.
[41] J. Loveridge, *The Constitution and Law of Guernsey* (1975; Guernsey, 1997 edn), p. 1.

At the time of Charles Mollet's birth in 1742, the Crown was represented in both Jersey and Guernsey by Governors. The office of Governor entitled its holder to local Crown revenues,[42] and was usually bestowed on a high-ranking British army officer at the end of his career, as a form of reward for long service. No Governor resided locally or performed his duties in person after the early eighteenth century. These duties were instead delegated to resident Lieutenant-Governors, whom Governors appointed themselves and paid from their own revenues. The responsibilities of Lieutenant-Governors were chiefly military. They were in overall command of both the British garrison and the local militia. In addition, they had specific duties relating to foreigners and security, and acted as conduits for communication between British and insular authorities. At the time of Mollet's birth, the monarch's power over the Channel Islands was chiefly exercised through the Privy Council. After the Home Office was created in 1782, insular affairs were primarily handled by this department, with the Privy Council as intermediary.

As regarded finances, Guernsey was largely self-funding. The British government (which was responsible for the island's defence) limited its spending to the military sphere, paying the expenses of the garrison, partly funding the militia, and contributing towards the construction and upkeep of some (though not all) coastal fortifications. All local domestic needs were met exclusively from local sources: parochial expenses were funded from parish rates, and all-island expenses were funded from a combination of harbour dues, import duties, and island-wide general taxes.[43]

In Mollet's day, Guernsey's government fell into three tiers. Much basic work was done by the island's ten parishes, which exercised civil as well as ecclesiastical functions. Aside from their duties in respect of parish churches and churchyards, they also bore responsibility for parochial policing, parochial poor relief, parochial schools, and parochial roads and sea walls. Each parish possessed a body elected by its *Chefs de Famille* (adult male

---

[42] Crown revenues came principally from dues and tithes on Crown fiefs, which Governors appointed local Receivers to collect in return for a percentage of the sums collected. Towards the end of Mollet's life, these revenues amounted to c.£2,800 annually.

[43] There was also a tax on innkeepers from 1780, and, from 1814, a duty on locally sold spirits known as the *impôt*.

ratepayers) which was known as the Douzaine.[44] The Douzaine was the parish's governing body. With it lay the power to select and approve the objects of parochial expenditure, and to decide how much should be raised through the rates. It was also the interface between the inhabitants of the parish and higher authorities.

At the apex of parish structure were two *Connétables* or Constables, who were elected by the *Chefs de Famille* and served for a minimum of one year.[45] As well as maintaining public order, these two parish Constables also acted as parochial treasurers and executive officers of their Douzaines, and occupied a seat in the States.[46] This made a Guernsey Constable's office highly prestigious, so that parochial Constables were exclusively drawn from the leading families of their parish. Usually elected to this role as young men (as Mollet himself was), many of them were later also elected to the Douzaine.

The Royal Court, which operated at island-wide level, formed the next tier of government. This Court exercised both a judicial and legislative function. It was composed of the Bailiff (who acted as Court president); twelve lay magistrates or Jurats (leading citizens who acted as judges in judicial cases and deliberators in legislative sittings); the Procureur and Comptroller (lawyers who acted as public prosecutors and advisers to the Crown, Court and States); a Greffier (who kept the Court's records); and executive officers known as the Prévôt and the Sergeant. In Mollet's day, the Bailiff, Procureur, Comptroller and Greffier were Crown appointees, and the Sergeant was appointed by the Governor. The Prévôt and Jurats were elected (see below for the electing body). The titles of all of these officers, save the Jurats, were usually prefixed with the designation *du Roi*, as in *le Procureur du Roi*.[47]

---

[44] Douzeniers were twelve in number in all parishes aside from the Vale, which had sixteen, and St Peter Port, which had twenty. Although service was nominally for life, Douzeniers were allowed by convention to retire at sixty.

[45] From 1736, St Peter Port had an additional four 'assistant constables' chosen annually by the Douzaine from the ranks of shopkeepers and tradesmen, to serve under the parish Constables' direction.

[46] States functions are described below. There was only one States seat for each parish, so the two Constables usually took it in turns to attend States meetings, where they voted in accordance with the instructions of their Douzaine, who met to discuss the agenda before the States meeting took place.

[47] Or, later, in English, 'HM Procureur'.

In its judicial role, the Royal Court had sole cognizance of all criminal matters arising in Guernsey as also sole jurisdiction over most civil matters.[48] In its legislative role, it promulgated local laws known as *Ordonnances* (Ordinances) at thrice-yearly sessions called *Chefs Plaids* (Chief Pleas). These Ordinances concerned such matters as the regulation of markets, the import and export of produce and livestock, weights and measures, public thoroughfares, taverns, hunting, the foreshore, and much else of routine domestic import. Sometimes they could also be declaratory of existing law and custom.

The States represented the highest tier of local government. This body appears to have arisen in the fifteenth or sixteenth century as an afforcement of the Royal Court convened to deal with matters felt to require a wider measure of consultation than could be achieved by the Court alone. During Mollet's lifetime, the States were composed of thirty-two members: the Bailiff (who as well as presiding over the Royal Court, also presided over the States),[49] HM Procureur, the twelve Jurats, ten parish Constables, and eight parish Rectors.[50] During the eighteenth and early nineteenth centuries, the States met a few times each year to deal with such high-level matters as the control of food supplies in times of want, the maintenance of St Peter Port harbour, the initiation and management of public construction projects, and the purchase of arms and equipment for the militia. Most States' decisions were given force by Ordinance of the Royal Court, but any legislation which embodied new taxes, altered the customary law, or made new substantive law had to be submitted for approval by the King in Council (a form of oversight to which Ordinances were not subject). Such legislation was uncommon in Mollet's day.

Aside from its legislative role, the States also had an elective role. In this capacity, its usual thirty-two members were increased to 184 by the addition of both Constables and the entire Douzaines of each parish. In this augmented form, it elected the Jurats of the Royal Court and HM Prévôt.[51]

With this brief summary of Guernsey's politics and administration – important not least because of Mollet's participation at every level – we close

---

[48] Some seigneurial courts shared jurisdiction over contractual and landholding matters on their fiefs.

[49] This made the Bailiff Guernsey's *de facto* civic head.

[50] The ten parishes had just eight Rectors between them because St Sampsons/the Vale, and Torteval/the Forest each formed one living.

[51] The elective iteration of the States was later known as the States of Election.

our exposition of the broad background against which the diarist lived his life. We shall now narrow our focus to the person of Charles Mollet himself. Chapter 2 will look in detail at Mollet's antecedents, his siblings, the extent of his property, and his general place within local society. The account will begin long before Mollet's birth.

2

Charles Mollet – Personal Background

The name 'Mollet', like many other Channel Island names, is French in origin. By the time Charles Mollet was born, there had been Mollets in Guernsey for centuries, and the identities of those who first introduced the name are unknown. Mollets were fairly thick on the ground in the 1700s. An inspection of church register indexes shows that there were around two hundred Mollet baptisms in St Peter Port during the eighteenth century, and the same again in the country parishes. Only Torteval and St Peters had no Mollet baptisms at all.

Charles Mollet's branch of the family originated in town. His great-grandfather, Pierre Mollet, was a miller, an occupation which seems to have been a family calling.[1] In 1657, Pierre Mollet married Michelle Ollivier of St Saviours. The baptisms of seven children followed between 1658 and 1666, all in St Peter Port. Our Charles Mollet was descended from the couple's second son, also named Charles, who was born in 1660.[2] This Charles, Mollet's grandfather, moved to the Castel parish in the early 1680s, probably drawn by the opportunities the parish offered to millers. Records show that, by the early 1700s, this Charles Mollet had interests in all three of the watermills in the area now known as the King's Mills. At various times (sometimes simultaneously), he was the tenant of the le Grand Moulin du

---

[1] Occupations were not usually specified in Guernsey's seventeenth-century church registers, but it is a measure of the relative importance of millers at that time that Pierre Mollet's occupation was given in a number of entries concerning him (as was also the case for others sharing the Mollet name).

[2] For the diarist's family tree, see Appendix 2.

Roi and le Moulin du Milieu, and had a share in the tenancy of le Moulin de Haut.[3]

Charles Mollet married Margueritte Henry in the Castel parish in 1683. He had seven children by her, of whom five died in infancy or childhood (confusingly including two boys by the name of Charles). The survivors were Margueritte (1686–1757) and Rebecca (1688–1732). The former married Pierre Griffon, also a miller. The latter married farmer Daniel Le Cheminant, and gave birth to a number of Le Cheminant cousins whom our own Charles Mollet mentioned regularly in his journals.

In July 1695, Margueritte Henry died at the age of thirty-five. Her husband, busy at his mills and with children on his hands, remarried that same year. His second wife was Margueritte Lihou, the daughter of Nicolas Lihou and Thomasse Le Lacheur. With his second wife, Charles Mollet had a further six children, of whom four survived into adulthood. Two of these were daughters: Marie, (1697–1735) and Rachel (1712–46). The other two were sons. The elder son was Thomas, born in 1696, and the younger son was yet another Charles, born in 1706. This Charles was our Charles's father.

In July 1719, our Charles's grandfather died aged fifty-nine (his second wife had died two years earlier). As his eldest surviving son, Thomas Mollet was Charles's principal heir. In January 1720, the Castel Parish Register recorded twenty-four-year-old Thomas being allocated his *préciput*, or eldership, by the Castel Douzaine.[4] A short time later, the young man acquired a further addition to his patrimony. His father had used some of his profits from milling to put out to loan, and most of these loans were secured on his debtors' personal and real estate. One such loan had been made to James Collenette, the owner of a property in the Castel known as le Déhuzet,

---

[3] Mollet's tenancy of le Moulin du Milieu and le Moulin de Haut (also known, respectively, as le Moulin Main and le Moulin Susain) are recorded on pp. 100–1 of the Rental of William Le Marchant of L'Hyvreuse, who owned these mills (AQ 0680/01, Island Archives). Evidence of Mollet's tenancy of le Grand Moulin du Roi comes from HM Receiver's Books in the De Sausmarez Collection at Guernsey's Greffe (No. 2.2, 'Farm of the Mill of les Grands Moulins', p.12).

[4] 7.1.1720, Castel Parish Register, 1664–1764 (AQ 1083/01, Island Archives). According to Guernsey inheritance law, the eldest son was entitled by way of *préciput* to a single enclosure of about one-sixth of an acre, usually containing the main dwelling, before the rest of the estate was divided between the siblings (two-thirds to males, one-third to females). The Douzaine were responsible for determining the location and extent of the eldership.

and when Collenette's heirs were unable to repay the loan, his property was forfeited to Thomas Mollet.[5]

This property was to remain in the hands of the Mollet family for a century and forms the setting for our Charles Mollet's diaries.[6] Thomas Mollet, however, enjoyed it for only a short time, as he died in January 1739. Since Thomas had never married and had no children, his only brother Charles (the diarist's father) inherited the property.

At the time of his succession, Mollet's father was aged thirty-three and living in Jersey. He had perhaps gone to join his sisters Marie and Rachel, who had both married Jerseymen and moved to the larger island.[7] How he was earning a living is unknown, but it may have been connected to the sea and to trade. By the time of Thomas's death, Charles had probably been living in Jersey for at least four years, since, in October 1735, he had married twenty-seven-year-old Marie Le Vavasseur dit Durell at Jersey's Trinity parish church.[8] Marie, one of the eight children of Abraham Le Vavasseur dit Durell and Marie Romeril, was undoubtedly an advantageous match for Charles, as the Durell family were well-off and influential in their home island.

In November 1736, Charles and Marie's first child, a daughter also named Marie, was baptised in Jersey's Town Church. This was our Charles's eldest sister. The death of her uncle Thomas when she was two years old evidently brought her father and his household back to Guernsey, as the Mollets' next daughter, Marthe, was baptised at the Castel parish church in the spring of 1740. A son, doubtless much longed for, was also baptised at the Castel church on 25 August 1742. This was the diarist himself. No further Mollet children are recorded.

The infant Charles Mollet's baptismal entry is interesting in that, although his mother is identified as *Dame* Marie Durell, his father is not a *Monsieur* but a *Sieur*. It seems likely that Marie Durell's personal status elevated not only that of her husband but also that of her children, perhaps giving them access to social circles they would not otherwise have entered. Charles's parents secured a prestigious set of godparents for their baby son. These were the siblings Charles, James and Rachel Andros, the adult offspring

---

[5] 1.3.1720, Amerci en Plaids, Greffe.

[6] For the location and extent of this property (later known as 'Woodlands', though not in the diarist's lifetime), see Maps 4 and 6.

[7] Marie Mollet married Nicolas De Ste Croix in 1722. Rachel Mollet married Thomas Cartault in 1732.

[8] This marriage is also recorded in the Castel church register.

of Jurat Charles Andros of les Piques, who was one of Guernsey's leading country parishioners.

Returning to the island to take up his Castel estate, Charles Mollet senior was an eminently suitable candidate for parochial office. In January 1741, he was elected a Constable, and the following year a Douzenier.[9] Over the next few years, Mollet senior (who was evidently imbued with a strong business sense) added to his assets by putting money out to loan and purchasing *rentes*.[10] Like others of his contemporaries, he probably also took out shares in privateers and trading vessels. The profits from these investments enabled him to enlarge his landholdings.[11] By 1762, when our own Charles Mollet came of age, his father was the wealthiest man in the Castel parish in terms of real and personal property assessed for rates. Though still designated a *Sieur*, his property was valued at 310 quarters, which in monetary terms,

---

[9] 15.1.1741, 12.5.1742, Castel Parish Register, 1664–1764 (AQ 1083/01, Island Archives).

[10] Several loans and purchases of *rentes* made by Mollet senior are recorded in vol. 34 of Contrats pour Lire et pour la Date at Guernsey's Greffe. Richard Hocart also mentions a loan of 3,512 *livres tournois* (about £250 stg) made by Mollet senior to Jurat Jean Andros in the 1730s (R. Hocart, *The Country People of Guernsey and their Agriculture, 1640–1840* (Guernsey, 2016), p. 155). The term *rente* requires a detailed explanation, as it will feature elsewhere in this book. *Rentes* derived from the local mode of buying and selling real property in the eighteenth and earlier centuries. When a property was sold, the price was normally converted into a perpetual mortgage expressed in terms of wheat, as most purchasers had insufficient money for a cash purchase. The purchaser undertook to pay the agreed quantity of wheat annually at Michaelmas (either in kind, or in cash at a rate set each year by the Royal Court). This was known as a *rente*. The agreement was also binding on a purchaser's heirs and successors in title, and so long as they continued to pay their *rentes*, they continued to hold their property as freehold (on a vendor's death, *rentes* originally payable to him became payable to his heirs). The owner of a *rente* could sell it to a third party, or leave it to someone as a bequest. A *rente* could be redeemed at any time in return for money by the person who owed it, but only if the owner of the *rente* agreed to the sale. Alternatively, a property-owner could free himself of a *rente* by purchasing a *rente* of equal value and assigning it to the person to whom he owed the original *rente*. Most of Guernsey's eighteenth-century property-owners both owed and owned *rentes*.

[11] This is evidenced by new entries in Mollet's name in the 1750 Livre de Perchage for the Fief des Vingt Bouvées du Villain Fief le Comte, where most of his property was situated (AQ 1330/02, Island Archives). Livres de Perchage were surveys of landownership taken every ten or twenty years in order to assess landowners for the annual feudal charge known as *chefrente*, which was calculated on the basis of a property's area.

equated to about £6,200.[12] His nearest rivals were Elizée Le Marchant of la Haye du Puits and Jean Guille of St George, both *Messieurs*, who were assessed at 280 quarters (£5,600) and 250 quarters (£5,000) respectively.[13] Charles Mollet senior died on 20 May 1770. As well as his Guernsey property, he also left £1,000 in British Government stock.[14]

Before Mollet senior passed away, he had the satisfaction of seeing his two daughters make excellent marriages. In 1754, his elder daughter, Jersey-born Marie, married the St Helier merchant and ship-owner Philippe Lerrier. She was to remain in Jersey for the rest of her life and bore her husband thirteen children. A decade later, Mollet's younger daughter Marthe married the St Peter Port merchant Peter Mourant. Marthe remained settled in Guernsey, and she and her four children played an important part in our diarist's life.[15]

Marthe's husband Peter Mourant, though he became very wealthy, was not from Guernsey's traditional elite. His was a seafaring family which appears to have moved from Jersey two generations before his birth in 1740.[16] His father had been a sea captain, and at least two of his brothers also followed this profession. In 1780, Peter Mourant's assets were valued for tax purposes at 1,400 quarters (£28,000), making him the fourth wealthiest individual in St Peter Port.[17] In the early 1780s, Mourant used some of the wealth he was accumulating to commission the building of a new house on land which he owned to the north-west of town. This house, which Charles Mollet knew as 'Candie', was also to play a large part in the diarist's life.[18]

The Mourants' family was complete long before they moved into 'Candie'. The couple's eldest child Martha (whom Mollet always called Patty)

---

[12] A quarter was a measure of volume containing about 6,530 cubic inches. It was used *inter alia* for measuring dry wheat grain. Since property was valued in wheat for the purpose of sale and purchase, it was also valued in wheat for assessing liability to parish rates. It was accepted that one quarter was equivalent to £20.

[13] Tax List dated 11.2.1762, Castel Parish Register, 1664–1764 (AQ 1083/01, Island Archives).

[14] 26.10.1770 and 4.1.1771, Stock Ledger, 1765–71 (AC27/6731, Bank of England Archives).

[15] See Appendix 3 for detail on Charles Mollet's sisters, their spouses and their descendants.

[16] His father, Etienne Mourant, was born in Guernsey in 1683. His grandfather, another Etienne, was born in Jersey in 1651.

[17] St Peter Port Tax Book, 1797–1803 (AQ 1004/01, Island Archives). For an account of Peter Mourant's commercial activities, see G. Stevens Cox, *The Guernsey Merchants and their World* (Guernsey, 2009), pp. 110–14.

[18] For Victorian images of the house and gardens, see Plates 15 and 16. 'Candie' currently houses Guernsey's Priaulx Library.

was born in 1765. Another daughter, Mary (whom Mollet occasionally called Polly), followed in 1767. A third daughter, Anne (to whom Mollet referred as Nancy) was born in 1769, and a son, Peter junior, was born in 1770. Mollet's sister Marthe was only thirty when Peter was born. She went on to have a long and tiring series of stillbirths, all documented in Mollet's diary.[19]

Peter Mourant senior's ever-increasing wealth ensured that Patty, Mary, Nancy and Peter junior all married into top-tier families. Patty went first, marrying the well-to-do merchant Bonamy Dobrée, ten years her senior, in 1783. Mary and Nancy followed in 1784 and 1786 respectively, marrying brothers Henry and William Brock. These were first cousins of the future Major-General Sir Isaac Brock and Bailiff Daniel De Lisle Brock.[20] Henry Brock, four years Mary's senior, was eventually elected a Jurat. William Brock, thirteen years older than Nancy, moved his family to Exeter in 1798. Peter Mourant junior waited until 1807 before taking a wife. At the age of thirty-seven, he married twenty-three-year-old Sophia Carey, the daughter of wealthy Jurat and merchant Jean Carey. Peter and Sophia never had any children, and neither did Mary and Henry Brock. Patty and Bonamy Dobrée and Nancy and William Brock however more than made up the deficit. Patty had nine children, of whom seven survived, and Nancy had at least seventeen, of whom nine are known to have reached adulthood. Mollet's diary documented the childhood and eventual marriages of many of his great-nieces and great-nephews.

What of Charles Mollet's own childhood? Evidence suggests that he spent frequent holidays in his mother's native Jersey: his journals recorded ten visits to Jersey between 1771 and 1796, during which he interacted with many old friends and acquaintances (the majority of them in high places).[21] Charles Mollet may also have spent part of his school-days in France. Sending children to France for their education seems to have been a common practice in Mollet's Jersey family. His brother-in-law Philippe Lerrier is known to have sent his ward William Chepmell to school in Caen.[22] Although Charles Mollet nowhere mentioned being educated in France, his diary documented

---

[19] This subject will be addressed in Chapter 8.
[20] See Appendix 4 for the composition of the Brock and Dobrée families.
[21] Mollet's travels will be discussed in Chapter 8.
[22] Chepmell, who later moved to Guernsey, was Lerrier's nephew. While in Caen, he was briefly kidnapped by some nuns. This bizarre episode is recounted in C. Ozanne, 'Adventures of a Channel Islander in France in the 18th century', *Transactions of la Société Guernesiaise*, 3 (1928), pp. 275–83.

four sojourns in Normandy, during which he visited several families with whom he already seemed to be acquainted.

By 1767, at all events, Charles Mollet was permanently settled on the family farm at le Déhuzet. In December that year, aged twenty-five, he was elected a churchwarden of the Castel parish, an office which he occupied for the next two years.[23] Following his father's death in May 1770, Mollet became a farmer in his own right. He first appeared on the Castel tax list in 1771. Designated *Sieur* like his father, his real and personal property was valued at 100 quarters (£2,000).[24] The discrepancy between this valuation and the assessment of his father's property ten years previously probably reflected the division of paternal assets, money spent on marriage portions, and possibly the repayment of paternal debts. Charles's mother was also taxed in her own right for the first time in 1771, in her case on 54 quarters (£1,080).

Mollet junior clearly lacked Mollet senior's economic dynamism, for his wealth never regained the heights of his father's. In 1793, the year after his mother's death had transferred some of her assets to him, he was taxed at 190 quarters (£3,800).[25] By this point, he was designated *Monsieur* in the tax lists. In 1801, his wealth reached its maximum – 200 quarters (£4,000).[26] It then plateaued at that level for the remainder of his life. In 1819, the last year Mollet was taxed, seven parishioners were rated higher than him. These included Jean Guille of St George (650 quarters or £13,000) and Josias Le Marchant of la Haye du Puits (550 quarters or £11,000).[27] If Mollet had not gone down in the world, then – unlike his Guille and Le Marchant neighbours – he had certainly not gone up.

This brings us back to the question posed in the previous chapter regarding Charles Mollet's position in society. There is no doubt that his father's wealth and his mother's rank had placed him in the upper bracket at birth, as also that the advantageous marriages of his sisters (and later his nieces) had buttressed his position. This made Mollet a figure of importance in his own parish, as well as enabling him to associate freely with all the leading members of the little polity that was Guernsey. His status might not

---

[23] 23.12.1767, 22.12.1769, Castel Parish Register, 1748–1835 (AQ 1083/3, Island Archives).
[24] 6.4.1771, Castel Parish Register, 1764–1809 (AQ 1017/8, Island Archives).
[25] 4.12.1793, Castel Parish Register, 1764–1809 (AQ 1017/8, Island Archives).
[26] 23.1.1801, Castel Parish Register, 1764–1809 (AQ 1017/8, Island Archives).
[27] 19.2.1819, Castel Parish Tax Lists, 1808–28 (AQ 155/1, Island Archives).

have been sufficiently grand to propel him to the Jurats' bench, but as it was, Mollet never showed any ambition to occupy this office. He also stood out among his entrepreneurial contemporaries in not furthering his financial and commercial interests with any conspicuous zeal. This lack of enthusiasm may partly have been due to the fact that Mollet was unmarried and did not have any futurity to provide for. It was perhaps also because he was as uninterested in commerce as he was unsuited to it. Whatever the case, Mollet's lack of economic success (coupled with his lack of successors) meant that, as he grew older, he became an increasingly peripheral figure, respected always, but no longer a personage of any great significance. This is perhaps where he preferred to be. In the next two chapters we will focus in greater detail on economic matters. Given the centrality of farming to Charles Mollet's life, Chapter 3 will begin by investigating how Mollet exploited his farm.

3

Economic Life, Part 1: Farming

Financially speaking, Charles Mollet did not need to farm, as he had sufficient resources to live respectably in town, had he so chosen. However, the farm was not only his patrimony, it was also the embodiment of his identity. The property was located in the southern half of the Castel parish, about 1½ miles from Vazon Bay on the west coast and 4 miles from town on the east.[1] As noted in Chapter 1, the farm occupied 26⅓ acres in total, making Charles Mollet what agricultural commentator Thomas Quayle once jokingly described as 'a capital farmer'.[2]

The core fields Mollet inherited from his father in 1770 were le Courtil des Eturs, le Courtil Robin, le Pré du Pommier, le Courtil Brulin, and part of a large field named la Sencière (all contiguous to his farmstead) together with two detached fields at nearby Mont d'Aval.[3] Over the next fifteen years, Mollet made further purchases at la Sencière, la Domaillerie, les Vallées, le Préel and les Tuzets.[4] In addition to his own land, Mollet for several years rented a large field from the Moullin family of le Ponchez.[5] At other times, he let out fields of his own to third parties.[6]

All of Mollet's fields, and even portions within them, were separated by earthbanks. These earthbanks, like those of most his contemporaries, would

---

[1] See Map 6.
[2] Relevé des Propriétaires du Castel, May 1817 (SG 23/43, Island Archives); T. Quayle, *General View of the Agriculture and Present State of the Islands on the Coast of Normandy subject to the Crown of Great Britain* (London, 1815), p. 249.
[3] *Courtil* = field; *pré* = meadow. The fields contiguous to the farmstead are depicted in Map 4, as also on the back cover of this book. Closer to his house, Mollet had a number of smaller fields and gardens, which he named *inter alia* le Marquet, le Carré and le Ruquet.
[4] Records of these are to be found in Guernsey's Greffe: in chronological sequence, 26.12.1770, Contrats pour Lire; 28.8.1773, Contrats pour la Date; 19.8.1780, Contrats pour Lire; 9.2.1784; 10.2.1785, Contrats pour la Date. The properties at la Domaillerie, les Vallées and le Préel included houses. By the time of his death in 1819, Mollet had sold his property at le Préel, les Vallées and le Mont d'Aval (Diary, 26.11.1791; Conveyance of 19.1.1816 (Island Archives, AQ 1133/021); 17.10.1818, Contrats pour Lire, Greffe).
[5] This field was known as le Neuf Courtil (Diary, 22.5.1776).
[6] Diary, 26.9.1773, 19.10.1779, 8.9.1790, 9.2.1801, 10.3.1812, 30.12.1816.

have been about 4½ feet in height and 3 feet wide at the top.[7] Many of Mollet's older earthbanks were topped with trees or covered with bracken. On the new earthbanks he had built himself, he usually sowed gorse or planted blackthorn.

Mollet's house, the main part of which is estimated to have been built around 1540, faced north.[8] It was accessed along a short drive from the lane now known as Les Vallées. His outbuildings were extensive. They included a barn and a cartshed (one or the other of which was joined to the house by a covered passageway); a press-house (for cider-making); horse stables; several cowsheds and pigsties; a slaughter-house; a dairy; a wash-house; an outdoor privy; and a wine and cider store. The roofs of all these buildings, including the pigsties, were thatched. Mollet's farmstead also contained pens and coops for his poultry; accommodation for his pigeons and bees; a lime-pit for grain storage; and a stackyard with staddle stones for his hay- and corn-stacks. Further away from the house were three field-wells; three ponds; a clay pit; a gravel pit; and a small quarry situated at la Sencière.

Mollet's agricultural equipment was locally made to traditional designs – 'the same kind of plough, harrow, and every implement of husbandry, used some centuries back,' as the Englishman William Berry described it.[9] An auction of some of Mollet's belongings after his death listed for sale (among other things) one large and one small cart; one large and one small plough; two harrows with accompanying traces.[10] The large cart would have been what locals called *un laong tchériot*, low-sided and open at the front and back, with a curved rave to hold hay and corn.[11] The small cart would have been *un taombré* or boxcart. Mollet had his carts renewed or repaired several times over the five decades covered by his journals. New ones were made at the farm by rural carpenters, usually with materials Mollet provided himself.[12] Mollet's ploughs and harrows were also made and repaired at his farm.[13] John

---

[7] T.F. Priaulx, 'Our hedges', *The Review of the Guernsey Society* (Summer 1977), pp. 46–8.
[8] J. McCormack, *Channel Island Houses* (Guernsey, 2015), p. 793.
[9] W. Berry, *The History of the Island of Guernsey* (London, 1815), p. 284. Berry lived in Guernsey c.1810–15.
[10] Auction catalogue (n.d.), Box 18, De Sausmarez Collection, Greffe.
[11] See Plate 22.
[12] See, for instance, Diary, 10.12.1806.
[13] For ploughs, see Diary, 20.1.1778, 14.12.1801, 29.1.1817. For harrows, see 19.1.1809.

Jacob, who settled in Guernsey after Waterloo, described such local productions as 'clumsy and heavy'.[14]

The bulk of Mollet's everyday farm work was not, however, executed by horse-drawn implements but by men armed with tools of wood and iron. Locally made scythes were used for cutting hay and corn.[15] The traditional Guernsey spade (a 14-inch blade on an ashen shaft) was used for digging.[16] The Guernsey *sarcloir* (an 8-inch blade on a short dog-leg-shaped handle) was used for most weeding, which was done on hand and knee.[17]

As well as reaping, digging and weeding, threshing was also done manually. In the first two years after coming into his property, Mollet had his corn threshed and winnowed on other people's premises. This was probably a perpetuation of his father's practice. In 1773, he began threshing and winnowing his grain crops at home, usually delegating the task to freelance labourers for a piece-rate. Threshing (the separation of ears from stems) could be done two ways: by beating the sheaves on *un ch'va* (a large piece of tree trunk on four legs) or striking them repeatedly with flails on the barn floor. It is not clear from the diary which of these two methods Mollet used, but whichever it was, the work was certainly done by hand.

Winnowing (the separation of grain from chaff) was a different matter. Here, machines were made use of, at least for part of Mollet's farming career. Mollet first mentioned ownership of a winnowing machine in 1788.[18] He also recorded buying a new one from England in 1806.[19] These hand-powered machines were the only mechanical devices in use on Mollet's farm.

In an age before chemical fertilisers, Charles Mollet used only natural substances as manure. Dung from the stables and cowsheds was collected and

---

[14] J. Jacob, *Annals of some of the British Norman Isles constituting the Bailiwick of Guernsey* (Paris, 1830), pp. 179–80.

[15] Diary, 27.6.1817.

[16] Quayle, *General View*, pp. 256–7.

[17] *Ibid.*, p. 256. Hoes were sometimes also used, though less often and usually only where garden vegetables were growing close together. For an instance of hoeing, see Diary, 11.5.1775.

[18] Diary, 29.10.1788. Winnowing machines separated ears from chaff using a blast of air directed at threshed grain poured through a hopper. They were introduced to Britain from the Netherlands in the early 1700s (G.E. Fussell, *The History of the Farmer's Tools: British Farm Implements, Tools and Machinery AD 1500–1900* (1952; London, 1981 edn), pp. 158–60).

[19] Diary, 14.2.1806. The new machine cost him 3 guineas.

stored for future use in a number of heaps around the farm.[20] Pig waste was periodically removed from pits adjacent to the sties and carted to the fields.[21] Guano from poultry coops and runs was shovelled into baskets and taken away for use in vegetable beds and cold frames.[22] Mud and animal droppings from the roads bordering Mollet's property were scraped off to be spread on fields and gardens.[23] Nothing useable was wasted. Mollet even recycled sludge from the bottom of his ponds.[24]

Mud and dung were not, however, Mollet's most important fertilisers. This function was fulfilled by seaweed, available in much larger volumes. Seaweed was the prized asset of all island farmers and smallholders. Anyone was at liberty to collect driftweed between sunrise and sunset all year round.[25] This could be taken from the piles of weed which formed naturally on the beaches or raked up while still floating in the sea. It was particularly plentiful after autumn and winter storms, which is generally when Mollet sent his labourers to collect it. In the spring of 1818, Mollet noted that his men had collected 106 cartloads of seaweed since the previous September.[26] Four or five cartloads of seaweed normally sufficed to manure half an acre.[27] Small amounts of seaweed were also sometimes added to dungheaps.[28]

As well as the gathering of driftweed, the cutting of live seaweed was also permitted. This was however restricted to two periods in early spring and summer.[29] The spring cutting ran from the first spring tide after 2 February to 15 March. The summer cutting ran for two tides following the first spring tide after 24 June.[30] Most people left their summer seaweed to dry on the

---

[20] In the summertime, these were covered with sand to prevent them drying out.
[21] Diary, 27.9.1774, 7.1.1778, 12.10.1810. This is likely to have been combined with human waste, since pits which took waste from pigsties generally also took waste from privies (J. McCormack, 'Guernsey pigs', *The Review of the Guernsey Society* (Summer 1994), p. 41).
[22] Diary, 9.2.1779, 21.10.1807, 15.1.1817.
[23] Diary, 6.11.1772, 20.2.1793.
[24] Diary, 26.12.1817.
[25] *The Guernsey and Jersey Magazine*, 3 (1837), pp. 118–19.
[26] Diary, 13.3.1818.
[27] *The Guernsey and Jersey Magazine*, 1 (1836), p. 275.
[28] Diary, 26.4.1779, 16.5.17.
[29] For detail on seaweed-cutting, which was the subject of many Ordinances, see Quayle, *General View*, pp. 274–5; E.F. Carey (ed.), *Guernsey Folk Lore from MSS by the late Sir Edgar MacCulloch* (London, 1903), p. 78.
[30] The first week of the summer cutting was reserved for poor people without a cart or horse, who were allowed to cut as much as they liked, provided they brought it up to the top of the beach in a sack on their own backs.

dunes, after which some took it home to use as winter fuel, and others burned it on outdoor fires in order to make ashes. These seaweed ashes were greatly valued as fertiliser and were usually sold for money. Mollet occasionally sent his men to participate in the spring and summer cuttings.[31] Sometimes, he burned seaweed to make ashes of his own. More frequently, however, he purchased the ashes he needed from his less well-off neighbours. In an average year, he would buy ashes from five or six sellers, in quantities of 20 to 50 bushels. The price he paid for a bushel of seaweed ashes rose from 2 *sous* (about 1¾d) in the late eighteenth century to 7 *sous* (6d) in the post-Napoleonic era.[32] Mollet would apply these ashes to his cornfields before sowing (sometimes mixed with driftweed), or scatter them directly around a growing crop.[33]

As well as seaweed, Mollet occasionally sent his men to fetch barrels of sea water. This seems to have had two uses. Sometimes, Mollet applied it directly to the soil as a fertiliser.[34] He also sprinkled it around trees or on paving stones as a moss-killer.[35] Sand, too, was brought from the beach in large quantities. Its main agricultural use was in lightening heavy soil. Sometimes it was spread directly over field surfaces before ploughing; sometimes it was mixed with dung before spreading.[36] Mollet used a number of other soil conditioners in addition to sand. The most important of these was burnt lime,[37] but he also occasionally used asafoetida,[38] powdered salt,[39] and even powdered dried peas.[40]

Mollet kept regular records of the weather and its effects on his farming. Living at the tail-end of what is known as 'the little ice age',[41] he documented conditions distinctly colder than in Guernsey today. The highest temperature mentioned in Mollet's diary was 82 degrees Fahrenheit (27.8 degrees Celsius), recorded on Friday 19 July 1793. Mollet called this 'extreme [...] a

---

[31] Diary, 14.2.1794, 18.2.1817, 9.6.1817.
[32] Diary, 12.1.1795, 21.4.1817.
[33] Diary, 10.3.1777, 22.2.1787.
[34] Diary, 24.1.1777, 14.9.1795.
[35] Diary, 18.5.1795, 12.1.1801.
[36] Diary, 7.6.1771, 15.9.1808.
[37] Diary, 14.11.1771.
[38] Diary, 6.10.1773.
[39] Diary, 22.11.1786.
[40] Diary 24.2.1803.
[41] This ran approximately from the mid-1500s to the mid-1800s (B. Fagan, *The Little Ice Age* (New York, 2000), pp. 47–55).

temperature similar to Madras in India.'[42] A more usual maximum was 73 degrees Fahrenheit (22.8 degrees Celsius), recorded in 1796.[43] Winters were correspondingly colder, with frosts commoner than they are now. In many years there were regular frosts from December to March, and even the odd one in October or May.[44] These frosts were not as damaging as the protracted severe frosts experienced in France or Britain, but Mollet often had to take measures to protect his tender flowers and vegetables.[45] Snowfall was also recorded in almost every one of the forty-two years covered by Mollet's journal, although usually of limited volume and duration. That said, some years were markedly worse than others: 1771, 1786, 1795, 1807 and 1811 in particular. The worst of these was perhaps 1771, when snow lay on the ground for nearly six weeks.[46]

Also of interest in the context of temperature are Mollet's observations for 1816, 'the year without a summer', when the climate is thought to have been disrupted by the eruption of Mount Tambora in the Dutch East Indies.[47] Mollet knew nothing of this event, but he recorded unseasonably cold, wet and overcast weather throughout the spring and summer, which resulted in a markedly delayed harvest. On 18 July 1816, he wrote:

> Heavy rain between 8 o'clock & midday. The rest of the day was very damp. The ground is saturated. Water is flowing down the channel in the hillside garden, just as it does in the winter. It has even overflowed into the trees. We have had a stiff, cold south-westerly wind since noon yesterday. It is very rare for us to have such a cold & wet summer as this.

The year 1816 was also marked by storms, some of which caused damage to coastal areas.[48] Damaging storms, however, were by no means uncommon in any year, Guernsey being situated in the western approaches and fully exposed

---

[42] Diary, 19.7.1793.
[43] This was recorded on 24 July 1796 and published in Anon., *Almanach Journalier à l'Usage de l'Ile de Guernesey pour l'Année 1797* (Guernsey, 1797).
[44] See for instance Diary, 25.10.96, 15.10.09, 31.10.10, 16.5.02, 1.5.08, 5.5.10.
[45] Diary, 2.1.1795, 30.11.1809.
[46] Diary, 9.1.1771–15.2.1771. This is corroborated by Elisha Dobrée's journal, which *inter alia* recorded 25-foot drifts in which two people froze to death (J.P. Warren, 'Extracts from the diary of Elisha Dobrée', *Transactions of la Société Guernesiaise*, 10 (1929) p. 498).
[47] Fagan, *Little Ice Age*, pp. 54–5. The eruption of Mount Tambora was the largest observed volcanic eruption in recorded history. The main eruption took place in April 1815, but ejections continued for many months afterwards.
[48] Diary, 15.5.1816.

to Atlantic gales. Mollet recorded serious storm damage to his grain crop in 1773;[49] to his blossoming apple orchards in 1800;[50] and countless occasions where trees were blown down and portions of roofing thatch torn off.[51]

Mollet also experienced a number of drought years over the course of his lifetime. In an island whose only water sources were streams and wells, protracted droughts could be problematic. Judging by Mollet's records, the most serious drought years were 1775, 1778, 1784/5, and 1802/3, with 1784/5 the worst of all. On 18 April 1785, Mollet wrote:

> Between 20 September & 1 November last year, there was no rain at all, & the winter has in general been exceptionally dry. The usual winter streams did not appear, & some streams which flow all year dried up. This has made it very difficult for the millers, & stunted the growth of grass.

A few months later, on 5 September 1785, he observed:

> We have had no rain since 5 February (30 weeks ago last Saturday), save a little on 24 February, 18 April, 20 & 29 May. Everyone has had difficulty feeding their livestock & there has scarcely been any hay, nor barley, nor clover among the barley.

As if the weather were not enough to contend with, Mollet also had perennial problems with pests. His worst enemies were the rats which stole his grain; the rabbits which devoured his young crops; the birds which pecked at the fruit on his bushes and trees; the dogs which attacked his poultry; and even, occasionally, egg-stealing weasels. Traps were set for rabbits and rats;[52] fruit trees were netted against birds;[53] marauding dogs were unceremoniously shot.[54] To a modern reader, weasels are perhaps the most interesting of these pests, as they are now extinct in Guernsey. In the winter of 1803, a weasel nesting in Mollet's cartshed took some 180 eggs from under his hens before being evicted, although Mollet did not note having killed it.[55] Wasps, not an agricultural pest as such, were also a problem in some years. Mollet's diary

---

[49] Diary, 19.8.1773.
[50] Diary, 17.5.1800. Note the comparatively late date of what must have been peak blossom.
[51] Diary, 26.2.1773, 9.11.1800, 2.12.1806, 18.12.1808, 10.11.1810, 12.3.1818.
[52] Diary, 4.4.1810, 30.8.1817.
[53] Diary, 21.7.1802.
[54] Diary, 12.9.1794, 9.9.1797, 2.3.1817.
[55] Diary, 7.1.1803, 8.1.1803, 9.1.1803, 18.2.1803.

regularly recorded the destruction of large numbers of wasps' nests in late summer – as many as twenty-seven of them in the drought year of 1785.[56]

Mollet himself participated in the destruction of these wasps' nests, and indeed he was no stranger to work around the farm. Many of his diary entries recorded him digging, weeding, sowing, picking fruit, taking cuttings, re-potting plants, etc. He did not however do this on a daily basis, nor did he do the really hard work, such as digging a whole parsnip field with a spade or cutting a hay meadow with a scythe. Mollet essentially worked when he felt inclined to, out of a desire for exercise or out of personal interest in his plants and flowers.

This left the real work of the farm to be performed by Mollet's farm servants and day labourers. Mollet always had at least one live-in farm servant, and in some years even two or three. Mollet's farm servants lived in his house (not in an outbuilding) and took all their meals in his kitchen. They were expected to be available to do his bidding twenty-four hours a day, and had only a fortnightly Sunday afternoon off. Mollet's diaries record more than forty different live-in farm servants by name. The majority of them were young unmarried men from the Castel parish, whom Mollet took on in their late teens or early twenties. He also employed fifteen French and six English live-in farm servants. The amount Mollet paid his native farm servants ranged from the equivalent of about £9 15s a year in the 1770s to £15 in the early 1800s.[57] Non-native farm servants tended to come cheaper. Englishman Thomas Andrews was paid about £7 15s a year in 1800, and Frenchmen Georges and Jacques Nicolet £8 a year in 1802.[58] Although farm servants were notionally hired by the year, most of Mollet's farm servants worked only a few months for him before moving on, particularly the English and French ones. Only six of Mollet's live-in farm servants stayed with him for more than two years. These were all Guernseymen. With four of these men – Pierre Gavet, Abraham Machon, Daniel Ferbrache and Jean Cateline – Mollet formed significant relationships. These will be considered at length in Chapter 9.[59]

Mollet complemented his live-in farm servants with day labourers and piece-workers, of whom he employed well in excess of one hundred during

---

[56] Diary, 28.9.1785.
[57] Diary, 22.1.1771, 6.5.1811.
[58] Diary, 15.7.1800, 14.10.1802.
[59] For biographical details on these men, see Appendix 5.

his lifetime. In any given year, Mollet might have up to a dozen of these workers on his books.[60] Mollet's day labourers usually only worked two or three days a week for him, devoting the rest of their time to their own land or to other employers. The total number of days they collectively worked depended on how many live-in farm servants Mollet had at the time. In a year with more than one live-in servant, his day labourers might put in between 300 and 500 man-days. In years when he had only one farm servant, the number of man-days could be much higher – around 700 in 1771, for instance, and nearly 900 in 1818.[61]

Mollet's day labourers and piece-workers were of all ages. Some were only boys, but some were in their seventies. Over the course of five decades, Mollet employed multiple generations of the same Castel families as day labourers, piece-workers and farm servants – sons succeeding fathers, nephews succeeding uncles, grandsons succeeding grandfathers.[62] One particular individual worked for Mollet throughout the entire five decades covered by his diaries. This was the smallholder Etienne Lihou, who, born in the same year as Mollet, was still labouring for him in his seventies and eventually outlived him by thirteen years. In addition to these local men, Mollet employed fifteen named British soldiers as occasional labourers (as also two French soldiers from an *émigré* regiment). These soldiers were usually taken on at peak times, and generally only worked a few weeks to supplement their military pay.

Mollet employed fewer piece-workers than day labourers. Piece-workers performed discrete tasks such as digging, weeding, furze-cutting, or threshing, which they fitted in as and when they could. They were paid by the area they dug, weeded or cut, or the number of sheaves they threshed, at rates which might equate to between one and three shillings per day, depending on how quickly they worked and whether or not they required food and drink. In some cases, they were paid not in money but with a share of the product of their work. In 1778, for instance, Jacques Sarre threshed fifty sheaves of

---

[60] Before beginning his diary for any particular year, Mollet left a few blank pages which he filled with notes as he went along. These pages always included a sort of table or grid in which Mollet kept a tally of days worked by each of his workers.
[61] Diary, Notes relating to 1771 and 1818.
[62] Appendix 6 depicts the inter-relatedness of many of Mollet's employees.

barley for Mollet in return for the straw.[63] In 1800, Jean Ferbrache lopped Mollet's trees in return for firewood.[64]

Labourers employed by the day generally worked from dawn till dusk. On work days (which ran from Monday to Saturday), these labourers had breakfast, dinner and supper in Mollet's kitchen and were supplied with cider at intervals during the day. Pay varied with age and experience, and also with the seasons. In the early nineteenth century, Mollet's standard rate for his regular labourers was about 1s 2d per day rising to 1s 8d in the summer, when daylight hours were longer and more work was done.[65] However, a soldier like Thomas Wilford might receive just 10d a day,[66] and a sixteen-year-old like Henry Blondel might get as little as 8d a day.[67]

In most years, Mollet's tally of occasional workers also included some craftsmen employed to maintain and renew his farm gear and buildings. Mollet normally provided these craftsmen with materials and also paid them by the day. Performing their work on site, they took their meals with other workers around Mollet's kitchen table and were similarly supplied with cider. They were usually from the country parishes, most of them with smallholdings of their own. The tradesmen most frequently called upon by Mollet were carpenters, whose skills encompassed a broad range of tasks: sawing tree trunks into planks; making carts and ploughs; laying wooden floors; making roof frames; making furniture such as tables, bedsteads and wardrobes.[68] Stonemasons were equally multi-skilled. They erected walls and gateposts; laid flagstones and drains; re-made wells and earthbanks; built new stables and cowsheds.[69] At regular intervals, Mollet also engaged thatchers to work on the roofs of his houses and outbuildings, parts of which required regular re-thatching.[70] Coopers and basket-makers were called upon with similar regularity – coopers to re-hoop Mollet's stock of barrels and casks;[71] basket-makers to make and repair the baskets, hampers and horse-panniers in

---

[63] Diary, 14.2.1778.
[64] Diary, 5.4.1800.
[65] See Diary, Notes relating to 1809.
[66] Diary, Notes relating to 1810.
[67] Diary, 5.10.1816.
[68] For examples of carpenters' varied work, see Diary, 28.5.1772, 15.7.1773, 29.5.1779, 20.3.1795, 20.1.1798, 30.8.1806, 10.12.1806, 30.5.1816.
[69] Diary, 4.5.1772, 29.9.1772, 3.3.1773, 2.12.1795, 15.9.1801, 14.6.1811.
[70] Diary, 22.12.1774, 6.8.1785, 6.3.1793, 11.12.1800, 31.7.1811, 12.12.1815, 22.7.1818.
[71] Diary, 2.10.1776, 21.10.1794, 11.11.1797, 13.10.1802, 14.12.1815,

daily use around the farm.[72] Tradesmen could command better pay rates than labourers, although there was a distinct hierarchy of trades. In the early nineteenth century, Mollet might typically pay a stonemason or a carpenter 3s per day,[73] a thatcher 2s 3d,[74] a cooper 2s,[75] and a basket-maker just 1s 9d.[76]

Mollet had a further source of labour aside from that for which he paid with cash. This was mutual aid, which was very much the order of the day among Guernsey's small farmers. Mollet co-operated to a greater or lesser degree with all of his neighbours,[77] but he also had a number of preferred partnerships. In the late eighteenth century, he often partnered with the Le Pelley family.[78] In the early nineteenth century, he partnered for almost two decades with Nicolas Breton of le Mont d'Aval.[79] Mollet and his partners regularly assisted one another with seaweed-gathering, ploughing, sowing, reaping, carting, and many other agricultural tasks. There was also an ongoing exchange of horses, oxen, carts, ploughs, and other equipment.[80] The journal shows that this was not done haphazardly. Mollet was scrupulous in noting when, how much, and by whom help had been given, and he always ensured that it was appropriately reciprocated.[81]

Charles Mollet, like most of his local contemporaries, practised mixed farming. He kept livestock, grew cereals and root crops, maintained orchards, cultivated soft fruit and table vegetables – but all on a limited scale. The primary object of all of this cannot really be said to have been commercial. Although Mollet did sell produce in the market and elsewhere, he does not seem to have produced systematically for the market. Rather, the first object

---

[72] Diary, 8.10.1774, 22.6.1798, 21.8.1802, 11.5.1810, 13.5.1812, 29.7.1817.
[73] Diary, Notes relating to 1810, 5.1.1818.
[74] Diary, 18.12.1815.
[75] Diary, 22.12.1815.
[76] Diary, 4.8.1817.
[77] Save, notably, his wealthy contemporaries the Guilles of St George and Le Marchants of la Haye du Puits.
[78] This family consisted of the widowed Susanne Le Pelley and her four sons, Jean (born 1753), Denis (1755), Nicolas (1757) and Thomas (1760). They initially all lived at Les Pelleys, a farm just up the road from Mollet's.
[79] According to the 1817 Relevé des Propriétaires du Castel (SG 23/43, Island Archives), Nicolas Breton (1763–1829) farmed 4 acres and owned a horse, an ox and five cows.
[80] The following diary entries contain a few examples of mutual aid, but it is no exaggeration to say that they occur on almost every second page of Mollet's diaries: 21.4.1795, 3.8.1785, 23.8.1792, 4.9.1797, 6.1.1800, 23.6.1800, 19.8.1806.
[81] See, for instance, Diary, 3.8.1785.

of his farming was self-sufficiency. In the next few paragraphs we will consider the main categories of Mollet's agricultural output in detail.

Livestock

The number of animals Mollet kept on his farm was modest, but he kept an interesting variety of them. Bees were the smallest living things which Mollet kept. There are references to hives and colonies in almost every decade.[82] He also kept pigeons. Their management is seldom mentioned, but now and again he gave away pigeons as gifts, and he periodically noted renewing their nesting boxes and cages.[83] Ducks and chickens were a permanent fixture in Mollet's farmyard (intermittently joined by geese, turkeys and peacocks). The ducks had their own shallow scrape and moveable pen, while the chickens enjoyed the amenity of a permanent coop. Every August or September, Mollet recorded taking batches of ducklings and pullets to feed on spilt grain in his fields after harvest.[84] At other times, he fed them barley grain complemented with table slops, brewers' draff, and even slugs and limpets.[85] Most of these birds and their eggs seem to have been consumed at Mollet's own table, since he rarely mentioned selling them at market.[86] On the few occasions when he did,[87] they were sold by his female servants, whose exclusive task it was to take all produce to market (save only red meat, which was restricted to male servants).

Mollet also seems to have kept dogs, though they not feature often in his journal. Large dogs, like the one named Keeper, may have been farm dogs.[88] The ones he referred to as Sappho and Volage were almost certainly pets.[89]

The only large quadrupeds kept by Mollet were horses, dairy cattle and pigs. Horses were used both as draught animals and personal transport. Mollet usually had two or three of them in his stables at any one time.

---

[82] Diary, 17.9.1774, 6.8.1777, 20.10.1795, 20.7.1799, 27.8.1799, 15.6.1807. There are, however, no mentions of honey or beeswax.
[83] Diary, 30.4.1775, 7.10.1776, 16.12.1776, 14.10.1811, 3.6.1817.
[84] Diary, 19.8.1797, 21.8.1797. One thing Mollet never mentioned was the post-harvest gleaning of grain by human beings.
[85] Diary, 11.5.1793, 28.5.1794, 15.12.1794, 9.2.1818.
[86] Mollet entertained extensively, as Chapter 7 will demonstrate.
[87] See, for instance, Diary, 22.2.1817, 27.6.1818.
[88] Diary, 17.3.1792.
[89] Diary, 24.6.1818.

Guernsey-bred horses were considered inferior as gentlemen's mounts, so Mollet preferred to source his saddle horses from Jersey, France or England.[90] Such horses were expensive. Their prices ranged from about £17 in the 1770s to as much as £42 in the early 1800s.[91] With this in mind, Mollet usually purchased mares from which he could breed. At intervals, he would pay for them to be serviced by his neighbours' stallions (about 5s a time in the early 1800s),[92] and either keep or sell the resulting foals. Draught horses were cheaper and more expendable than saddle horses. Mollet sourced them locally and often kept them for long periods of time. He purchased one such horse – Jack – from a neighbour for £8 8s in 1776 and used him to pull carts, ploughs and harrows for nearly twenty years, only having him put down in 1797, at the age of twenty-six.[93]

Oxen were also used as draught animals, and Mollet normally kept at least one of these for heavy work, such as deep-ploughing for parsnips and pulling seaweed-laden carts.[94] Like good horses, they were expensive to buy, especially when trained to the yoke. In 1809, Mollet recorded buying a three-year-old ox for £15.[95] Where he could, he would rear his own from the calves produced by his dairy cows, breaking them to the yoke when they were about two years old.

Mollet's cows were among his most valuable assets. He normally had a complement of five or six milking cows, which would be serviced yearly by bulls on neighbouring farms. They were not what are now known as 'Guernsey' cows, whose distinctive colour was only produced by selective breeding in the nineteenth century.[96] Mollet began systematically to note the colour of his cows in 1794, and they were of a variety of hues from brown, to black, to red and white. These, too, he normally reared from calves of his own. On the rare occasions when he bought a cow or a heifer, he could expect to pay a fairly high price. In 1777, he bought a six-year-old cow for the equivalent of about £11; in 1785, he bought an eighteen-month-old pregnant

---

[90] Diary, 25.10.1773, 27.10.1773, 14.7.1792, 12.5.1803.
[91] Diary, 25.10, 1773, 1.3.1812. Note that, in both instances, this was far more than a farm servant could have earned in a year.
[92] Diary, 13.5.1818.
[93] Diary, 10.9.1776, 25.1.1797.
[94] See Plate 22 for oxen pulling a cart.
[95] Diary, 5.4.1809.
[96] R. Hocart, *The Country People of Guernsey and their Agriculture, 1640–1840* (Guernsey, 2016), p. 109.

heifer for about £7 15s.[97] Most of Mollet's purchases were of local animals, but he once recorded buying a Jersey cow and twice recorded imports from Alderney.[98]

Not only did Mollet's cows provide his household with valuable dairy products, they also brought in welcome cash. As the travel writer Henry Inglis observed a few years after Mollet's death, 'on all properties and farms of tolerable size, the dairy is [...] the most profitable part of farming.'[99] This was essentially because of the butter, which always achieved a ready sale at market, and indeed was often the only product Mollet's servant had to sell.[100] Butter was not sold all the year round, as there was an annual gap of two months or so when milk was diverted to new-born calves. In July 1816, Mollet recorded that the farm had begun to sell butter again after just such a gap. Between January and May, they had sold 121½ lb, which had made them £11 9s 5d. At a selling price of 13d per pound, Mollet calculated that, if they sold a similar amount between July and December, butter would make the farm a total of £23 over the course of the year.[101]

Mollet's calves also brought in some income. Every year, he would sell two or three bull calves for veal. He generally kept them only between four and six weeks and had them slaughtered at the farm.[102] His farm servant would then take the carcases to town, where they would be weighed at the King's Weights for a small fee, professionally butchered for a further fee, and a separate 'market' fee paid on top. The farm servant would then stand in the marketplace and sell off the various cuts piecemeal. In 1796, Mollet recorded that the two calves sold at market that year had brought in a total of about £5 10s, with the joints selling for around 8d per pound, and the other parts (such as head and feet) for lesser prices.[103]

From time to time, Mollet would also sell adult cows for meat, usually because they were dry, old, or even suffering from sickness. In these cases, he would sell the animal direct to a butcher. In 1787, butcher Robin Johnceline

---

[97] Diary, 7.4.1777, 25.8.1785.
[98] Diary, 27.8.1776, 7.11.1793, 1.10.1794.
[99] H.D. Inglis, *The Channel Islands*, 2 vols (London, 1834) 2, p. 77.
[100] Diary, 28.10.1809, 18.1.1817, 27.12.1817.
[101] Diary, 13.7.1816. This was significantly more than the female servant who sold the butter could herself expect to earn over twelve months.
[102] The slaughtering (as all slaughtering) was done by a local specialist, not one of Mollet's own men.
[103] Diary, Notes relating to 1796.

bought a sixteen-year-old cow from Mollet for £9.[104] In 1811, Mollet sold a four-year-old sick cow to butcher Mrs Lye for around the same amount.[105] On these occasions, Mollet would usually retain the offal (liver, kidneys, tripe, sweetbreads, etc.) for himself. From time to time also, Mollet would fatten and sell an ox. Oxen could achieve weights in excess of 1,000 lb and were also sold directly to butchers. In 1805, Mollet sold a nine-year-old ox weighing 1,221 lb to butchers Gardner and Hannam. They paid him more than £36 for it, and he retained all the offal.[106]

Now and again, Mollet would sell live cattle too. A bargain might be privately struck with a neighbour, or an animal might be taken to the livestock fair which was held every quarter about a mile from Mollet's farm.[107] Here, it was both female and male servants' job to sell the animal, having previously been instructed not to go below a certain price. Very often they came back having failed to make a sale owing to this stricture. Sales they did make included a four-year-old black bullock for £12 10s at Michaelmas 1799, and a three-year-old red bullock for £15 at Easter 1801.[108]

Between 1795 and 1815, Mollet also recorded the sale of five live cattle for export.[109] Four of these beasts were destined for England. The best price Mollet achieved for a cow heading north was 18 guineas, paid by a ship's captain from Newcastle in 1812.[110] The best price Mollet made on any of his exported animals was 20 guineas, paid by Thomas De Sausmarez for a cow to provide fresh milk on a sea voyage to India in 1810.[111]

Commensurate with their value, Mollet and his employees treated their cattle with considerable care. In the colder months, the beasts would generally be kept indoors and fed on hay leavened with a few parsnips and the occasional outing to graze. The months between early spring and late autumn were spent out in the fields, on pastures of grass (or sometimes lucerne or clover). Adult cows were usually tethered in these cases, both for ease of milking and to make best use of scant land.[112] After harvest-time, Mollet

---

[104] Diary, 30.3.1787.
[105] Diary, 12.8.1811, 13.8.1811.
[106] Diary, 19.12.1805.
[107] This was Guernsey's only livestock fair. It was held at the crossroads in front of the Castel parish church until 1803, when a nearby field was purchased to host it instead.
[108] Diary, 26.9.1799, 7.4.1801.
[109] Diary, 22.10.1795, 23.1.1810, 25.3.1812, 17.10.1815, 25.9.1817.
[110] Diary, 25.3.1812.
[111] Diary, 23.1.1810.
[112] Diary, 3.10.1815, 4.5.1818.

would let younger beasts loose in his furzebrakes and cereal fields, where they grazed on the after-grass and sometimes a few late oats sown specifically for their benefit.[113]

Cattle which suffered accidents or had difficulty calving were conscientiously attended to. Local cattle doctors, Nicolas Du Four of the Forest and Jean Duquemin of St Saviours, would be sent for in the most serious cases.[114] Mollet's servants, male and female, would stay up all night, or even several nights, with a distressed animal.[115] When a one-year-old bullock became stuck in a pond in 1816, a dozen men, women and children from the neighbourhood came together to pull him out and bring him home.[116]

Pigs were no less vital than cows to Charles Mollet – as indeed they were to all of his local contemporaries. According to the 1817 agricultural census of the Castel parish, 87 per cent of households owned at least one pig. Mollet himself had six pigs; his wealthy neighbours the Guilles of St George had five; and Admiral Lord James Saumarez, who also lived in the Castel parish, had nine pigs.[117] Pigs were important not for commercial reasons, but because they were central to a household's food economy. This was because pig meat formed the basis of ordinary people's daily diet, which consisted largely of soups or stews enhanced with small amounts of salt pork.[118]

Initially, Mollet kept only the local breed of pig, but from 1803, he began to breed from some 'Chinese' sows which had been given to him.[119] Every autumn or winter, he would have two sows serviced on neighbouring farms, the piglets from which would be born in the spring. Generally Mollet would keep two female and five or six male piglets, sell one or two piglets to his neighbours, and either eat or give the rest away to friends.[120] Once weaned, the piglets Mollet had retained would be kept over the summer in one of his furzebrakes. In the autumn, he would bring them into the sties and fatten them up on parsnips. The parsnips would be served raw at first and then

---

[113] Diary, 9.11.1798, 3.10.1815.
[114] Diary, 15.3.1806, 9.6.1809.
[115] Diary, 22.3.1806, 21.4.1818.
[116] Diary, 20.12.1816.
[117] Relevé des Propriétaires du Castel, May 1817 (SG 23/43, Island Archives).
[118] L.L. Clarke, *Redstone's Guernsey & Jersey Guide* (1841; Guernsey, 1843 edn), pp. 67–8.
[119] Diary, 12.1.1806. John Jacob wrote a few years later that the admixture of Chinese and English breeds had 'much improved' the local stock of pigs (Jacob, *Annals*, p. 177).
[120] The parish Rector was also entitled to a share of the progeny as tithe (see, for instance, Diary, 20.2.1809).

cooked as the pigs tired of the raw ones.[121] Early the following year, when the parsnips ran out, Mollet would have all his pigs (save the two young sows selected for breeding) slaughtered on the farm. The resulting carcases (scraped, eviscerated and halved lengthwise) were then thoroughly salted on Mollet's dedicated salting bench. Kept on a rack over the kitchen hearth, the preserved carcases would typically furnish Mollet's servants and labourers with an annual supply of salt pork in excess of 1,000 lb.[122]

In keeping with the fact that pigs were primarily for domestic use, Mollet recorded only seven occasions when he sent a pig to be sold at market.[123] Like the calves he sent to town, these were professionally butchered, and, in the early nineteenth century, the cuts typically fetched between 5d and 9d per pound, which was roughly the same as his veal.

Cereals

Respondents to Guernsey's early nineteenth-century agricultural census were asked to provide information on the area they devoted to cereals. The return for the Castel parish showed that Charles Mollet had cereals on about five of his 26⅓ acres in 1817.[124] The area he devoted to grain crops varied over time, but it was never very extensive. Generally speaking, the existence of tithes and *champart* in Guernsey (by which every eleventh sheaf went as tithe, and every twelfth as *champart*) meant that, by the eighteenth century, grain was normally grown only for domestic use and paying *rentes*.[125] That said, Mollet in particular was enabled to reduce his grain-growing by virtue of the very fact that, for many years, he was a tithe-collector himself. Between 1773 and 1787, and again between 1800 and 1818, Mollet sub-contracted with the

---

[121] Diary, 5.11.1806, 25.9.1816.

[122] Diary, 14.2.1817.

[123] Diary, 18.3.1808, 26.11.1808, 31.12.1808, 29.12.1809, 16.12.1815, 11.1.1817, 27.2.1818.

[124] Relevé des Propriétaires du Castel, May 1817 (SG 23/43, Island Archives).

[125] *Champart* was a seigneurial due owed to individual fiefs. The tithe was originally an ecclesiastical due, but passed to the Crown in the fifteenth century. In the 70 per cent of land which was in Crown fiefs, the collections were united and leased out by HM Receiver to parochial tithe-farmers (Hocart, *Country People*, pp. 28, 117). For *rentes*, see Chapter 2, n. 10.

tithe-farmers of the Castel parish to collect the tithe from certain districts.[126] In this way, he was able to supplement his home-grown cereals with tithe grain for a total of thirty-four years.[127]

On his five or six acres of grain-producing land Mollet grew a combination of wheat, barley and oats (the latter to an increasing extent as time went on). Oats were principally used to feed livestock; barley was used to make bread for Mollet's servants and labourers;[128] wheat was used to pay Mollet's *rentes* and make the white loaves and pastries eaten by Mollet and his guests. Mollet did not trade in cereals commercially, although he did sell the odd bushel to his workmen, friends, neighbours and family members.[129] While serving on the Board of the Country Hospital between 1771 and 1781, he also sold small amounts to that institution.[130]

Mollet sowed his wheat in December or January; his oats in March or April; and his barley in April or May. Mixed in with his barley and oats (following the traditional practice in Guernsey), he usually sowed some other seed. In 1777, for example, he mixed the barley he was sowing in eleven strips at le Courtil Robin with clover in six of the strips, turnip in three, and kale and cabbage in the remaining two.[131] In 1817, he sowed cabbage and turnip along with his barley at la Sencière, and clover along with his oats.[132]

Based on a brief local residence in 1812, Thomas Quayle described a five-year cereal-based rotation which he said Guernsey farmers practised 'with few exceptions': first year wheat; second year barley and clover; third year clover; fourth year wheat: fifth year parsnips.[133] Mollet, though he did practise a form

---

[126] Diary, 7.1.1773, 26.8.1800, 11.3.1818. The parish was divided into seven districts (known as *quêtes*) for the purpose of tithe collection: les Grantez, les Vallées, le Villocq, les Houmets, le Nanage, les Hougues, le Grand Fil. Mollet's involvement, at various times, encompassed the last three.

[127] *Rentes* received in kind would also have supplemented Mollet's own produce, though to a lesser extent.

[128] For the customary consumption of barley bread by Guernsey's lower ranks, see T. Dicey, *An Historical Account of Guernsey* (London, 1751), p. 23.

[129] Such sales were usually recorded on the pages Mollet left blank between the end of December one year and the start of January the next. When selling these commodities to workmen, Mollet seems to have deducted the payments from their wages.

[130] Mollet's largest-ever cereal sale to the Hospital was 5 quarters and 1 bushel of barley in 1779 (Diary, Notes relating to 1779).

[131] Diary, 13.5.1777.

[132] Diary, 28.4.1817.

[133] Quayle, *General View*, pp. 255–6.

of rotation, was not so systematic. In 1817, for instance, he recorded preceding barley with peas, oats with potatoes, and peas with wheat.[134]

Mollet usually began harvesting cereals in mid-August and was finished by the end of September. Barley was generally pulled up by the roots and wheat cut with a scythe, although the journals contain examples of the reverse.[135] The rationale for pulling up barley in this way was that more of the straw was preserved, as also that the soil disturbance benefited the co-plantings of clover, turnips, etc. Quayle however observed that it made the flour gritty.[136] As noted above, Mollet never mentioned post-harvest gleaning, though he did take poultry to scratch among the stubble.

The harvested sheaves of wheat, barley and oats were stored in stacks in Mollet's stackyard. Threshing and winnowing were done at intervals throughout the autumn and winter. Winnowed grain was taken to one of several local watermills to be ground into flour.[137] In years when he had a surplus, Mollet would put wheat grain into his lime-pit for long-term storage.[138] In years when his own supply ran short, Mollet would purchase additional stocks on the open market.[139] In years of poor harvests and high prices, Mollet would occasionally buy rice for grinding and mixing with barley flour to make his household's daily bread.[140]

Other field crops

Aside from cereals, the other main field crops grown by Mollet were, in order of importance, parsnips, potatoes, brassicas and peas. Parsnips are thought to have been grown in Guernsey from the mid-seventeenth century.[141] They were not grown for table use, but as animal fodder. Each year Mollet sowed

---

[134] Diary, 3.2.1817, 12.3.1817, 28.3.1817, 4.3.1818.
[135] There are many examples of barley being reaped with a scythe. It was less usual for wheat to be pulled out by the roots, but it did happen from time to time (see, for instance, Diary, 12.8.1785).
[136] Quayle, *General View*, pp. 257–8.
[137] Mollet noted in 1777 that he owned three miller's sacks, all marked 'C.M.L.' (Diary, Notes relating to 1777).
[138] Diary, 7.12.1771, 10.12.1777, 13.12.1815, 8.1.1817.
[139] Diary, 13.1.1771, 8.7.1773, 23.11.1780, 2.6.1801, 7.2.1807.
[140] There are examples of such purchases in 1810, 1811, 1816 and 1818. Mollet recorded their purpose in his Notes for 1811.
[141] Hocart, *Country People*, p. 91.

two or three acres of parsnips for his pigs, cattle and horses. Parsnip cultivation was very labour-intensive, and this use of the root was only economic because labour was so cheap. In his early years, Mollet had all stages of cultivation done manually: preparation of the soil by deep digging; broadcast sowing; three rounds of weeding on hand and knee; lifting from September onwards. In 1786, 1798 and 1805 Mollet experimented with ploughing rather than digging.[142] Ploughing for parsnips required the use of a special plough, which is believed to have been introduced to Guernsey in the 1750s or 1760s.[143] This plough was unusually large and heavy, and needed up to four oxen and eight horses to draw it, and nine or ten men to control them and direct the plough.[144] As a result, Mollet had to borrow animals, workers and, at first, the plough itself from neighbouring farms. After 1805, Mollet went over exclusively to ploughing for parsnips and acquired a large plough of his own. Sowing, weeding and lifting continued to be performed manually. Mollet never recorded selling any parsnips, but he frequently purchased parsnips from other farmers, usually buying them by the perch while they were still growing, and having them lifted by his own men.[145]

In the late summer, Mollet often sowed turnips in ground from which earlier crops had been harvested, and he supplemented his parsnips with these in the winter diet of his livestock. From his earliest years as a farmer, he also used potatoes for this purpose.[146] In his first two decades, Mollet grew mainly what he termed *cosnu* potatoes. This variety has not been traced, but the tubers seem chiefly to have been used to feed animals. As time went on, potatoes became more popular as a human food, and from the 1790s, Mollet introduced more table varieties – round red potatoes, early Irish whites, kidney potatoes, Scillonian potatoes. He mainly sold these to private customers such as friends and family members, but latterly also took some to market: in 1816, for instance, his servant Elizabeth Machon sold a bushel of new potatoes at the market for 10d per denerel.[147] On a single occasion towards the end of his life, Mollet even sold potatoes for export. In 1817, he

---

[142] Diary, 30.1.1786, 8.2.1798, Notes relating to 1805.
[143] Carey (ed.), *Guernsey Folk Lore*, p. 40.
[144] Quayle, *General View*, pp. 259–60; Jacob, *Annals*, pp. 179–80, 183.
[145] There are many examples of such purchases, but see Diary, 24.11.1796, 15.10.1799. The Guernsey perch was equivalent to 49 square yards.
[146] Potatoes had been grown in Guernsey for about forty years by the time Mollet inherited his farm (Hocart, *Country People*, p. 93).
[147] Diary, 6.7.1816.

recorded that Elizabeth Machon had arranged the sale to Messrs La Serre and Co. of 60 bushels for export at 2s per bushel. This represented some 3,600 lb of potatoes and made Mollet £6.[148]

The main brassica crops Mollet grew in his fields were cabbages and kale.[149] He also grew what he called *broccolis*, by which he may sometimes have meant cauliflowers.[150] Mollet frequently bought these brassicas in the form of seedlings, which his men pricked out in large numbers from spring to autumn (1,000 seedlings in May 1786, for instance).[151] Such large numbers seem to indicate a commercial intention, but brassica were mainly for household use. Only on one occasion did Mollet mention taking cabbages to market.[152] In an era without chemical pesticides, the large numbers probably signal an expectation of spoilage. Sometimes he recorded giving over-mature cabbages away.[153]

Thomas Quayle asserted in the early nineteenth century that peas were only grown in small quantities in Guernsey, and never 'as an article of culture apart'.[154] Mollet's journal seems to belie this statement, as he regularly grew field crops of peas. These were for drying, rather than eating green, and were usually sown in the early spring.[155] They were left in the ground until the end of the summer, then pulled up and bundled when dry. The bundles were brought into the barn and threshed in the same way as cereals (indeed, Mollet and his contemporaries always thought of peas as another type of corn). Again, these peas were essentially for household use, but Mollet now and then sold small amounts to friends and relatives.[156]

---

[148] Diary, 15.3.1817, 17.3.1817.
[149] Mollet always distinguished between *choux* and *caboches*. In his *Dictionnaire Franco-Normand* George Metivier defined the *guernésiais* term *chaou* as a loose-leaved cabbage, and *caboche* as a cabbage with a tight head (G. Metivier, *Dictionnaire Franco-Normand ou Recueil des Mots particuliers au Dialecte de Guernesey* (London, 1870), pp. 97, 122). Following Metivier, I have translated *choux* as kale and *caboches* as cabbages.
[150] In her dictionary, Marie De Garis gives *broccôlu* as a translation of cauliflower (M. De Garis, *Dictiounnaire Angllais-Guernesiais* (1967; Chichester, 1982 edn), p. 25). In the first years of his diary, Mollet occasionally referred to *choux-fleurs*, but after 1795, there are only two references to these, and very many to *broccolis*.
[151] Diary, 8.5.1786.
[152] Diary, 30.5.1812.
[153] Diary, 30.5.1812.
[154] Quayle, *General View*, p. 259.
[155] Diary, 22.2.1771, 17.3.1786, 20.3.1799, 8.3.1806, 23.3.1809, 22.3.1816, 28.3.1817.
[156] In 1807, Mollet also sold 2 quarters of peas to the Town Hospital (Diary, 3.10.1807).

Orchards and cider

Richard Hocart has estimated that orchards covered about 4 acres of Charles Mollet's land.[157] Mollet usually referred to them as *jardins* or gardens. This was because the normal designation for an orchard in Guernsey was *jardin à pommes* (and it was by no means inapt, since most Guernsey orchards contained garden crops under the trees). Some of Mollet's *jardins* were devoted exclusively to cider apples. Others held a variety of dessert apples and pears, typically Pippin, Russet and Nonpareil apples, and Chaumontel, Swan Egg and Rousselet pears.[158] Mollet's pears, especially his Chaumontels (some of which weighed as much as ¾ lb individually), were popular as gifts, and each year Mollet gave away large numbers of them.[159] Mollet would also sell early-maturing fruit at the market, where they fetched premium prices. In 1798, Mollet recorded having made nearly £2 between 24 July and 11 August from sales of New York Early Pippins. Interestingly, he noted that this was his 'most profitable' early apple harvest yet.[160] His remaining eating apples and pears were carefully put into store at the farm, where they were used piecemeal throughout the long winter.

The largest proportion of Mollet's orchards was, however, dedicated to cider apples. Cider was his household's common beverage, so Mollet needed to be self-sufficient in it.[161] His cider apples were gathered over a period of weeks in October and November, usually by local children, in several 'sweeps'. In the autumn of 1804, Charles Mollet recorded having paid six children the equivalent of about 5d a day for working sixty-two man-days gathering cider apples.[162] The annual amount gathered was immensely

---

[157] Hocart, *Country People*, p. 102.

[158] More than seventy named apple and pear varieties grown by Mollet are listed in Appendix 9. He also grew plums, cherries, medlars and quinces in his orchards.

[159] Chaumontel pears were a Norman variety which grew well in Guernsey. For a specimen weighing ¾ lb, see Diary, 28.9.1798.

[160] Diary, Notes relating to 1798.

[161] Richard Hocart notes that cider had superseded locally brewed beer as islanders' daily drink in the late seventeenth or early eighteenth century, as the Royal Court encouraged local cider production in order to limit the outflow of French coins as payment for imported French cider (Hocart, *Country People*, pp. 123, 144–5).

[162] Diary, Notes relating to 1804. A tithe on these apples was payable to the parish Rector.

variable. In a good year, Mollet might gather sufficient to make seventy or eighty barrels of cider; in a poor year, he had only enough for three or four.[163]

The apples were pressed between November and March. Like all Guernsey farms of any size, Mollet's had its own stone apple-crusher as well as a cider press, which was accommodated in an outbuilding Mollet called his *pressoir*.[164] As his main purpose was to provide his household with cider, he generally only sold what he had to spare. His sales varied from a maximum of thirty-seven barrels in 1771 to just one barrel in 1817.[165] In the short term, the selling price of a barrel of cider depended on the supply available locally in any one year. In the long term, it seems to have followed a generally rising trend. At the start of Mollet's farming career in the 1770s, a barrel might sell for the equivalent of 13s–15s stg. By the end of his career, prices had risen to 35s–40s. A peak was reached in 1815, when Mollet managed to sell six barrels to a local blacksmith for 45s each.[166] Most of Mollet's sales were local, but he sometimes sent a few barrels to contacts in Alderney and Jersey, and – on four occasions – he exported small quantities to England.[167]

Like other Guernsey farmers, Mollet managed all his fruit trees proactively. There are constant references to grafting in his diaries, usually carried out by his workmen Eleazar Ingrouille and Etienne Lihou, who seem to have been specialists in grafting.[168] Grafted trees which were surplus to Mollet's requirements were often sold.[169] Mollet also experimented with new

---

[163] For good years, see Diary, 18.4.1785, 14.2.1795. For poor years, see Diary, 24.10, 1809, 4.11.1815. A Guernsey barrel (*barrique*) held 55 gallons.
[164] For the equipment and processes involved in cider-making, see T.F. Priaulx, 'Cider-making', *Transactions of la Société Guernesiaise*, 15 (1953), pp. 286–292. For a photograph of what was probably the very apple-crusher used by Mollet, see Plate 20.
[165] Notes relating to cider sales 1771–3 (at the back of the first volume of Mollet's diary); Notes relating to 1817.
[166] Diary, 21.8.1815.
[167] For Alderney, see Diary, 17.2.1785; for Jersey, 5.9.1794; for England 11.6.1798. Exports to England were invariably initiated by third parties, rather than Mollet himself. The export (of four barrels) which took place in 1798 was, for instance, organised by a Captain Deschamps, who provided the barrels himself.
[168] Grafting is a way of propagating new fruit trees using buds or twigs ('scions'). A scion from an existing tree is fused on to a branch or stem of another tree (the 'rootstock') by cutting and binding. The fruit produced by the scion will be the same as that on the tree from which the scion was taken.
[169] In the file of Mollet Correspondence and Memoranda at the Priaulx Library are fragmentary accounts showing that, in 1795, he sold a total of 63 grafted trees at prices varying between 1s and 1s 6d.

apple and pear varieties of his own by sowing pips in nursery beds and raising the resulting seedlings.[170] If he liked the fruit they produced, he would give them a name.[171] If not, he used them as rootstock.

Soft fruit and table vegetables

Mollet grew a profusion of soft fruit, table vegetables and herbs in orchards and other gardens around his house. As regarded soft fruit, strawberries and raspberries were his mainstays but he also grew whitecurrants, redcurrants, gooseberries and, for a time, melons (on hotbeds and under frames). In addition to these, he recorded the cultivation of twenty-three different kinds of table vegetable: asparagus, broad beans, carrots, celeriac, celery, chickpeas, chicory, colocynths,[172] cress, cucumbers, French beans, globe artichokes, green peas, Jerusalem artichokes, leeks, lettuce, onions, pimientos, radishes, salsify, scarlet beans, scorzonera, shallots, and squash. The range of culinary herbs Mollet grew was more limited, but among those he mentioned were chervil, coriander, dill, mint, peppermint and thyme. In an era without pesticides, companion planting was standard practice: chrysanthemums grew between rows of asparagus, and annual flowers among lettuces.[173]

Mollet consumed much of his garden produce at his own table, as well as in gifts for friends. A proportion was, however, sold at market. The first strawberries and fresh peas of the season usually fetched a good price.[174] Asparagus, artichokes and lettuces also appear to have sold well.[175] Later in the summer, Mollet recorded sales of raspberries, gooseberries and redcurrants.[176]

---

[170] Apples and pears do not reproduce true to type, meaning that the tree grown from seed will produce fruit almost certain to be different from the apple or pear from which it came – a new variety that is a hybrid of the parent tree and some unknown other tree.
[171] Some of Mollet's own named varieties of apple and pear are recorded in Appendix 9.
[172] A climbing plant of the gourd family bearing pulpy fruit.
[173] Diary, 31.3.1772, 1.9.1775.
[174] Diary, 10.6.1797, 6.6.1798, 29.6.1799. In the late eighteenth century, early strawberries typically sold for about 5d per pound and green peas for 7½d per pint.
[175] In his Notes for 1799, Mollet noted that he had made nearly 25s on asparagus sold in the market between 4 May and 22 June.
[176] Diary, 16.7.1808, 8.7.1809, 27.7.1816.

Non-food crops

Mollet's principal non-food crops were grass, clover, lucerne and, in certain years, vetch.[177] These were primarily for grazing, but Mollet also made hay to use as winter fodder. Hay-cutting usually began in mid-June and finished in mid-July. Mollet's men tended the hay daily as it dried in the field, cocking it whenever rain threatened. When it was ready for carting, it was raked into rows and pitched into a low-sided cart. A full load might be as much as ten feet high. This hay was then either stacked in the stackyard or stored in Mollet's hay-lofts. In 1806, an average year for hay, Mollet noted that his men had cut eighteen large cartloads (including 6½ of lucerne hay).[178] At 14 or 15 hundredweight per cartload, this equated to a total hay harvest of approximately 13½ imperial tons.[179] In 1811, which seems to have been an exceptionally good year, Mollet reported harvesting 20 tons.[180]

Like his cider, Mollet needed his hay for his own purposes and only sold it when he had a surplus. His prices varied between 4s and 4s 6d per hundredweight.[181] In low-yielding years, Mollet sometimes ran out of hay at the tail-end of winter, and was then obliged to buy in supplies from his neighbours.[182]

Charles Mollet also maintained a large range of woodland trees on his farm. As well as serving as shelter belts and hedging, these trees were harvested for timber, firing and thatching. Every year, Mollet would lop some of his trees to obtain a supply of logs, faggots and spar gads.[183] Occasionally, he would fell a mature tree, which would be de-barked, squared off and sawn into planks for future use in building and carpentry projects. He also sold mature trees for shipbuilding. These were invariably large elms which buyers had to fell and process themselves. His main customers were the ship carpenters Alexander Thom, Laurence Vaudin and Barry Le Patourel. Mollet

---

[177] Mollet only recorded growing vetch in eight years (1774, 1777, 1780, 1787, 1804, 1811, 1812 and 1816).
[178] Diary, 5.8.1806. Lucerne was usually cut two or three times in the course of a summer.
[179] The weight of a large cartload is given in Diary, 24.7.1816.
[180] Diary, 20.7.1811.
[181] Notes relating to 1795; Diary, 13.3.1795, 17.4.1796.
[182] Diary, 15.2.1776, 4.4.1777.
[183] Spar gads were fashioned from thin, flexible branches. They were used for pinning down thatch.

sold this timber by length, at prices which gradually increased from 1s 2d per foot in the 1770s to 3s per foot thirty years later.[184]

Mollet maintained and expanded his stock of trees by raising seedlings in a number of nurseries and plantations. At various times he mentioned growing alder, ash, beech, blackthorn, birch, chestnut, cypress, elm, hawthorn, holly, hornbeam, lime, oak, pine, plane, poplar, rowan, sycamore, willow and yew. Mollet sourced some of his young trees from outside the island, such as the 300 birch, beech and hornbeam saplings he imported from Normandy in 1792.[185] More often, however, he would laboriously grow his own from acorns, beech mast, chestnuts, haws, sloes, sycamore keys, etc. Like his fruit trees, he regularly sold young broadleaf trees to neighbours and friends.[186]

In addition to these broadleaf trees, Mollet had several plantations of osier, a low-growing willow whose stems (known as withies) were used in basket-making and cooperage.[187] Mollet had the withies cut every December or January when the plants were dormant. He stored a proportion of them for renewing his own baskets and panniers, but, prior to the Anti-Smuggling Acts of 1805 and 1807, he also sold several hundred bundles each year to town-based coopers. At prices rising from about 5d per bundle in the 1770s to 12d per bundle in the early 1800s, Mollet's annual takings from osier seem to have peaked at around £12 in 1802.[188] As the Anti-Smuggling Acts took effect, however, sales began to drop off. By the end of his career, Mollet was chiefly disposing of his withies to a crabpot-maker and neighbouring farmer.[189]

Charles Mollet also grew hemp, which he had cut, pounded and dried every August. Mollet sometimes gave his hemp away, but he never recorded selling any. It was chiefly made into twine for use around the farm, in particular for binding grafts.[190]

---

[184] Diary, 26.7.1779, 5.3.1792, 4.11.1794, 14.10.1810, 11.9.1811, 29.2.1812.
[185] Diary, 3.3.1792.
[186] See, for instance, Diary, Notes relating to 1796.
[187] Coopers used split withies to fasten together the ends of the wooden hoops holding barrel staves in place.
[188] Mollet systematically recorded his osier sales between 1794 and 1802 at the beginning of volume 4 of his journal.
[189] Diary, 24.1.1817. See also Notes relating to 1817.
[190] Diary, 19.8.1816.

The 1817 agricultural census showed that 2 acres of Mollet's farm were covered by furzebrakes (*jaonnières*).[191] These were not mere wasted space, as furze (otherwise known as gorse) was an essential commodity in eighteenth-century Guernsey. It was chiefly used for pre-heating bread ovens. Mollet had his furze cut and bundled every autumn, left it to season over the winter and stacked it or stored it in the spring. He seems to have harvested between 400 and 500 bundles each year.[192] Most of this furze was consumed in his own ovens, though his diaries record occasional sales to workmen, neighbours and – in later years – to town-based friends and relatives. The price of 100 bundles ranged from about 14s 4d in the late eighteenth century to 25s in 1818.[193]

The bracken which grew on Mollet's earthbanks was also cut and bundled annually. This was a task performed every autumn by women and children and typically yielded around 200 to 250 bundles.[194] Dry bracken was used as animal bedding; as a covering for hay- and corn-stacks; and as a filling for *jonquières*, a crude sort of couch which almost all rural parishioners had in their kitchens.[195] In the last decade of his life, Mollet often supplied friends and relatives in town with bundles of bracken. However, he omitted to record the price he was charging (if any).

Finally, we should mention the shrubs, ornamental trees, annual and perennial flowers which were Mollet's personal passion. These he usually took care of these himself, using pots, cloches, cold frames and – not least – his greenhouse. It is interesting that, although Mollet's brother-in-law Peter Mourant is usually credited with introducing greenhouses to Guernsey, Mollet frequently mentioned his own *serre* or *orangerie* from the mid-1770s onwards. This structure, which seems to have been contiguous with his house, had a thatched roof until 1806, when the thatch was replaced with tiles.[196]

---

[191] SG 23/43, Island Archives.
[192] Diary, Notes relating to 1793, 11.4.1811.
[193] Diary, Notes relating to 1792, 26.5.1818. In the entrepôt era, furze was also in demand for breaming the hulls of vessels, but Mollet did not record selling any for this purpose.
[194] Diary, 11.9.1806, 4.10.1810, 21.9.1815, 28.9.1815.
[195] This consisted of an oblong wooden base on legs containing a thick layer of bracken (and other dry vegetation) covered with some sort of fabric (Carey (ed.), *Guernsey Folk Lore*, p. 216).
[196] Diary, 20.7.1774, 2.11.1774, 1.9.1780, 24.11.1786, 29.11.1787, 30.8.1806, 1.9.1806, 4.9.1806.

For filling his hotbeds, Mollet made his own compost.[197] For filling his plant-pots, he used both compost and a special sandy soil obtained from the garden of an acquaintance who lived near the coast. Mollet recorded fetching this light soil by the cartload, in exchange for cartloads of heavier soil from his own property.[198]

Mollet recorded growing more than fifty different types of annual and perennial flowers in his beds and borders, ranging from narcissi and tulips in the spring, to dahlias in the summer and chrysanthemums in the autumn. His ornamental shrubs and trees formed a constantly expanding backdrop to his flowers. These included camellias, fuchsias, laburnums, lilacs, magnolias, myrtles, rhododendrons, and much besides.

Mollet was always actively adding to his ornamental collection. He had contacts with nurseries in England and Holland from which he regularly obtained seed, bulbs and young plants.[199] When he travelled, he made a point of visiting botanical gardens and nurseries and usually made a number of purchases.[200] Many of Mollet's peers were equally interested in ornamental flowers and shrubs, so that seeds, bulbs, cuttings and offsets were widely given and exchanged.

Mollet also had a special sideline in Guernsey lilies (*nerine sarniensis*). These bulbiferous flowering plants are native to South Africa but were introduced to Guernsey in the 1660s, long before they made their way to Great Britain. For a time in the seventeenth and eighteenth centuries, Guernsey was the sole source of exports to the United Kingdom.[201] Charles Mollet planted several large beds of Guernsey lilies in 1773 and continued adding to them over ensuing years.[202] Every autumn, he sent twenty or thirty boxes of bulbs across the Channel. Some of these were undoubtedly intended as gifts. However, it seems likely that Mollet sold at least a proportion of them for money. The only record of a price came in 1809 when he mentioned

---

[197] Diary, 30.3.1786, 23.4.1801, 6.5.1817.
[198] Diary, 26.3.1804.
[199] In the early years, Williamsons in England were frequent suppliers (Diary, 13.8.1771, 29.11.1771). The name of Mollet's Dutch contacts is elusive, but he regularly mentioned 'florists' in Haarlem (Diary, 3.8.1793, 11.10.1797).
[200] On a visit to Caen in 1790, he purchased several new specimens from le Jardin des Plantes (Diary, 2.10.1790).
[201] A.H. Ewen and A.R. De Carteret, 'The Guernsey lily', *Transactions of la Société Guernesiaise*, 19 (1973), pp. 269, 285; Quayle, *General View*, p. 271.
[202] Diary, 7.9.1773.

selling 14 dozen bulbs to a sea captain's wife for 3s per dozen.[203] Mollet also appears to have sold cut flowers. He never recorded taking any to market, but in 1808 and 1809, he did make references to cash earned from such sales.[204]

Conclusion

Charles Mollet's crops and farming methods changed little over the five decades of his journal. In this, he perhaps merited William Berry's criticism of local farmers for being 'too bigoted in long-rooted principles to think improvement possible'.[205] A modern reader, on the other hand, might admire the sustainability of his farming. Mollet's inputs were all natural and renewable, and nothing was ever wasted. Through all of this, his primary aim seems to have been self-sufficiency – in food for his household, fodder for his livestock, fuel for his fire, and materials for making equipment and maintaining buildings. It was only when such primary needs were met that Charles Mollet sold anything for money. Mollet almost certainly kept accounts, but he kept them separately from his diaries and they have not survived. It is therefore impossible to tell exactly how much money he did make from farming. The crucial point to bear in mind is that Mollet possessed a variety of other financial assets, which lessened his need to make money from agriculture. In the next chapter we will look more closely at Mollet's non-agricultural resources and activities.

---

[203] Diary, 14.9.1809.
[204] Diary, 5.9.1808, 1.4.1809.
[205] Berry, *Island of Guernsey*, p. 284.

4

Economic Life, Part 2: Investments and Enterprises

Investments

Wheat *rentes*, many of them inherited, featured prominently among Mollet's resources.[1] Evidence from his journals and Guernsey's Greffe shows that, at various points between 1771 and 1819, Mollet was owed *rentes* by at least forty-one people. These were nominally payable in October each year, either in kind or in cash.[2] As far as it is possible to tell, the highest-value *rente* owned by Charles Mollet was one of 3 quarters and 2 bushels, which in 1810 would have brought Mollet a return of £6.[3] The lowest-value *rente* owned by Mollet was one of just half a bushel. Daniel Trachy owed Mollet this *rente*, and in 1818 paid him 10s 6d for three years.[4] Those who owed such small *rentes* did not usually trouble to pay them each year, and ensuring their eventual payment often required action on the part of the owner. In January 1787, Mollet recorded calling on several individuals in the upper parishes to request payment of *rentes* which had been due the previous October.[5] In some instances, recourse to the Royal Court was required. In the autumn of 1787, Mollet initiated an action against Jean Falle for payment of seven years' arrears of his *rente* of 6 bushels.[6] For some reason, the action did not produce the desired result, and by 1794, Falle owed Mollet fourteen years of arrears amounting to more than 250 *livres tournois* (about £18). Only in September 1795 did Mollet note that Falle had finally paid off the arrears.[7]

---

[1] For *rentes*, see Chapter 2, n. 10.
[2] At a rate set annually by the Royal Court based on the average sale price of wheat the previous year.
[3] This *rente* was owed to Mollet by an individual named Pierre Le Ray (Diary, 14.10.1810).
[4] Diary, 22.2.1818.
[5] Diary, 28.1.1787.
[6] Diary, 19.11.1787.
[7] Diary, 26.9.1795.

Mollet himself owed *rentes* to at least thirty people at various points, some of which had resulted from property purchases he himself made in the 1770s and 1780s. The value of the *rentes* Mollet owed to others appears on average to have been higher than the value of those which others owed him. He owed the Le Pelley brothers a *rente* of more than 13 quarters, for instance, and he owed his wealthy neighbour Jean Guille of St George a *rente* of 22 quarters.[8] At 24 *livres tournois* per quarter in 1810, a *rente* of 22 quarters required Mollet to pay Guille (whom he always paid in cash) about £37.

Mollet recorded purchasing twelve new *rentes* in the five decades between 1771 and 1818. Significantly, nine of these were *rentes* he himself owed to others, and he was buying them back in order that he might extinguish them.[9] He also recorded selling ten *rentes* to people who owed them to him, again to allow them to extinguish them.[10] It may have been the case that, for individuals like Mollet who both owed and owned many *rentes*, income so little counterbalanced disbursements that they were often more trouble than they were worth. At all events, he and others went through considerable convolutions to free themselves of them. In May 1817, Charles Mollet made the following diary entry:

> I went to town & passed contracts with Sr Ab. Naftel, from whom I bought 2 bushels & half a denerel of wheat *rente* which I owed him over & above the two quarters which he has owed me since buying, on my advice, the ten bushels & half denerel I owed the late Frederick Price (he bought them from Sr Thos Trachy, an authorised representative of Mr Price's creditors). These two *rentes* are thus now extinguished.[11]

Rentes clearly lacked the attraction for Mollet that they had for his father and grandfather, and the same may also be said of loans as a form of investment. Although Mollet did lend money to other people, he generally did so as a favour to the borrowers, only lending them small sums short-term and not charging them interest. Many of these small loans were to his workmen, such as the £4 he lent to Pierre Gavet in 1800, or the £3 he lent

---

[8] Diary, 27.4.1801, 27.10.1815.
[9] Diary, 10.9.1785, 3.12.1785, 17.12.1785, 7.3.1796, 29.12.1798, 1.1806, 8.9.1810, 17.6.1816, 7.5.1817.
[10] Diary, 29.4.1780, 27.5.1780, 15.7.1780, 16.6.1787, 22.10.1796, 3.1.1801, 4.12.1802, 4.5.1816, 7.5.1817, 26.3.1818.
[11] Diary, 24.5.17.

to Pierre Machon in 1808.[12] These loans were usually repaid within months. On the one occasion when Mollet noted having lent out money at interest, the venture proved a failure. In 1791, he lent James Torode 144 *livres tournois* (about £10 4s) at 5 per cent interest. Torode made no repayments whatever until 1811, when he paid off the intervening years' interest and enough to reduce the principal to 120 *livres*. He then paid nothing more for the next five years, and Mollet was obliged to apply to the Court to have his goods arrested in the spring of 1816. In the autumn of that year, when Torode's effects had been sold and the legal costs paid, Mollet found to his dismay that he had actually recouped less than he was owed (147 *livres*, on an outstanding sum of 170 *livres*).[13]

During the War of American Independence, Mollet invested in a number of privateers. He bought small shares (typically one-sixty-fourth) in nine named vessels: the Vulture, the Hunter, the Swift, the Hero, the Tartar, the Duchess of Kingston, the Arbuthnot and the Kite.[14] Mollet did not mention how much he paid for these shares, but Richard Hocart has observed that Peter De Havilland (a friend of Mollet's) paid about £50 for a one-sixteenth share in the Duchess of Kingston in 1778.[15] Extrapolating from this one instance, we might hazard a guess that Mollet's total outlay on privateers was in the region of £150.

Mollet also omitted to record how much prize money his shares eventually brought him. Alan Jamieson has pointed out that although privateering 'retained the unfailing attractions of a gamble [...] it brought wealth to only a tiny handful of investors.'[16] Jamieson added as an illustration that, although the Hunter (in which Mollet had a share) captured five French vessels in August 1778, investors received no prize money at all, as the High Court of Admiralty judged that the vessels had been taken when the Hunter did not have a commission to take them, so all five were forfeit to the Crown.[17] Jamieson similarly pointed out that, although the Duchess of Kingston took

---

[12] Diary, Notes relating to 1800, 15.2.1808.
[13] Diary, 1.2.1791, 31.3.1811, Notes relating to 1811, 18.4.1816, 20.7.1816, 9.10.1816.
[14] Diary, 26.1.1778, 28.1.1778, 9.5.1778, 5.10.1778, 29.7.1779, 18.12.1779. He also bought shares in two or three other privateers whose names he did not record.
[15] R. Hocart, *Peter de Havilland: Bailiff of Guernsey, A History of his Life, 1747–1821* (Guernsey, 1997), p. 26.
[16] A.G. Jamieson, 'The return to privateering: Channel Island privateers, 1739–83, in A.G. Jamieson (ed.), *A People of the Sea: The Maritime History of the Channel Islands* (London, 1986), p. 172.
[17] *Ibid.*, pp. 169–70.

more than one prize before being sold in 1779, payment of prize money was significantly delayed.[18] Charles Mollet's diary shows that the Duchess's accounts were not finally signed off until 1791 (a full twelve years later), but again he did not specify what gain, if any, he had made from this speculation.[19] Mollet recorded no further investments in privateers.

Mollet's investments as detailed so far seem singularly unremunerative, but he did in fact make one very sound investment choice. This was his decision to acquire further real property. His first acquisition appears to have come to him without his even seeking it. In July 1771, Mollet's uncle, Jean Le Vavasseur dit Durell, transferred ownership of a house in Jersey to Mollet on condition that his nephew should provide him with suitable board, lodging and spending money for the rest of his life.[20] Mollet let the house out to tenants, and was still receiving rental income from it twenty years later.[21] Mollet's purchases in the Castel parish have already been noted.[22] In addition to these, he bought two warehouses and surrounding land in St Peter Port in early 1780.[23] Mollet retained all but one of these properties for the remainder of his life, and derived a steady rental income from them. In 1794, he also purchased a four-seater pew in St Peter Port's Bethel Chapel, and from 1802 rented it out to a group of spinster sisters (the Miss Perchards).[24]

La Domaillerie, which Mollet bought in 1773, was situated to the west of Mollet's farm and contiguous with it. The property consisted of two orchards, a field, a house and an outbuilding.[25] It was almost certainly purchased for the sake of the land rather than the buildings, which were in a dilapidated condition from the outset. Nevertheless, shortly after his purchase, Mollet set carpenters and masons to tidy up the house and in 1774

---

[18] *Ibid.* pp. 162–5. See also Hocart, *Peter de Havilland*, p. 26.
[19] Diary, 1.4.1791, 11.4.1791.
[20] Contract dated 2.7.1771, book 53, p. 7b, series D/Y/K4 (Public Registry), Jersey Archive; Diary, 2.7.1771. Jean Le Vavasseur dit Durell (1720–93) was the youngest brother of Mollet's mother. He appears to have had mental health problems.
[21] Diary, Notes relating to 1791.
[22] Chapter 3, n. 4.
[23] 15.1.1780, Contrats pour la Date, Greffe. See also Diary, 24.12.1779, 31.12.1779. Mollet bought the St Peter Port property from Peter De Havilland, whose wife Carterette had inherited it from her grandfather, the late Elizée Le Marchant of la Haye du Puits.
[24] Diary, 19.9.1794, Notes relating to 1802.
[25] La Domaillerie (which Mollet always spelled *Daumaillerie*) is visible some distance to the left of Mollet's farmhouse on the detail from the 1787 Gardner map reproduced on the back cover of this book. There is a (romanticised) pictorial representation of it in Plate 18.

let it out to Pierre Le Lievre and his family at a rent of 48 *livres tournois* per year (about £3 8s).[26] It is not known how long the Le Lievres lived there, as Mollet's diary for 1781–4 is missing. By 1785, at all events, Pierre Le Lievre had disappeared, and his wife and children were living in another of Mollet's houses.[27] It does not seem as if la Domaillerie was ever tenanted after this, and it appears to have become increasingly ruinous.[28] In later years, Mollet recorded storing potatoes and other commodities in the house, and even mentioned keeping chickens in it.[29]

Perhaps the chief interest of la Domaillerie (though not immediately concerning Mollet) is that it formed the subject of a later 'legend'. Louisa Lane, whose father bought Mollet's farm after his death, had an interest in folklore and a colourful imagination.[30] In 1836, she submitted an article to a local magazine entitled 'The Domaillerie Cottage – A Guernsey legend'.[31] The 'legend' concerned a 'fairy-like' girl given to 'wild plaintive music' who inhabited la Domaillerie with an 'extraordinary old woman' who often read to her from a 'thick, black-looking volume'. The girl vanished at the age of sixteen with a mysterious stranger who might or might not have been the devil, causing the old woman to die of grief. The pair are said to have rented the house from a foreigner named Dubois who, after the old woman's death, 'gladly parted with it to the owner of the Woodland estate'.[32] Mollet's diary contains not a word about fairy-like girls or extraordinary old women, and he in fact purchased la Domaillerie not from a foreigner named Dubois, but from Nicolas Brouard whose elderly father James had previously owned it. Louisa Lane (who by then had become Louisa Lane Clarke) repeated her 'legend' in an 1841 guidebook, and it was later picked up by other writers.[33]

Mollet's property at le Préel also contained a house as well as land. It was only in Mollet's possession between 1784 and 1791. We do not know the circumstances of its purchase as this occurred during a period for which the

---

[26] Diary, 11.9.1774.
[27] Diary, 14.12.1785.
[28] In 1806, its chimney collapsed, taking part of the gable with it (Diary, 18.12.1806).
[29] Diary, 21.1.1807, 15.10.1815.
[30] Louisa Lane (1812–83) was the daughter of Colonel Ambrose Lane and Elizabeth Le Mesurier.
[31] *The Guernsey and Jersey Magazine*, 1 (1836), pp. 359–63.
[32] After purchasing Mollet's property, Colonel Lane renamed it 'Woodlands'.
[33] L.L. Clarke, *Redstone's Guernsey & Jersey Guide* (1841; Guernsey, 1843 edn), pp. 183–8. See also T. Bellamy, *Guernsey Pictorial Directory and Stranger's Guide* (Guernsey, 1843), p. 112–13.

diary is missing. By 1785, however, Pierre Le Lievre's wife and family were living in the house. In 1787, Mollet recorded letting the dwelling and attached garden to Nicolas Mauger for seven quarters of wheat annually (which roughly equated to £5 5s). Mauger was still in residence as sitting tenant when Mollet sold the property to Etienne Le Noury four years later.[34] Mollet appears to have sold it to realise funds for building work he was having carried out in town (see below).

The property at les Vallées, just across a cart-track from Mollet's farm, was owned by Charles Mollet for a much longer period. It consisted of a house on a sizeable plot containing an orchard and gardens. In due course, Mollet acquired the habit of referring to the house as the 'upper' house. Mollet let out rooms in this house to multiple tenants – the 'large kitchen' to one individual, the 'large bedroom' to someone else, the 'small bedroom' to yet another person, sometimes in combinations of more than one room. Most of the tenants also had a share of the land, which they cultivated in their own right. Jean Roussel and his family occupied two rooms in the upper house for more than twenty years.[35] When they moved out in 1808, they were paying a rent of £5 per year.[36] Jacques Ozanne and his family occupied another couple of rooms for at least sixteen years from 1798, also for £5 a year.[37] Many other tenants came and went: Daniel Brouard, Thomas Mauger, Nicolas Le Page, Denis Le Pelley, even the French Royalist *émigré* Henri Delaroche-Vernay.[38]

In 1786, Mollet set a new trend for the upper house when his farm servant Pierre Gavet married his house servant Marie Nicolle, and he decided to move them from his own house to the upper house, treating the accommodation as part of their pay.[39] This arrangement lasted until they left Mollet's employ a year later.[40] In 1798, Mollet repeated the arrangement with another newly-wed servant couple, Abraham Machon and Elizabeth Le Ray.[41] In this case, the couple (Ab and Lisabo, as Mollet called them) continued working for

---

[34] Diary, 28.12.1787, 26.11.1791. The house (no. 549 on Map 4) remains in existence today.
[35] Diary, 12.1.1781, 20.9.1808.
[36] Diary, Notes for 1808.
[37] Diary, Notes relating to 1798.
[38] Diary, 27.9.1791, 8.9.1791, 20.7.1796, Notes relating to 1795 and 1796.
[39] Diary, 23.8.1786.
[40] Diary, 29.9.1787.
[41] Diary, 22.3.1798.

Mollet until his death in 1819. Throughout their residence at the upper house, they assiduously worked their share of the garden, and kept pigs there, selling vegetables, piglets and meat on their own account. This enabled them to save, and by 1815, having accumulated sufficient resources, they were able to purchase the entire house from Mollet, and remained there for the rest of their lives.[42]

Turning now to Mollet's St Peter Port properties: the two warehouses Mollet bought in 1780 were located on the western outskirts of town in a street known as la Profonde Rue, which roughly followed the course of the present St James Street. Frederick Lukis (born nine years after Mollet made his purchase) described la Profonde Rue as a 'deep cutting' bounded by 'a high falaise or earthy cliff', narrow, unpaved, and fit only for one cart at a time. He went on specifically to say that Mollet's property stood at the upper end of la Profonde Rue, where a lane named le Coffinot branched off towards the top of Berthelot Street.[43] Lukis added that, after Mollet's death, his property was bought by the Collings family, who demolished the earlier structures and erected a new residence by the name of Bonamy House. This ochre-coloured building still exists.

In the first few years following his acquisition of the warehouses, Mollet seems to have used the lower one for storing items of his own, and rented the upper one out. He also let out part of the land which surrounded the warehouses, as well as a stable attached to the upper warehouse. His early tenants for the upper warehouse included HM Receiver John Harris and Bailiff William Le Marchant.[44] By 1790, Mollet seems to have been making an income of about £16 a year from his town property.[45] In 1791, at a point where he had no income from farming, Mollet decided to convert the lower of the two warehouses into two dwelling houses.[46] This conversion appears to have been financed by the sale of Mollet's property at le Préel. Building work was not complete until 1793, but almost as soon as the two houses were finished, Mollet found tenants for them. One was let to Dr Jean De Sausmarez for 20 guineas a year, and the other to a Mr Andrew Mitchell for

---

[42] A copy of the conveyance (dated 18.5.1815) is preserved in AQ 1133/021 at the Island Archives.
[43] F.C. Lukis, 'Reminiscences of Former Days in Connection with Guernsey' (unpub. MS, Priaulx Library).
[44] Diary, 4.5.1787, 15.8.1787, Notes relating to 1789, 17.6.1790.
[45] Notes relating to 1790.
[46] Diary, 23.5.1791. Reasons for this lack of agricultural income will be explored below.

£18 a year, thus bringing Mollet a combined annual income approaching £40.⁴⁷ Mollet also continued to rent out his upper warehouse as a store.

This warehouse appears from Mollet's diary to have been a simple structure, consisting of a vault, a ground-floor store, and a loft under a thatched roof. Mollet usually rented out two of the floors and kept the other one for himself. He had many different tenants over the course of the years, including Solomon Lauga, Nicolas Dobrée, William Combs, David Watson, John Tupper, George White and John Brock. The last of these, a merchant like most of the others, rented the vault and ground-floor store between 1815 and 1818 for £19 a year.⁴⁸

Mollet also continued renting out part of the stable and some of the land adjacent to the remaining warehouse. Tenants of the stable (in which Mollet reserved a stall for his own horse) included Pierre Rabey, Jean Maindonal, Advocate John Jeremie and a Mr Macey. The usual rent seems to have been 4 guineas a year.⁴⁹ The land was at some point divided into three plots. In 1804/5, a Mr Lewis was renting the larger plot for 5 guineas per year; Monsieur Pierre Bardel (a French merchant and auctioneer) was renting the smaller plot for 2 guineas; and Mollet himself was growing parsnips in what remained.⁵⁰

By the early nineteenth century, the whole complex might collectively have been earning Mollet around £95 a year, as the annual rent for the two dwelling houses had risen. From 1799, a Mr Ebelling and his family rented the lower house for £30, and from 1803 a Mr Studdart rented the upper house for £25.⁵¹ Ebelling and Studdart were reasonably reliable tenants and caused Mollet few problems. Both however departed in 1812/13,⁵² after which their replacements proved more problematic. Guernsey's economy had received a shock from the imposition of the Anti-Smuggling Acts, and work had become scarcer and less remunerative. Mollet's new tenants, the

---

[47] Diary, Notes relating to 1793. The French Revolutionary War had just begun, and Dr De Sausmarez wished to use Mollet's house as a naval hospital (Diary, 22.3.1793). Note that Dr De Sausmarez's surname sometimes also appeared as 'Saumarez'; see Appendix 4.
[48] Diary, 16.10.1815, Notes relating to 1817.
[49] Diary, Notes relating to 1804.
[50] Diary, 18.3.1803, Notes relating to 1804.
[51] Diary, Notes relating to 1799, 9.1.1803.
[52] For Studdart's departure, see Diary, 18.3.1812. We have no precise date for Ebelling's departure which took place during a period for which the diary is missing.

Kennedys and the Newells, both defaulted on their rent, and in 1816 Mollet resorted to the Court in order to recover what they owed him.[53]

In that same year, Mollet himself was also on the receiving end of Court action. His warehouse roof had been damaged by repeated storms, and, in having it re-thatched, he inadvertently fell foul of a new law which prohibited the repair (or new roofing) of buildings with thatch in certain parts of St Peter Port.[54] Theoretically, Mollet would have been liable to a fine of 300 *livres tournois* (about £21 8s); however the Court agreed not to fine him in view of his ignorance of the recently promulgated law. Instead, they gave him three years to remove the thatch, by which time Charles Mollet had passed away.[55]

By 1816, the Napoleonic War was over, the garrison had been cut back, and Guernsey was entering a period of depression. Demand for rental accommodation was slack, and it took Mollet a while to find tenants for his houses after the Kennedys and Newells had left. In 1817, however, he was able to re-let them both to a Mr and Mrs Christian, an English couple who kept a public house. Nevertheless – in a sign of the depressed times – the rent Mollet was asking for both houses combined was just £30.[56] Unfortunately, he was not able to take receipt of it for long: 1818 brought a further complication, when the Christians declared their intention to keep the lower house but relinquish all save the kitchen of the upper house. In a renters' market, Mollet agreed to this arrangement, but it put him to the trouble of finding tenants piecemeal for the vacated portions of the upper house.[57] This was a complication Mollet could well have done without in his mid-seventies, and if 1819 had not brought his demise, he might well have decided to end his career as a St Peter Port landlord.

Enterprises

We saw in the previous chapter that Charles Mollet would sell farm produce whenever he was able to. In his early days, he also sold other things. In 1771, while still in his twenties, Mollet had the idea of importing hats to Guernsey. The idea seems to have come to him while on a visit to London, and he

---

[53] Diary 18.4.1816, 30.4.1816, 27.9.1816, 28.9.1816, Notes relating to 1816.
[54] Ordinance of 29 October 1816.
[55] Diary, 3.11.1816, 4.11.1816, 7.12.1816.
[56] Diary, 4.3.1817, 30.3.1817.
[57] Diary, 25.2.1818, 1.4.1818, 15.4.1818, 25.6.1818.

purchased a number of hats from Messrs Fort & Benson for the price of £39 3s.[58] These were in all probability simple round hats, of the sort his labourers might wear. On return to Guernsey, Mollet had his hats advertised in country churchyards after Sunday morning service.[59] His price per hat was 5 *livres* 16 *sous* (about 8s 3d). This may possibly have been too high, as the hats did not sell as quickly as he had anticipated. A few were bought by labourers and tradesmen, and one was even purchased by the future Lieutenant-Bailiff Eleazar Le Marchant (though it was clearly not to his taste, as he sent it back).[60] Thus, after six or seven years, Mollet still had many unsold hats on his hands. Not knowing what to do with them, he entrusted them in 1778 to a departing sea captain, to be sold, he wrote, 'in Madeira or America'.[61] Mollet never mentioned these hats again.

During the mid-1780s, Mollet entered a form of sharecropping arrangement with the wealthy merchant Pierre Dobrée (1722–1808), whose son Bonamy had recently married Mollet's niece Patty Mourant. In 1784, Dobrée took out a lease on a large field in the Castel parish, and recruited Mollet to cultivate it for him. The agreement entitled Dobrée to a specified amount of the produce, for which he paid Mollet a set price, leaving Mollet the remainder to use or sell as his fee for working the land. Mollet recorded having made a profit of about £5 15s from this arrangement in 1785. It is possible that Dobrée did not obtain the value he had expected from the agreement, or perhaps Mollet found it more trouble than it was worth. Whatever the case, the sharecropping arrangement lasted only three years.[62]

Another short-lived partnership was that which Charles Mollet entered with Jean Carré in 1788. This was mercantile rather than agricultural in nature. According to the agreement, Mollet was to import timber and iron from the Baltic, and Carré was to sell it, with Mollet taking two-thirds of the profits, and Carré taking one-third.[63] In the three years for which the partnership lasted, Mollet only reported the arrival in Guernsey of two consignments of timber and iron (from Messrs Arfvidson of Gothenburg).[64]

---

[58] Diary, 28.10.1771, 13.1.1772.
[59] Diary, 3.11.1771, 8.11.1771. Parish notices were read out in the churchyard after divine service on Sundays.
[60] Diary, Notes relating to 1772, 1775, 1777.
[61] Diary, 27.1.1778.
[62] Diary, 1.1.1785, Notes relating to 1785 and 1786.
[63] Diary, 31.1.1788, 15.4.1788.
[64] Diary, 2.8.1789, 29.7.1790.

It is not clear what profits, if any, were made. When Mollet lost interest and withdrew from the partnership in 1791, he ceded what remained of the timber and iron (stored at his warehouse) to Jean Carré to dispose of as he might.[65]

Of longer duration than the preceding ventures was Mollet's foray into distilling. He became interested in this after making the acquaintance of an *émigré* Capuchin friar in the late 1790s. The friar's religious name was Frère François Marie and his civil name Jean Mortier (although Mollet usually referred to him as 'Monsieur Marie').[66] The friar was a skilled herbalist and maker of cordials, which he sold through High Street grocers Joseph Davy and Thomas Bowls. These cordials were flavoured with essential oils distilled from aromatic plants. Having sampled the friar's cordials, Mollet decided to try making some himself and bought an alembic still of his own in 1799.[67] To begin with, the still was operated by Frère Marie, a regular visitor to Mollet's home. In 1800, Mollet recorded sending six bottles of rose water distilled by the friar from the petals of roses grown on his farm to a St Peter Port shop for sale at 21 *sous* per bottle (about 1s 6d).[68] In time, Frère Marie taught Mollet's servant Lisabo Machon the art of distilling, and Mollet purchased a much larger still, which was installed in his wash-house.[69] Lisabo became adept at distilling in her own right and, in the last decades of Mollet's life, turned out hundreds of bottles of rose water, *eau de menthe* and *eau de noyau* (distilled from peach leaves) each year. Mollet was obliged to send his servants to collect the peach leaves from other people's gardens, but he produced his own roses, mint and peppermint from beds planted specifically for that purpose. Mollet sold some of his cordials at the market, some through St Peter Port shops, and some via private sale to friends and relatives.[70] He also accepted consignments of plants and herbs to distil for other people, for which service he charged 6d per bottle.[71] Whether Mollet's distilling venture brought him an appreciable return is unknown. It is clear from the diaries

---

[65] Diary, 27.8.1791.
[66] Jean Mortier made Guernsey his permanent home and died in the island in 1826. He was from La Flèche in the Loire Valley.
[67] Diary 31.8.1799. The still, which came from London, had a capacity of five gallons and cost Mollet five guineas.
[68] Diary, Notes relating to 1800.
[69] Diary, 6.2.1807. This still was locally sourced and cost Mollet just over £9.
[70] Diary, 26.12.1815, 3.9.1816, 7.11.186, 22.2.1817.
[71] Diary, 2.9.1808, 30.8.1816.

that he gave countless bottles – which formed ideal gifts – away. The still consumed vast amounts of firewood, and the sugar he bought in large quantities was not cheap.[72] Mollet however became well-known for his cordials, and this gentle pastime seems to have been more to his taste than buying and selling ironmongery.

By the time he started distilling, Charles Mollet was clearer as to his own ambitions than he had been earlier in life. He had experienced something of a watershed at the end of the 1780s, when he spent two years as a merchant in Alderney. This is one of the most interesting episodes in Mollet's life, so it will now be considered in detail.

Charles Mollet turned forty-six in 1788. Quite why he decided to abandon farming that year and embark on a mercantile career is a mystery. Perhaps his decision was born of dissatisfaction with his own lack of financial progress. It may even have been at the prompting of his wealthy brother-in-law Peter Mourant. Mollet's good friend, Lieutenant-Governor William Brown, was at any rate against the project and tried to dissuade Mollet from it, even offering 'to do something' for him if he desisted.[73] Mollet had however made up his mind, and Brown's wise counsel went unheeded.

It is likely that Charles Mollet was well acquainted with Alderney long before 1788. From its opening in 1771, his diary shows him socialising regularly with members of Alderney's ruling Le Mesurier family, in particular Jean Le Mesurier, who was the island's hereditary Governor between 1743 and 1793, and his son Peter who occupied the position between 1793 and 1803.[74] Alderney, an island just over three square miles in area, is located thirteen miles north-east of Guernsey, ten miles west of France and fifty-five miles south of England.[75] In the late eighteenth century, it was essentially what Gregory Stevens Cox has called a 'counter' visited by English smugglers.[76] The island was inhabited by between 1,000 and 1,200 people, many of whom were involved in the import and sale of wines, spirits and tobacco.

---

[72] £11 for 316 lb of loaf sugar in 1809, for instance (Diary, 21.10.1809).
[73] Diary, 6.10.1787. There will be more on William Brown in later chapters.
[74] Diary, 27.2.1771, 23.7.1771, 29.7.1778, 13.1.1780, 24.5.1780. On the Alderney Le Mesuriers in general, see E.F. Carey, 'Peter Le Mesurier, Governor of Alderney, 1793–1803', *Transactions of la Société Guernesiaise*, 10 (1926), pp. 45–61.
[75] See Map 8.
[76] G. Stevens Cox, *The Guernsey Merchants and their World* (Guernsey, 2009), p. 28.

Mollet initially envisaged spending a term of six years in Alderney. In November and December 1787, he rented out his fields at the Castel, sold off his livestock, and came to an agreement with his former workmen Pierre Gavet and Eleazar Ingrouille by which they were jointly to rent his house and gardens for six years at £50 per annum.[77] Mollet next entered into a formal partnership with forty-year-old Thomas Marett.[78] Under the terms of the partnership agreement, the two men were to trade in Alderney under the style of 'Messrs Charles Mollet & Co.', as importers and sellers of wines, spirits and other luxury goods.[79] To complete his preparations, Mollet took out a six-year lease on Mouriaux House (Peter Le Mesurier's recently built Alderney home) at £30 per year, as also on the two stores at Alderney's Braye harbour from which Le Mesurier ran his own smugglers' supply business, again for six years at £40 per year.[80]

Having thus tied himself up for the next six years, Charles Mollet arrived in Alderney on New Year's Day 1788, declaring it his intention to make the island his 'general place of residence throughout this period'.[81] There was then a four-week hiatus before the partnership made their first sales.[82] This delay had been caused by Thomas Marett's late arrival in Alderney and Peter Le Mesurier's continuation of the smugglers' supply business on his own account until Marett was present.[83] The failure to hand over directly to Mollet hints at Mollet's lack of business experience and his subordinate role as regarded the practical side of the enterprise. At all events, Mollet only mentioned sales three times in the whole of his sojourn, and never again after 19 February 1788.

Mollet recorded going to the stores at Braye only seventy-eight times during his entire two years in Alderney, notwithstanding that were 627 weekdays on which he could potentially have worked there. He moreover scarcely even mentioned what he did in relation to the enterprise. It was evidently Thomas Marett who took the leading role at Braye, and the

---

[77] Diary, 25.11.1787, 1.12.1787, 2.12.1787, 10.12.1787, 13.12.1787. Mollet reserved the use of a bedroom at the house, and also retained the option to take everything back after four years on provision of three months' notice.
[78] Although Marett is a Jersey name, Thomas Marett had been born in St Peter Port in 1747. His father was another Thomas Marett and his mother was Elizabeth Day.
[79] Diary, 14.11.1787, 16.11.1787, 23.11.1787.
[80] Diary, 31.12.1787. For a twentieth-century photograph of Mouriaux House, see Plate 26.
[81] Diary, 1.1.1788.
[82] Diary, 29.1.1788.
[83] Diary, 26.1.1788.

partnership probably also employed a clerk. Anyone reading Mollet's 1788/9 diary for information on the smugglers' supply business will therefore find little in his daily entries. For more detailed information, we must look a few years further on in Mollet's journal, where data on Mollet & Co.'s business activities has survived by accident rather than by design. Before resuming our account of Mollet's experiences in Alderney, we will pause to review these data.

Charles Mollet was never one for waste, and he wrote his diary for 1808–12 in a partly-filled account book from his Alderney days. The first eighty-three pages of this volume contain old stock-lists and invoices, with the diary proper only beginning on the eighty-fourth page. Many of the old inventories and invoices were pasted over (after Mollet's death) with pictures cut out of Victorian children's books. Such of them, however, as are visible between or on either side of the pastings do shed much useful light on the partnership's business activities. At the very beginning of the volume is part of a list of goods left in Peter Le Mesurier's stores when Mollet and Marett took them over in January 1788. The goods Le Mesurier left behind became part of Mollet & Co.'s stock-in-trade, and Mollet and Marett paid Le Mesurier for them. The list occupies three pages in total, but unfortunately only the first page is visible. This page recorded the presence in the stores of 1,238 gallons of rum, 712 gallons of cognac and 244½ gallons of brandy. Collectively, these were worth £235 13s 6d. If the other two pages listed goods of similar value, the full three pages might possibly have recorded stock worth more than £700. Further on in the old ledger, there is an intact list of stock remaining in the stores on 31 December 1788, after Mollet & Co.'s first year of trading. This included 7,418 gallons of liqueurs, 4,304 gallons of brandy, 1,180 gallons of cognac, 1,050 gallons of rum, 844 gallons of gin, 6 hogsheads of red and white wine, and some chocolate. Collectively, this stock was worth £929 11s 11d.

The invoices in the ledger all relate to purchases (sales must have been recorded separately). They provide evidence of the purchase and importation of wines and spirits from Valencia, Rotterdam, Ostend, the West Indies, Montpellier, Toulon, Lorient, Roscoff, and Guernsey. The wines and spirits arrived in Alderney in large containers such as puncheons, pipes and hogsheads. Mollet & Co. (who also imported materials for cooperage) had them decanted into small kegs on arrival in the island.

Brandy usually came from France or Spain. An invoice dated 12 September 1788 shows the purchase of 28,807 gallons of brandy from Messrs

Burnett & Durand of Montpellier. These were imported on a ship named the Diligence, captained by John Andrews (identified as an Englishman). Together with a few other small items (such as three cases of almonds and two chests of soap), the bill for this cargo came to £695 10s 3d (this total, as everything else in the ledger, is given both in sterling and *livres tournois*). Another invoice dated 20 December 1789 shows the purchase of £376 9s worth of brandy from Roze & Reboul of Toulon. Yet another, dated 22 May 1790, is for £488 11s worth of brandy from Vague & Boneli of Valencia (to be carried on the Friendship, Captain Timothy Silvers).

Gin came principally from the Low Countries. An invoice of 17 February 1789 shows the purchase of gin to the value of £105 3s from Jas & Jas Le Marchant & Co. of Rotterdam (both Guernseymen). It was to be carried to Alderney on the Jessie of Greenock, Captain James Rodgers. Another invoice dated 9 October 1789 shows the purchase of gin (and barrel hoops) worth £199 9s also from Jas & Jas Le Marchant & Co., to be carried on the Elizabeth, Captain Nicolas Mauger.

Rum came from the Caribbean. An invoice dated 10 May 1790 shows the purchase of 1,190 gallons of rum worth £114 13s 9d from Saint Croix (then one of the Danish West Indies but now a US Virgin Island). The cargo came to Alderney via Ostend on the Peggy, Captain Francis Giffard. Fragments of other invoices show that Mollet & Co. also bought a substantial proportion of their stock indirectly, via Guernsey-based merchants. Most prominent among these Guernsey merchants were Mollet's brother-in-law Peter Mourant, his niece's husband Bonamy Dobrée, and his friend William Chepmell.

Mollet's silence on his activities at Braye was not the only indication of his lack of engagement in trading. The focus of his Alderney diary was almost wholly on his garden and his social life. Mollet brought over a male and a female servant from Guernsey, and attempted to recreate the kind of life he had enjoyed in the larger island. The extensive garden at Mouriaux House was soon planted up with vegetables and flowers, and Mollet regularly sent for fruit, meat, dairy products and other foodstuffs from Guernsey. With provisions such as these, he entertained guests to dinner, tea or supper several times a week. Mollet's list of invitees reads like a late eighteenth-century 'who's who' of Alderney. As well as the Le Mesuriers, Mollet entertained (and was entertained by) the Alderney Judge Jean Gauvain; the resident surgeon Jean Colomez; the Anglican Minister Pierre Solier; and merchants such as Nicolas Barbenson, Joseph Lorani, James Ahier, Thomas Le Patourel and

Stephen Serane. One name which figured particularly frequently was that of Tom Williams. Thomas Williams (senior) was Alderney's Greffier between 1773 and 1819. He also held the office of Procureur for part of that time.[84] He was married to a Jerseywoman named Rachel De La Taste with whom he had two sons, Thomas, born in Guernsey in 1769, and Frederick, born in Jersey in 1775. In Mollet's diary entries, it is not always clear whether references are to the elder Thomas or his twenty-year-old son. However, context suggests that it was most often the latter, and indeed, there are occasional hints that it may have been the younger Thomas who filled the role of clerk to Charles Mollet & Co.[85]

Despite Mollet's resolution to the contrary, he ultimately spent a large amount of time away from Alderney during his two years there. This began just over twelve weeks after his arrival, with a stay in Guernsey between the 6th and 18th of April 1788. After this, his departures from Alderney became increasingly frequent, such that he left the island no fewer than twelve times in his twenty-four months there.[86] Mollet evidently missed his friends and relatives in Guernsey, as this is where most of his time away from Alderney was spent. However, he also undertook two voyages to France and two to England. Mollet's visits to England are of particular interest on the account of the information they provide on his Alderney customers. We shall consider these voyages in detail.[87]

Between the 31 October and 15 November 1788, and again between 21 April and 20 May 1789, Charles Mollet recorded what appear to have been debt-collecting journeys to south-west England. His smuggling clients usually obtained their supplies on credit, which allowed them time to sell the goods before settling their bills. Many other suppliers, including Mollet's brother-in-law Peter Mourant, employed agents in England to collect their debts for them.[88] Perhaps on grounds of economy, Mollet and Marett

---

[84] Williams was the son of the Reverend Thomas Williams, Rector of St Sampsons and Vicar of the Vale between 1730 and 1743, and Rector of St Saviours between 1743 and 1763.
[85] See, for instance, Diary, 13.2.1790, which recorded Thomas junior handing money to Mollet to cover his expenses on a business trip.
[86] In total, Mollet spent 133 days away from the island.
[87] The French trips will be discussed in Chapters 5 and 8, below.
[88] J.R. Johns, *The Smugglers' Banker: The Story of Zephaniah Job of Polperro* (1997; Clifton-upon-Teme, 2008 edn), pp. 85, 90.

forwent this convenience, and Mollet appears to have been designated the partnership's debt-collector.[89]

Charles Mollet's missions concentrated on the stretch of coast between Bournemouth and Brixham. He usually began his journeys by spending several days around the Hampshire villages of Burley, Ringwood and Kingston, where he saw, among others, 'Mr Tunks & Messrs Warne & Early'.[90] Mr Tunks has not been identified, but it is likely that Messrs Warne and Early were John Early and the brothers John and Peter Warne, who are known to have operated as smugglers in the New Forest area.[91] Mollet also saw many other individuals whom it has not been possible to trace: Mr Syms and Mr Richardson at Newton Bushel; Mr Rackstraw and William Efford at Brixham; James Trott and George Tozer at Seaton; John Lane and William Woodgate at Beer; Mr Green, Mr Woolfreys, Mr Napper Roper, Samuel Pope and Mr Whitfield at East Lulworth.[92] It is likely that most of these were smugglers too.

Some months later, when he had returned permanently to Guernsey, Mollet recorded his considerable resentment at Thomas Marett's having left it to him to collect the partnership's debts.[93] By then, however, the two men were hardly speaking to each other. The first sign of discord had come ominously early. Just three months into their partnership, Mollet recorded a dispute over a clause in their partnership deed concerning repairs. They had been on the verge of appointing arbitrators, but had eventually simply agreed to disagree.[94] From this time on, Marett was conspicuous in his long absences from Charles Mollet's guest list.

Even more ominously, there were also signs of a deterioration in Mollet's relationship with the Le Mesuriers. This initially seems to have arisen from a political contretemps in the spring of 1789. For reasons he did not record in his diary, Charles Mollet had omitted to put candles at his windows when instructed to do so to celebrate George III's recovery from mental illness, and

---

[89] Mollet went on three further such missions after he had returned permanently to Guernsey.
[90] Diary, 2.11.1788, 22.4.1789.
[91] G. Morley, *Smuggling in Hampshire & Dorset, 1700–1850* (1983; Newbury, 1990 edn), pp. 106, 109, 142–3, 150, 170; R. Platt, *Smuggling in the British Isles: A History* (2007; Stroud, 2011 edn), pp. 195–6.
[92] Diary, 8.11.1788, 10.11.1788, 13.11.1788, 7.5.1789, 10.5.1789.
[93] Diary, 27.6.1791.
[94] Diary, 4.3.1788.

as a result of this omission, had five of his window-panes smashed by the mob.[95] It was unseemly for the Le Mesuriers, who owed their position to a royal patent, to be associated with such dissent. A fortnight or so later, Mollet reported that Mr Le Mesurier had called at Mouriaux House to inform him that, on account of this incident, he would no longer be able to receive Mollet's visits, nor even acknowledge him in any way.[96]

This set the scene for an even graver contretemps five months later. On 23 September 1789, Mollet noted that he had 'had words' with Peter Le Mesurier at Braye harbour.[97] He did not record the subject of their argument, but felt sufficiently slighted by Le Mesurier to challenge him to a duel.[98] Six o'clock the following evening was appointed as the time for their encounter. Le Mesurier duly presented himself at the agreed place with a local man as his second, but Mollet arrived alone. He had been unable to persuade either Thomas Marett or Thomas Williams to act as second for him and could find no one else willing to do so.[99] This resulted in a postponement of the duel until early October, by which time both belligerents had travelled to Guernsey and returned with alternative seconds. Le Mesurier secured the Guernsey Procureur Hirzel Le Marchant as his second, and Mollet secured twenty-three-year-old Philip Fergusson, a relative of his by marriage.[100] The duel with Le Mesurier eventually took place on 7 October. Mollet's diary account of it was laconic to say the least: 'at 4 o'clock, Mr Le M. & I met at the appointed place, bringing our seconds with us. We both fired two shots, but without effect.'[101]

---

[95] Diary, 31.3.1789. It seems likely that Mollet's political sympathies lay with the Whigs, who had hoped that the Whig-supporting Prince of Wales would be made Regent should the King not recover. Favouring the Tories, George III had dismissed the Whig Prime Minister in 1783 and appointed the Tory William Pitt in his place. Many Whig sympathisers were concerned about the King's incipient 'despotism'.
[96] Diary, 17.4.1789. It is unclear whether 'Mr Le Mesurier' was Jean Le Mesurier or his son Peter, to whom Mollet sometimes referred as the Governor, even though he was actually the Lieutenant-Governor. On balance, it seems likelier that it was Peter, who had just returned from an absence in Guernsey.
[97] For a contemporary portrait of Peter Le Mesurier, see Plate 10.
[98] Diary, 23.9.1789.
[99] Diary, 24.9.1789.
[100] Diary, 6.10.1789. Fergusson was the nephew of Mollet's Jersey brother-in-law Philippe Lerrier.
[101] Diary, 7.10.1789.

It was fortunate (and perhaps intentional) that both men's honour had been satisfied without injury, but the duel with a member of Alderney's leading family made Mollet's position in that small island untenable. Over the following few weeks, he made arrangements for his departure, and on 2 January 1790, he returned to take up permanent residence in Guernsey. True to Lieutenant-Governor Brown's presentiments, the episode had been something of a disaster. Charles Mollet had, however, turned a corner: he had abandoned any idea of a mercantile career. On 8 May 1790, he formally dissolved his partnership with Thomas Marett.[102]

Mollet's agreement with Pierre Gavet and Eleazar Ingrouille precluded him from returning to his farm immediately, so he lived for the next two years with his sister and brother-in-law in their house at Candie. In June of the first year, Lieutenant-Governor William Brown fulfilled his earlier offer and made Mollet one of his aides-de-camp.[103] Presumably Mollet received payment for this, but his duties were light. He recorded having taken a census of St Peter Port with Captain John Waugh between January and March 1791,[104] but, aside from this, Mollet's work as an aide-de-camp seems mainly to have consisted of accompanying Brown to military reviews. He also attended many dinner parties given by Brown and was introduced to a number of military men, whose company he seems to have enjoyed.[105] Mollet did not record when his role as aide-de-camp came to an end, but it does not seem to have lasted more than eighteen months. At all events, he had many other occupations during his two years at Candie, not least collecting outstanding debts from his Alderney clients and supervising the conversion of his lower warehouse in la Profonde Rue. He also spent a significant amount of time at his Castel home, where he gardened, entertained friends and occasionally slept the night.

Mollet's rental agreement with Gavet and Ingrouille allowed him to terminate their lease after four years on provision of three months' notice. He took advantage of this facility, and began the process of moving back into his house at the end of 1791.[106] Having re-installed himself there and taken on a

---

[102] Diary, 8.5.1790. Mollet saw little of Marett after this, but he did record attending his funeral six years later (Diary, 26.2.1796).
[103] Diary, 2.6.1790.
[104] Diary, 12.1.1791, 11.2.1791, 31.3.1791.
[105] See, for instance, Diary, 24.6.1791.
[106] Diary, 14.9.1791, 23.10.1791.

farm servant,[107] he resumed his life as a farmer in January 1792, gradually acquiring more livestock and planting crops in his fields as the leases on them expired. By the end of 1793, it was as if the intervening six years had never happened.

Later in the 1790s, an episode occurred which suggests that Mollet was still dissatisfied with his lot (or perhaps he was again prompted by Peter Mourant). This concerned his application for the Crown Receivership. On 3 August 1797, eighty-year-old Field Marshal Sir Jeffery Amherst, Guernsey's Governor, died and was replaced by Earl Grey. Each incoming Governor appointed his own Receiver, and competition for the office was intense, this being a lucrative post. Spotting an opportunity, Charles Mollet sent off a flurry of letters to acquaintances in high places soliciting support for his candidacy.[108] Unfortunately, their influence did not prevail against that exercised by the incumbent Receiver (and future Bailiff) Robert Porret Le Marchant, who had held the post since 1794. Earl Grey confirmed Le Marchant in the post, and he was to retain it until well after Charles Mollet's death. Characteristically, however, Mollet did not express any resentment towards Le Marchant, with whom he had long maintained friendly relations.[109]

In the final decade of his life, Charles Mollet experienced two mysterious financial setbacks. Their precise nature is obscure, not only because his personal accounts do not survive, but also because parts of the journal which relate to them are missing. The first of these setbacks occurred in the period between 5 January and 12 February 1808, for which the diary pages have been cut out. The first indication that something negative had happened came in an entry for the following 11 March. In this entry, Mollet recorded that Robert Le Marchant's wife Marie (*née* Ozanne) had visited him at his home in order to make him 'a very gracious & liberal offer of pecuniary assistance' on her husband's behalf, adding that Le Marchant wished Mollet

---

[107] Diary, 15.12.1791.

[108] Diary, 8.8.1797. One of these letters survives in the National Archives at Kew: Charles Mollet to Philippe D'Auvergne, 7.8.1797 (PC 1/115/118C/16). See also Mollet to D'Auvergne, 21.8.1797 (PC 1/118C/94) and G. Fisher to Earl Grey, 16.8.1797 (GRE/A1166/1, Papers of Charles, Earl Grey of Howick, Durham University Library).

[109] Mollet's first mention of 'Bob' Le Marchant, as he then called him, came in 1774, when Le Marchant was nineteen and Mollet thirty-one (Diary, 24.4.1774). The two men actually developed a better acquaintance after the Receivership episode, as Le Marchant had a house – 'La Chaumière' – built not far from Mollet's in 1802, and they became neighbours (Diary, 4.2.1802, 3.9.1802).

to 'consider him as a brother'.[110] The nature of this assistance and whether Mollet took advantage of it are never mentioned. A few weeks later, however, notices appeared in the local press advertising Mollet's houses and land for sale.[111] These notices elicited no offers, but then again, Mollet's difficulties were perhaps not as dire as the notices suggest, since the next few months of his life seem to have rolled on much as ever.

Four years later, in 1812/13, Mollet appears to have suffered another financial setback. This time, however, the entire volume covering the period is missing. Given this gap in entries, the existence of a problem can only be inferred from another batch of newspaper 'for sale' notices.[112] On this occasion, proximity in time allows us to speculate that the problem may have been related to the collapse of the London banking agents William Brock & Benjamin Le Mesurier and attendant failure of Guernsey's two banks.[113] Certainly, Mollet expressed considerable dismay at Brock and Le Mesurier's insolvency 'amid deplorable circumstances' in 1811.[114] Whatever the precise cause of the setback, Mollet's advertisements seem again to have attracted no takers – with the single important exception, perhaps, of his servants Abraham and Elizabeth Machon, who purchased the 'upper' house from him in May 1815.[115] This transaction brought Mollet 1,650 *livres tournois* (about £120 stg) in cash, and six quarters and three denerels in annual wheat *rente*. Although £120 would certainly have replenished Mollet's coffers, it was hardly a fortune. This begs the question whether the sale was made entirely for financial reasons. Mollet was clearly attached to Ab and Lisabo, and the bargain seems to have ensured their ongoing service, enabling the septuagenarian to continue living in the same comfortable manner as he had done for decades.

Mollet died less than four years after this transaction with his farm still a going concern and his town properties continuing to produce income. Since he had no posterity to provide for, it is almost irrelevant that his assets at

---

[110] Diary, 11.3.1808.
[111] *Gazette de Guernesey*, 16.4.1808, 23.4.1808.
[112] *Le Publiciste*, 10.10.1812, 29.5.1813.
[113] These two banks, which were intimately linked with the London partnership of Brock and Le Mesurier, were 'The Bank of Guernsey', opened in 1804 by Abraham Bishop and Henry De Jersey, and 'The Guernsey Bank', opened in 1808 by Thomas MacCulloch, John Allaire and John Bonamy.
[114] Diary, 10.6.1811, 13.6.1811, 28.11.1811, 18.12.1811.
[115] See n. 42, above.

death were not appreciably greater than they had been fifty years earlier. Chance had dealt him a better hand than the majority of his fellow islanders. That hand had enabled Mollet to preserve till the end of his days the agreeable lifestyle he ultimately seemed to value above wealth. We will examine the nature of Mollet's lifestyle more closely in Chapters 6 and 7. Chapter 5, in the meantime, will revert to the 1770s, to begin an analysis of Mollet's civic life and his role in the insular community.

Plate 1. Mary Brock, née Mourant (1767–1852), Mollet's niece
Courtesy of the Priaulx Library

Plate 2. Anne Brock, née Mourant (1769–1838), Mollet's niece
Courtesy of the Priaulx Library

Plate 3. Peter De Havilland (1747–1821)
Courtesy of the Priaulx Library

Plate 4. Jean Carey of 'Choisi' (1748–1821)
Courtesy of the Priaulx Library

Plate 5. Thomas De Sausmarez (1756–1837)
Courtesy of the Priaulx Library

Plate 6. Jean Guille, jun. (1733–1820)
Courtesy of Guernsey Museums and Galleries

Plate 7. Sir Thomas Saumarez (1760–1845)
Reproduced by permission of Lawrences Fine Art Auctioneers Ltd, Crewkerne, Somerset

Plate 8. John Savery Brock (1772–1844)
From L. Kosche, 'Contemporary portraits of Isaac Brock: an analysis', *Archivaria*, 20 (1985)

Plate 9. Rev. Etienne Gibert (1736–1817)
Courtesy of the Priaulx Library

Plate 10. Peter Le Mesurier (1750–1803), Alderney Governor
ourfamily63.wordpress.com (by kind permission)

Plate 11. Sir Hew Dalrymple (1750–1830)
Alamy stock image

Plate 12. Mary Bruce (1740–96), Duchess of Richmond
Alamy stock image

Plate 13 Józef Boruwlaski (1739–1837), musician and writer
Alamy stock image

Plate 14. Jean-Pierre Blanchard (1753–1809), pioneer balloonist and showman
Alamy stock image

Plate 15. Candie in Victorian times
Courtesy of the Priaulx Library

Plate 16. Garden at Candie, 1830s
Courtesy of the Priaulx Library

Plate 17. Woodlands, 1840s
From T. Bellamy, *Guernsey Pictorial Directory and Stranger's Guide* (Guernsey, 1843)

Plate 18. La Domaillerie, 1840s
From T. Bellamy, *Guernsey Pictorial Directory and Stranger's Guide* (Guernsey, 1843)

Plate 19. Woodlands, 1950s
Courtesy of the Priaulx Library

Plate 20. Woodlands apple-crusher, 1950s
Courtesy of the Priaulx Library

Plate 21. Typical Guernsey kitchen hearth
Courtesy of the Priaulx Library

Plate 22. Cart with horses and oxen, late 18th century (Joshua Gosselin)
Courtesy of Guernsey Museums and Galleries

Plate 23. Château des Marais, late 18th century (Joshua Gosselin)
Courtesy of Guernsey Museums and Galleries

Plate 24. Ships in Guernsey roads, 1777 and 1778
From the Diary of Elisha Dobrée, Island Archives Service (AQ 1572/03)

Plate 25. Louis XVI at Cherbourg, 1786
Alamy stock image

Plate 26. Mouriaux House, Alderney
From C.E.B. Brett, *Buildings of the Island of Alderney* (Belfast, 1976)

5
Civic and Communal Life

Charles Mollet's participation in the public life of his community took two main forms: parochial office-holding and the performance of quasi-military duties. While both were in some sense a function of his status as a leading Castel parishioner, Mollet's military activities also arose from the peculiar geopolitical circumstances of his lifetime: for forty-two of his seventy-six years, Britain was at war with France, and the Channel Islands were strategic British outposts off a hostile French coast. These unusual circumstances also affected the nature of Mollet's parochial duties, on which the first part of this chapter will now focus in detail.

Parochial public office

As major landowners in their parish, Charles Mollet and his family were expected to play a part in parochial governance and administration. This usually meant service as churchwardens, Constables and Douzeniers, elective roles which, although unremunerated, affirmed and enhanced a family's status. It was noted in Chapter 2 that Mollet's father was elected a Constable and then a Douzenier of the Castel parish in the 1740s. It was also noted that Charles Mollet himself had already served two years as a churchwarden before the start of his journals in January 1771. Early in February 1771, Mollet recorded receiving a visit from three leading Castel parishioners enquiring as to his willingness to stand for the office of Constable in a forthcoming election. After some initial reluctance, Mollet agreed to stand, and on 27 February 1771, he was elected to the role by a narrow majority.[1] Eighteenth-century parish Constables were typically young men in the prime of their health and strength. Charles Mollet was twenty-eight when elected. The office of Constable was by custom annual, meaning that no-one was obliged to serve for more than a year. However, Mollet served for ten years without

---

[1] Diary, 20.2.1771, 27.2.1771. The parochial electorate comprised only adult male ratepayers. Just eleven of these voted at the Constable's election, six of whom voted for Mollet.

submitting himself for re-election. During this period, five other men served as Castel Constables alongside him. Their terms ranged from one to three years.[2]

Mollet discharged his responsibilities as Constable concurrently with his farming and other activities. Although he performed the role gratuitously, it occupied a significant proportion of his time, and he would not have been in a position to serve the office had he not enjoyed considerable leisure. His diary provides a unique insight into the multifarious activities of an eighteenth-century Guernsey Constable.

Charles Mollet's administrative duties as Constable took up as much of his time as did his public order duties. One of a Constable's main duties was to convene Douzaine meetings and summon Douzeniers to them. Mollet's diaries recorded some ninety-five Douzaine meetings over his ten years in office. The Douzaine had no permanent base, so meetings were usually held in public houses (notably one run by Mollet's cousin Daniel Le Cheminant). In previous centuries, Douzaines had often met in parish churches and churchyards, but Mollet recorded only one instance of a meeting in the churchyard, and none inside the church itself.[3]

The Douzaine met for a variety of purposes, the most important of which was to set parochial taxes. This was an activity which took place two or three times a year. The taxes set at Douzaine meetings fell into two main brackets: the poor tax (usually destined for the Country Hospital),[4] and the Constables' tax, which funded all other parochial purposes. The Constables collected the latter tax themselves.[5] They also had custody of the funds collected, and responsibility for disbursing them on the objects designated by the Douzaine.

---

[2] Jean Bailleul was already serving as Constable when Mollet joined him in 1771. Succeeding office-holders were André Cohu (1772–5), Nicolas Le Beir (1775–6), Daniel Moullin (1776–9) and Josias Le Marchant (1779–81). See Diary, 30.4.1772, 7.6.1775, 17.10.1776, 13.1.1779.

[3] The churchyard meeting took place in April 1779 (Diary, 6.4.1779). The Douzaine had attempted to meet inside the church in October 1772, but were barred from doing so by one of the churchwardens. Mollet and his fellow Constable mounted a Court challenge to this prohibition, but it was upheld by the Court (Diary, 21.10.1772, 22.10.1772, 24.10.1772).

[4] For more on rural poor relief, see R.-M. Crossan, *Poverty and Welfare in Guernsey, 1560–2015* (Woodbridge, 2015), pp. 58–9.

[5] For examples of Mollet's tax-collecting, see Diary, 29.4.1771, 7.6.1773, 10.6.1773. The Constables did not collect the poor tax, which was the responsibility of the parish Procureur des Pauvres (in charge of poor relief funds) and his Collecteurs.

At least once a year, the Douzaine would meet to inspect and approve the Constables' accounts.[6]

As well as Douzaine meetings, Constables were also responsible for convening parish meetings, which were open to all ratepayers. These were less frequent than Douzaine meetings, and Mollet's diaries recorded only ten during his decade in office. The usual venue for parish meetings – in contrast to Douzaine meetings – was the churchyard. This was probably because of the larger attendance expected, which would have made a public house unsuitable. Parish meetings were held to despatch extraordinary business, such as determining how much emergency grain to purchase for poor parishioners during times of food shortage, which was a particular feature of the 1770s and 1780s.[7] They were also convened to inspect and approve the accounts of the parochial churchwardens and Procureur des Pauvres.[8]

States meetings also occupied a fair amount of Constables' time. Guernsey's parishes were represented in the States by one Constable from each parish, who was obliged to cast his vote as his Douzaine instructed. Mollet, who took it in turns with his fellow Constables to attend States meetings, recorded attending twenty-five such meetings during his ten years of service. The time taken by the meetings themselves was only one aspect of the demand they made upon Constables. They were also obliged to fetch copies of the agenda (known as *Billets d'Etat*) from the Bailiff or his Lieutenant, and deliver them to the Douzeniers.[9] They then had to convene and attend a Douzaine meeting to discuss the proposed measures and note the Douzaine's instructions.

In addition to normal States meetings, Charles Mollet also attended sessions of a special iteration of the States held to elect the Jurats and the Prévôt.[10] There were eleven of these elective sessions during Mollet's time as Constable. They were attended by all the members of the deliberative States, together with both Constables and the entire Douzaines of each

---

[6] See, for instance, Diary, 8.4.1772, 4.5.1775.
[7] Emergency grain supplies were purchased by the Castel parish in 1772, 1774, 1782 and 1784. For more on this practice, see Crossan, *Poverty and Welfare*, p. 56. See also R. Hocart, *The Country People of Guernsey and their Agriculture, 1640–1840* (Guernsey, 2016), p. 139.
[8] See, for instance, Diary, 7.2.1772, 13.11.1777.
[9] As Constable, Charles Mollet had also to deliver a *Billet* to the parish Rector, who had his own *ex-officio* seat in the States (Diary, 11.12.1771).
[10] This was later known as the States of Election. See Chapter 1, n. 51.

parish. In these sessions Mollet had a free vote, though he rarely recorded how he cast it.[11]

As a rural parish Constable, Charles Mollet was additionally obliged to attend meetings of the Country Hospital Board, on which he had an *ex-officio* seat. These meetings were held on Sunday afternoons, and Mollet now and then mentioned missing church to attend them.[12] Membership of the Board put Mollet in a good position to further his personal interests, as he occasionally sold commodities such as peas, barley and cider to the Hospital.[13]

As Constable, it was also Mollet's duty, jointly with at least six Douzeniers, to grant *bornements* (approve the boundaries) of people wishing to enclose land along public roads or make changes in boundary walls abutting on to public roads.[14] In order to fulfil this duty, the Constables and Douzeniers had to go to the property in question and physically inspect the land. Mollet recorded participating in such a procedure on six occasions during his tenure as Constable.[15] He also recorded accompanying Douzeniers to the properties of deceased parishioners in order to grant *vingtièmes* due to their male heirs.[16]

Another of Mollet's duties as Constable (and not the least onerous) was that of ensuring the maintenance of parish roads. At this period, owners of properties bordering Guernsey's roads were legal owners of half the road which their properties bordered, and they were obliged by law to keep surfaces in repair and cut back encroaching vegetation.[17] Mollet and his fellow Constables inspected the roads of the Castel parish twice yearly, in

---

[11] Exceptionally, on 30.6.1772, Mollet reported voting for twenty-four-year-old Jean Carey, whom he knew socially.

[12] Diary, 1.3.1772, 4.10.1772, 5.2.1775, 2.11.1777, 7.11.1779, 2.9.1780. Poor relief being considered a Christian duty, Sunday Board meetings were not seen as profaning the Sabbath.

[13] Diary, 14.3.177, 21.1.1778, 25.11.1779, 15.1.1780, 14.2.1780, 12.1.1781. See also Diary, Notes relating to 1776, 1779 and 1780.

[14] The Royal Court had allocated this duty to Constables and Douzeniers in the early seventeenth century, after landowners erecting banks around their fields were reported to be encroaching on the roads (R. Hocart, *Guernsey's Countryside: An Introduction to the History of the Rural Landscape* (Guernsey, 2010), p. 44).

[15] Diary, 20.10.1771, 23.2.1774, 28.3.1775, 26.6.1776, 2.11.1779.

[16] For an example, see Diary, 8.10.1776. Male heirs to land outside St Peter Port were entitled to take one-twentieth (*un vingtième*) of the estate in a single location before the rest was divided, and the Douzaine was responsible for determining where this twentieth should lie.

[17] T.F. Priaulx, 'Guernsey's roads', *The Review of the Guernsey Society* (Winter 1974), p. 83.

winter and summer.[18] They took notes of all the unfilled potholes and uncut hedges, then delivered notifications to parishioners informing them of the remediation required.[19] If the necessary work were not carried out within a certain time, the Constables would have it done by contractors, whom Mollet, at least, would personally supervise.[20] The Constables would then be obliged to take the delinquent parties to Court in order to recoup the costs thus incurred.[21]

Mollet represented the Douzaine in Court in a wide variety of parochial matters. When in 1774 the parish authorities wished to prevent Jean Guille of St George from closing off a well-frequented lane through his land, it was Charles Mollet and his fellow Constable André Cohu who challenged Guille's application in Court. This action, as all parochial actions, was undertaken in the Constables' own names (which was potentially awkward as the Mollet family were friends of the Guilles). As it was, the Court granted Guille's application, and upheld it in the face of a further appeal lodged by Mollet and Cohu.[22]

Constables' frequent contact with the Royal Court made them something of a conduit for communication between the Court and the parishes, notably in relation to emergency grain imports in times of food shortage.[23] Having initiated the process in the dearth of 1771, the Royal Court requested Charles Mollet to ascertain from his fellow parishioners how much grain they would need. Mollet then convened a parish meeting to determine the amount, and relayed the information back to one of the Jurats.[24]

Constables were also conduits for orders and instructions from the Lieutenant-Governor. This aspect of Mollet's role came particularly to the fore after France entered the War of American Independence in March

---

[18] See, for instance, Diary, 11.6.1772, 5.1.1773.
[19] This did not enhance a Constable's popularity. Mollet recorded that, when he delivered such a notice to William Le Messurier in the spring of 1772, Le Messurier 'gravely insulted' him and 'attempted to strike' him (Diary, 25.4.1772).
[20] Diary, 5.5.1771, 6.10.1771, 6.10.1772, 8.10, 1772, 14.10.1772.
[21] Diary, 14.10.1772, 19.10.1772, 3.12.1772.
[22] Diary, 26.11.1774, 3.12.1774, 7.2.1775. For more on this episode, see R. Hocart, 'Monsieur de St. George: Jean Guille (1712–78)', *Transactions of la Société Guernesiaise*, 26 (2010), pp. 681–2.
[23] Such imports were usually organised on an all-island basis, even though parishes paid individually for what they required.
[24] Diary, 8.5.1771, 12.5.1771, 15.5.1771, 18.5.1771.

1778.[25] Early in April, Lieutenant-Governor Paulus Aemilius Irving issued an order forbidding boat-owners from conveying any foreigners out of the island. This was transmitted to the parish Constables, and Mollet, together with his fellow Constable Daniel Moullin, visited all parochial boat-owners to apprise them of the prohibition.[26] The following year, after an invasion scare which turned out to be a false alarm, Irving issued a general embargo (a ban against going out to sea). On this occasion, Mollet and his colleague not only took the news to boat-owners, but confiscated their oars and posted sentinels to guard their boats.[27]

Hostilities with France seem to have entailed a general increase in Constables' duties, particularly in relation to the local militia. Constables had had custody of the militia's guns and ammunition since 1744,[28] but Mollet's pre-war role in this regard was limited to occasionally fetching gunpowder and supervising the manufacture of cartridges.[29] After 1778, however, he and his fellow Constable became much busier, fetching gunpowder on a more frequent basis, making larger numbers of cartridges, issuing muskets and bayonets for training, drills and watches, and ensuring that equipment was returned in good condition afterwards.[30]

On one occasion, Mollet even had to deal with rioting militiamen. A serious outbreak of militia insubordination occurred in the summer of 1780, perhaps owing to the extra pressure on rural parishioners who were attempting to cultivate their fields and practise their trades while undergoing training and performing watch-duty. Mollet describes the incident thus:

> *Sunday 11 June 1780*: while I was at church in the afternoon, Richard Moullin came to report that a number of militiamen from St Martin were threatening to assault their officers. Mr Ozanne & I went to investigate. We had two men taken to the guardhouse: Sr Jaques Guille (for disrespect & disobedience to the Constables) & James Robert of les Rues (at the request of his Captain, Mr Thos Andros, son of James). Wm Thoume, son of [......] of les Blanches, & Jean le

---

[25] Britain declared war on France on 17 March 1778, after France formally recognised the United States as an independent nation.
[26] Diary, 2.4.1778.
[27] Diary, 5.5.1779. This invasion scare will be discussed in more detail below.
[28] In 1744, the British government had sent 1,000 muskets to the island for militia use and distributed them between the parishes. By Order in Council of 7 November 1744, these were put into the custody of the Constables.
[29] Diary, 10.6.1771, 18.6.1772, 17.6.1777. The cartridges were made of paper and contained the musket ball together with some gunpowder.
[30] Diary, 8.4.1778, 9.4.1778, 13.4.1778, 11.4.1778, 22.6.1778.

Page of les Mouillepieds refused to assist us, & Sr Thos le Retillé threatened to punch the Comptroller (who was giving me advice), calling him a bugger & telling him this was none of his business.

This incident obliged Mollet to attend Court on three occasions to give evidence against the offenders, who were variously prosecuted for assault, insubordination and denying assistance to the Constables. Of the five men prosecuted, James Robert and Thomas Le Retilley were the most harshly punished, each being fined 60 *livres tournois* (about £4 6s stg), required to pay costs, and compelled to make a public apology at the bar of the Court.[31]

The large wartime influx of regular soldiers imposed yet more duties on Charles Mollet. In 1780, Mollet noted the presence in Guernsey of more than 1,800 British troops.[32] Some of the men were housed in Castle Cornet and other forts, but by no means all, as Guernsey was short of military accommodation. An Order in Council of 1691 had given Guernsey's civil authorities the right to decide where soldiers who could not be housed in military premises would be quartered. Traditionally, as many as possible had been lodged in public houses, to which they were allocated by the parish Constables. Publicans had formerly been obliged to provide accommodation *gratis*,[33] but in 1779, the States decided that, in lieu of providing lodgings, publicans should instead pay a tax which would be used to fund alternative billets.[34] The town was ordered to accommodate fifty soldiers, and the country parishes one hundred. Constables were charged with administering the scheme.[35] Accordingly, in the autumn of 1779, Charles Mollet attended a meeting of all the island's Constables to determine the amount by which publicans would be taxed. The sum was set at 10 *sous* (8½d) per publican per week.[36] The Constables collected this tax themselves, and Mollet recorded regular collections from publicans throughout the last two years of his tenure.[37] Once collected, the proceeds of the tax were pooled. Constables then met quarterly to settle their respective parishes' expenses.[38] The country

---

[31] Diary, 8.7.1780. See also 12.6.1780, 13.6.1780.

[32] Diary, 10.6.1780.

[33] The rationale for this lay in the large profits publicans made from soldiers.

[34] R. Hocart, *An Island Assembly: The Development of the States of Guernsey, 1700-1949* (Guernsey, 1988), pp. 5-6, 10.

[35] G.E. Lee (ed.), *Actes des Etats de l'Ile de Guernesey, 1651-1780* (Guernsey, 1907), p. 379.

[36] Diary, 11.11.1779.

[37] See, for instance, Diary, 10.8.1780.

[38] Diary, 20.1.1780, 19.4.1780, 10.8.1780.

parishes collectively used spare capacity in their workhouse to accommodate their share of soldiers, as also an empty dwelling house which they fitted out for the purpose.[39] All parishes additionally contributed towards the cost of providing plank beds, blankets and cooking utensils for temporary camps set up under States auspices.[40]

The presence of troops in the Country Hospital, which was located in the Castel parish, exerted a considerable impact on Mollet's public order duties. In the early part of his tenure, these had been relatively light. The public order duty which had made the greatest call on his time was that of supervising local taverns. Until 1774, these were banned from serving alcohol on a Sunday, and the Constables regularly made spot inspections at all times of day, sometimes leaving church in the middle of services.[41] Between 1774 and 1777, three new Ordinances were issued which, by the latter date, permitted Sunday opening between noon and 9 pm.[42] After this, Mollet's visits were restricted to mornings and evenings. On premises where he found out-of-hours drinkers, Mollet had no compunction in summarily ejecting them.[43] He does not mention whether such ejections gave him any satisfaction, but he may well have derived more pleasure from a complementary duty, which was to sample publicans' cider to vouch for its quality.[44]

Mollet never recorded prosecuting anyone for the breach of a public house Ordinance, but he did record prosecutions for the breach of other Ordinances (about twenty in his decade as Constable). The majority of these prosecutions fell into two main categories: for allowing livestock to graze on the public highway (such as that against Thomas Gallienne in 1772), or else for obstructing the public highway with unattended carts or other encumbrances (such as that against Sr Jean Girard in 1780).[45] Prosecutions under

---

[39] Diary, 30.10.1779, 30.9.1780, 6.10.1780. St Peters had its own poorhouse and did not contribute to the Country Hospital until 1798. How its authorities interacted with those of the other country parishes as regarded the troops is unclear.

[40] Diary, 3.6.1778, 5.5.1779.

[41] For instance, Diary, 6.10.1771, 13.10.1771, 8.8.1772. The law in force in the early 1770s was an Ordinance of 15 April 1611, as confirmed by one of 4 May 1685.

[42] An Ordinance of 16 January 1774 allowed public houses to open after 4.00 pm on a Sunday. Another of 2 October 1775 set Sunday hours at 4.00 pm to 9.00 pm. A further Ordinance of 6 October 1777 brought opening time forward to noon while leaving closing time at 9.00 pm.

[43] See, for instance, Diary, 5.7.1777.

[44] Diary, 7.9.1772, 26.10.1777.

[45] Diary, 13.6.1772, 27.5.1780, 2.12.80.

Ordinances were carried out in the joint names of the Constable concerned and HM Procureur.[46] Those found guilty had to pay costs and were punished with a fine, half of which went to the Constable. If the prosecution failed, the Constable was liable for costs.[47]

Ordinance-related prosecutions were regarded as regulatory rather than criminal matters. Until the quartering of soldiers in the Country Hospital in 1780, Charles Mollet dealt with very little criminal business. Thefts among parishioners were not unknown, but they rarely resulted in prosecutions. In most pre-1780 cases recorded in his diaries, Mollet's involvement was limited to making a search for the stolen goods (for which he did not require a warrant). More often than not, however, the search was fruitless and the identity of the thief remained obscure.[48] In the two pre-1780 theft cases where Mollet did uncover evidence, he reported his findings to the Procureur and Bailiff, but they decided not to take the matter further.[49]

After the soldiers' arrival, the peace of country life was disrupted. As well as coping with rising numbers of thefts, Mollet found himself having to deal with deserters, whom he pursued, arrested and took to the town guardhouse.[50] It was, however, the escalating thefts which caused Mollet most aggravation, not least because his own property was targeted on more than one occasion. On 7 December 1780 he recorded:

> Pierre [Gavet] caught a man by the name of Mactavy stealing my cress & confiscated his basket & gun. Yesterday he found 4 men making away with my turnips & confiscated their sack. This evening Mr Moullin & I seized nearly a bushel of potatoes from two men who had just stolen them from Sr Jean le Pelley.[51]

---

[46] For more on prosecutions under Ordinances, see R.-M. Crossan, *Criminal Justice in Guernsey, 1680–1929* (Benderloch, 2021), pp. 92–3.

[47] How much this impacted on a Constable's own purse is unclear. It seems likely that the fines in successful prosecutions would have been added to parochial funds in the Constable's custody, as also that the legal costs in failed prosecutions would have been drawn from these funds.

[48] Diary, 1.5.1772, 19.10.1772, 6.12.1772, 22.12.1777.

[49] Diary, 13.1.1772, 18.1.1777. For procedure in such cases, see Crossan, *Criminal Justice*, pp. 78–81.

[50] See, for instance, Diary, 23.8.1780. Guernsey's parish Constables did not require a warrant from higher authority to make an arrest.

[51] Pierre Gavet was Mollet's farm servant at the time.

Mactavy and the others were probably soldiers. Earlier that same month, Mollet had come into direct conflict with the military authorities when attempting to arrest two soldiers whom he had found in possession of some stolen timber. On this occasion, the duty officer at the Country Hospital had not allowed Mollet to remove the men from the premises, upon which Mollet had complained to the Court. As a result of Mollet's complaint, HM Procureur and Comptroller were deputed to ask the Lieutenant-Governor to order that soldiers suspected of crimes against islanders should always be handed over to the civil authorities.[52] Charles Mollet did not record whether the Lieutenant-Governor made the order requested, but he did relate that an 'Ensign Crooks' of the 96th Regiment had written a letter of complaint about him (Mollet) to the Lieutenant-Governor. According to Mollet, this letter made a number of 'false allegations' about him, which he had 'positively denied'.[53] Mollet did not record the substance of these allegations, and the letter which contained them has not survived.

As tensions with the military mounted at the end of 1780, Mollet was in the process of assembling a number of fellow parishioners who were each to submit evidence to the Court regarding 'the thefts, depredations and threats we have suffered'.[54] Mollet's own account of the outcome is missing, as this volume of his journal terminated a few days later, and the next has not survived. However, Royal Court records show that, on 26 May 1781, Mess Sergeant James Brown was sentenced to 200 lashes and three years' banishment for organising the systematic plundering of fruit, vegetables and poultry from Castel parishioners over a period of months.[55]

Court records also provide evidence of a more serious case in which Mollet must have been involved later in 1781. This concerned the brothers Pierre and Abraham Collenette, who were neighbours and acquaintances of Mollet. The house where the brothers lived with their respective families was broken into by three soldiers of the 96th Regiment during the night of 4/5 May 1781. The house was ransacked, valuables were stolen, the brothers were ill-treated, and their wives (Marie Guilbert and Madeleine Le Page) were raped in front of them. The case came to Court in June 1781, and two of the soldiers were hanged in November.[56]

[52] Diary, 1.12.1780, 2.12.1780.
[53] Diary, 18.12.1780.
[54] Diary, 14.12.1780, 18.12.1780, 20.12.1780.
[55] 11.12.1780, 9.2.1781, 14.2.1781, 26.5.1781, Livres en Crime, Greffe.
[56] 9.6.1781, 3.11.1781, Livres en Crime, Greffe. See also Crossan, *Criminal Justice*, p. 198.

By this time, Charles Mollet had been serving as a Castel Constable for more than ten years. He must have valued the status and authority which the office conferred upon him, for otherwise he would not have continued in this role, which, as previously noted, was nominally annual. From the middle of his tenure onwards, however, his journals reveal signs of friction with parochial Douzeniers. On more than one occasion he convened meetings to which they did not turn up.[57] Further, following an election to replace his fellow Constable in 1775, Douzeniers attempted to have the new Constable, Nicolas Le Beir (for whom they had all voted), officially designated *Connétable d'Etat*, which would have given Le Beir a monopoly of the parish seat in the States and effectively excluded Charles Mollet. There was no insular precedent for this, however, and the Court refused to grant the Castel Douzeniers permission to do so.[58] In yet another sign of friction two years later, Mollet expressed his belief that the Douzeniers were withholding parish papers from him. He actioned Douzenier Thomas Falla in an attempt to force him to hand over the documents, and although he recorded the Court's appointment of Commissioners to arbitrate between them, he did not record the final outcome.[59]

In January 1778, tensions between Mollet and the Douzeniers came to a head when the Castel Douzaine petitioned the Royal Court for an Ordinance formally prohibiting parish Constables from serving more than one year.[60] On this occasion, the petition was rejected, but the Douzaine re-submitted it a few months later in company with the Douzaines of five other parishes. As a result, the Court finally issued an Ordinance regulating Constables' tenure.[61] Contrary to the Douzaines' wish, however, this Ordinance made a fresh election mandatory after three years, not one. Although Castel parish registers do not record the precise date of Mollet's resignation, they show that it had occurred by November 1781 at the latest, which was almost exactly three years after the issue of the Ordinance.[62] Interestingly, unlike his father, Charles Mollet was never elected a Douzenier, nor did he subsequently seek elective office as a Jurat or Prévôt.

---

[57] For instance, Diary, 21.3.1775, 20.5.1775, 27.5.1775.
[58] Diary, 7.6.1775, 17.6.1775.
[59] Diary, 8.11.1777, 15.11.1777, 6.3.1778, 14.3.1778, 13.6.1778, 20.6.1778.
[60] Diary, 19.1.1778.
[61] Ordinance of 5.10.1778; Diary, 5.10.1778.
[62] 26.11.1781, Castel Parish Register, 1764–1809 (AQ 1017/8, Island Archives).

Quasi-military activities

Guernsey had had a standing militia since the mid-fourteenth century. By the late eighteenth century, it was made up of four infantry regiments and four artillery companies.[63] The infantry regiments consisted of the First or Town Regiment (comprising men from St Peter Port and St Sampsons, with buff facings on their tunics); the Second or North Regiment (Castel and the Vale, green facings); the Third or South Regiment (St Martins, St Andrews and the Forest, blue facings); and the Fourth or West Regiment (St Saviours, St Peters and Torteval, black facings).[64] Each regiment had a command structure of part-time Colonels and subordinate officers drawn from the local elite. By custom, all native males aged between sixteen and sixty were obliged to serve; however, this was not always enforced for islanders of high status.[65] In 1771, Charles Mollet was asked by William Le Marchant, Colonel of the North Regiment, to accept the post of Adjutant under him.[66] Mollet declined.[67] Thereafter, the diaries contain no mention of Mollet's joining the militia in any capacity. He did, however, keep a number of firearms at his house, and now and again he recorded his presence at target-practice.[68]

In 1772, Mollet began regularly attending militia reviews at nearby Vazon or les Mielles (as a spectator rather than a participant). This was a practice he kept up until the turn of the century. He was at first perhaps obliged to attend these reviews on account of his service as parish Constable.[69] His continuing attendance beyond his period in office may have been related to his personal connections with successive Lieutenant-Governors. As Chapters 7 and 9 will show, Mollet entertained friendly relations with Lieutenant-Colonel Paulus Aemilius Irving (Lieutenant-Governor, 1770–83), Lieutenant-Colonel William Brown (1784–93) and Lieutenant-General Hew Dalrymple (1796–1802). Something of a precedent was created when, in 1779, Mollet began inviting Lieutenant-Governor Irving and his retinue to take

---

[63] E. Parks, *The Royal Guernsey Militia: A Short History and List of Officers* (Guernsey, 1992), pp. 5, 9–10.
[64] Mollet often referred to these regiments by colour alone.
[65] The sixteen-to-sixty obligation was not mentioned in any written law until the Militia Ordinance of 27.9.1794.
[66] William Le Marchant (1711–73) was the eldest son of Elizée Le Marchant of la Haye du Puits (1686–1779).
[67] Diary, 4.1.1771.
[68] Diary, 24.6.1772, 8.2.1774.
[69] Vazon and les Mielles were both in the Castel parish (see Map 6).

refreshments at his home before or after such reviews.[70] Mollet's house was conveniently positioned on the route between Vazon and town, and the sight of the military party processing towards it will only have enhanced Mollet's prestige among fellow parishioners. In ensuing years, Charles Mollet continued this practice with the other Lieutenant-Governors with whom he was socially acquainted.

During wartime, it was the practice of some Lieutenant-Governors to appoint two prominent gentlemen from each parish to play a co-ordinating role in case of attacks or alarms.[71] In the War of American Independence (the first bout of Franco-British warfare documented by Mollet), the capture of the Channel Islands was a minor French strategic goal, with the aim of stopping the Islands' privateering operations. There were two attacks on Jersey during the course of this war, both of which had their repercussions on Guernsey. The first took place in the early hours of 1 May 1779, when a large force under the command of the Prince of Nassau-Siegen attempted a landing at St Ouen's Bay but were successfully repelled by the 78th Regiment and Jersey militia.[72] Mollet recorded having observed a French fleet of fifty-three vessels from Guernsey's south-east coast that very day, and the next day he received the news of their attack on Jersey.[73] On Monday 3 May, there was an alarm (false, as it proved) that Guernsey itself was about to be invaded, and Charles Mollet sprang into action. This might have been because he was a parish Constable, or perhaps because he was one of the Lieutenant-Governor's nominated gentlemen. Whatever the case, he recorded the incident thus:

> *Monday 3 May 1779*: Danl Moullin came here at three in the morning to tell us there was an alarm. Beacons were lit & bells were rung in almost all the parishes. I went to various places before breakfast, & even as far as Plein Mont, but it seems it was a false alarm, since there was no fleet to be seen. Later in the day, I went to town & to several other places. In returning from the Vale between two & three in the afternoon, I caught sight of a fleet to the north of us, in which I counted more than 60 vessels. The Governor gave the alarm signal at about four, & we

---

[70] Diary, 11.7.1779 records the first such instance.
[71] Anon., *Almanach Journalier à l'Usage de l'Île de Guernesey pour l'Année 1797* (Guernsey, 1797) gives the names of men appointed to this role in 1796.
[72] *The Guernsey and Jersey Magazine*, 3 (1837), p. 371. See also, J. Duncan, *The History of Guernsey* (London, 1841), pp. 150–1; F.B. Tupper, *The History of Guernsey and its Bailiwick* (Guernsey, 1854), pp. 371–2.
[73] Diary, 1.5.1779, 2.5.1779.

remained under arms until seven, when it was confirmed that the fleet was an English one. This fleet, under Admiral Arbuthnot, had been on its way to New York when it received the message that the Islands were in danger, & it came to our aid on the Admiral's own initiative (for which I hope he will receive the thanks which he deserves). Our people showed themselves brave & alert. Some men from the local companies went as far as le Braie du Valle. I returned here after eight in the evening feeling rather tired. I was almost constantly in the saddle from three in the morning & changed horses several times. I think I must have ridden about 100 miles.[74]

Like his fellow islanders, Mollet also undertook regular spells of watch-duty during the War of American Independence, usually in the newly-built loophole tower at Vazon, or else at Pleinmont in the south-west corner of the island.[75] As well as taking his own turn on the watch, Mollet also undertook duty on behalf of his mother who, as a prominent parishioner in her own right, was obliged to provide a man to perform watches in her name.[76] Mollet seems to have enjoyed the comradeship of these occasions enormously. In the late summer of 1779, he wrote:

Mr Bob Marchant & I spent last night at Plein Mont, where we were on watch-duty for 24 hours, 16 of us gentlemen having agreed to do duty in pairs for 24 hours each. We were the last pair, the watch having begun 8 days ago. We had a tent, &c., & spent the time most agreeably.[77]

Mollet also enjoyed accompanying the duty militia officers to inspect the watch, an activity which he termed in his diary *le surguet*.[78] The officers were obliged to make a nightly round of the watch-houses, batteries and sentry posts, after which they signed a return which was delivered to the Inspector

---

[74] The Admiral alluded to by Mollet was Vice-Admiral Mariot Arbuthnot (1711–94), who was on his way to take up an appointment as commander-in-chief of the North American station.

[75] Guernsey's coastal defences had been strengthened by the construction of fifteen loop-hole towers and other fortifications following France's entrance into the War of American Independence.

[76] Diary, 11.8.1779, 17.6.1779.

[77] Diary, 3.9.1779. The 'Bob Marchant' referred to was twenty-four-year-old future Bailiff Robert Porret Le Marchant.

[78] Information on *le surguet*, as also on female parishioners' obligation to provide a man for watch-duty can be found in F.C. Lukis, 'Reminiscences of Former Days in Connection with Guernsey' (unpub. MS, Priaulx Library).

of Militia. Inspections usually ended at Pleinmont and were often followed by a visit to a nearby inn run by a Mr Le Huray.[79]

A second and more serious attack on Jersey took place on 5/6 January 1781. This was led by Baron Philippe de Rullecourt, who had been second-in-command in the invasion attempt of 1779. De Rullecourt's force landed during the night at Grouville Bay and marched as far as St Helier, where in the early morning the Lieutenant-Governor, taken by surprise, signed articles of capitulation. Later in the day, the militia and garrison troops, who had been assembling outside the town, retook St Helier after a battle in the marketplace, where de Rullecourt and the acting garrison commander Major Francis Peirson were both fatally wounded.[80] On receiving news of the attack on Jersey, Charles Mollet again sprang into action:

> *Saturday 6 January 1781*: word reached us between 2 & 3 in the afternoon that the French landed covertly in Jersey early this morning. They took the town by surprise at about 6 & seized the Governor at 7. The alarm was sounded here, & the Regiments remained on high alert all night.
>
> *Sunday 7 January 1781*: I made several patrols through the parish & 4 journeys into town, spending the rest of my time with the officers at Anneville. The alarm remained in force from yesterday evening until 10 o'clock this morning, when an express arrived from Jersey to inform us that our troops had recaptured the town & freed the Governor the previous evening with the loss of 50 men killed & 25 wounded. On the French side, there were several hundred killed, 50 wounded, & 500 taken prisoner.[81]

On this occasion, Mollet's anxiety was especially acute because his seventy-three-year-old mother was staying with his sister Marie Lerrier in St Helier. He made several attempts to travel to Jersey in the immediate wake of the attack but was unsuccessful owing to bad weather.[82] On 13 January 1781, he wrote:

---

[79] Diary, 2.8.79, 4.8.79, 24.8.79, 26.8.79, 15.9.79, 31.8.80.
[80] This episode is recounted in *The Guernsey and Jersey Magazine*, 3 (1837), pp. 371–3. See also Duncan, *History of Guernsey*, pp. 151–6; Tupper, *Guernsey and its Bailiwick*, pp. 372–6.
[81] F.B. Tupper gave British casualties at what became known as 'the Battle of Jersey' as sixteen killed and sixty-five wounded; French casualties as seventy-eight killed, seventy-four wounded, and 417 taken prisoner (Tupper, *Guernsey and its Bailiwick*, p. 375).
[82] Diary, 12.1.1781.

today we received a letter from my brother[in-law] giving us news of everyone. No-one was hurt at his house, although nearly all his windows were broken & his doors were pierced by gunshot. Baron de Rullecourt, the French General, died at his brother's house.[83]

His fears partially allayed, Mollet gave up his bid to travel to Jersey and sent his servant Pierre Gavet there instead. Any further information Pierre might have brought back is missing, as this volume of the diary ended five days later and the next has not survived. When the diary resumed on 1 January 1785, Britain was at peace with France.[84]

This peace continued for four years and encompassed Charles Mollet's sojourn Alderney. In a foretaste of things to come, however, the French Revolution occurred during his second year in that island. Mollet made his first allusion to the Revolution on 22 July 1789, eight days after the storming of the Bastille. His reference was to news received in Alderney of 'a mutiny' at nearby Cherbourg. Cherbourg was in the grip of a food shortage at this time, and the rioting populace had forced open the grain stores, as also the municipal prison, from which – in an echo of the Bastille – the prisoners were set free.[85] This knowledge did not however deter Mollet from visiting the port city a few weeks later, where he witnessed the ceremony pledging 'fidelity to the Nation and King' which Cherbourg, along with all French municipalities, was ordered by the Assemblée Nationale to perform, in a measure intended to assuage the anxieties of respectable citizens following the tumultuous events of July:

> *Sunday 23 August 1789*: I accompanied Monsieur Du Long Prey to le Calvaire in the morning, where the militia was assembled. We then followed the first militia company as far as the Basin, where about 4000 soldiers & militiamen were

---

[83] Mollet's statement regarding Lerrier's brother's house is puzzling, as Philippe Lerrier's only brother appears to have died in infancy. It is possible that Mollet may have written *frère* for *fils*, as Lerrier's son, another Philippe Lerrier (1755–1823), was a doctor by profession, and Rullecourt is known to have been tended in his final moments by the doctor in whose house he died.

[84] The American War of Independence had ended with the Peace of Paris in September 1783.

[85] G. Lefebvre, *Cherbourg à la Fin de l'Ancien Régime et au Début de la Révolution* (Caen, 1965), pp. 141–65.

gathered in order to take the Oath of Fidelity to the Nation & the King, &c. The Oath was followed by a Mass & the singing of the Te Deum (inside a tent).[86]

Mollet did not record his political views in his diary, but like many of his peers, he may initially have been sympathetic to the Revolution, seeing it as a welcome move towards more enlightened government.[87] In 1790, once he had moved back to Guernsey, Mollet re-visited France. This time he stayed for nearly six weeks, touring Normandy and Brittany and meeting a range of people with differing views. One of these was the Canon Law Professor Jérôme Dom Costin (1759–1825), who later became an ardent supporter of the revolutionary cause.[88] In a sign of the unquiet times, however, Mollet, who was travelling without a passport, was twice arrested during his stay in France and detained by officials who may have mistaken him for a spy.[89]

As noted in the previous chapter, Charles Mollet served as Lieutenant-Governor William Brown's aide-de-camp for at least eighteen months after his permanent return from Alderney. This was probably his most sustained period in a quasi-military role. As it happened, it was uneventful, as it fell almost entirely during peacetime – albeit the uneasy peace immediately preceding the guillotining of Louis XVI.

The French king's execution on 21 January 1793 brought a number of significant changes to British (and local) public opinion, which saw it as a sign that France had descended into a state of violent chaos. On 24 January 1793, Britain responded to the regicide by expelling the French ambassador, and on 1 February the National Convention retaliated by declaring war on Britain. Hostilities with France were to continue for the next twenty-two years.[90] Charles Mollet, who was in his fifty-first year when the French

---

[86] For the ceremony and the decree of 10 August which mandated it, see Lefebvre, *Cherbourg*, p. 186.
[87] For a similar attitude on the part of Peter De Havilland, see R. Hocart, *Peter de Havilland: Bailiff of Guernsey, A History of his Life, 1747–1821* (Guernsey, 1997), pp. 35–6. It is interesting in this regard that Guernsey's only newspaper of the period, *la Gazette de Guernesey*, carried the full text of *La Déclaration des Droits de l'Homme et du Citoyen* and the whole of the new French Constitution in successive weekly instalments.
[88] Diary, 7.10.1790, 11.10.1790, 14.10.1790, 16.10.1790, 17.10.1790, 18.10.1790. Mollet's travels will be further discussed in Chapter 8.
[89] Diary, 22.10.1790, 24.10.1790, 25.10.1790.
[90] With a thirteen-month break following the signing of the Treaty of Amiens in 1802, and an eleven-month break between Napoleon's abdication in April 1814 and his return from Elba in March 1815.

Revolutionary War began, was in his seventy-third year when the Napoleonic War finally ended.

At the outbreak of the Revolutionary War, Guernsey once more became a frontline outpost, with all the disruption that this entailed. Mollet recorded the reinstatement of mandatory watches on 2 February 1793 and the arrival of the first regular military reinforcements on 18 February.[91] Although the influx this time was larger than ever,[92] there was no quartering of soldiers in workhouses. A new military headquarters at Fort George on the outskirts of town accommodated many of the troops, and barracks were also erected at Amherst, Delancey Hill, Vale Castle, L'Erée, Richmond, Hommet, Grandes Rocques and Jerbourg.[93]

As in previous wars, the new war saw a number of invasion alarms. Rumours were particularly rife in 1793/4, when French War Minister Lazare Carnot was thought to be planning an attack on the Channel Islands.[94] The attack, which was scheduled for February 1794, never in fact took place. It was initially postponed due to bad weather, and a second attempt in June 1794 is thought to have been thwarted by a naval action close to Guernsey's west coast. This action – involving a squadron under the command of Sir James Saumarez – was subsequently the subject of much local pride.[95] Mollet does not appear to have observed the action in person, but others did, and Mollet wrote an account of it from their testimony:

> *Sunday 8 June 1794*: Early this morning 5 French frigates gave chase to 3 English frigates (of superior strength) to the north of the Island. Towards noon, two of the English vessels made a dash to escape via les Hannois, & Sir James Saumarez in the Crescent narrowly avoided capture by sailing close to the rocks north of le Houmet, where he was fired on by 4 of the French vessels. Happily, he sustained

---

[91] Diary, 2.2.1793, 18.2.1793. The first regiment to arrive was the 54th (West Norfolk) Regiment.

[92] According to F.B. Tupper, more than 50,000 British soldiers passed through Guernsey between 1793 and 1814 (Tupper, *Guernsey and its Bailiwick*, p. 403).

[93] *Ibid.*, p. 391.

[94] Diary, 18.3.1793, 24.4.1793. See also C.H. De Sausmarez, 'Lazare Carnot's plan for the invasion of the Channel Islands, 1794', *Transactions de la Société Guernesiaise*, 19 (1974), pp. 416–34.

[95] For Saumarez and his family, who were friends of Charles Mollet's, see Appendix 4.

no damage (owing to the French sailors' lack of skill). The 3 English vessels reached the safety of the roadstead in the afternoon.[96]

The Lieutenant-Governor at the time of the 1794 alarm was Major-General John Small. At Small's death in March 1796, Mollet noted 'I never made his acquaintance.'[97] Perhaps this was a matter for regret, as Small had been a popular figure among islanders. Whatever the case, Mollet hastened to make himself known to Small's replacement, Major-General Hew Whitefoord Dalrymple, who was sworn in as Lieutenant-Governor in April 1796.[98]

Less than a month after Dalrymple entered into office, there was another invasion scare. Charles Mollet, perhaps missing the role he had played under Lieutenant-Governors Irving and Brown, spontaneously sprang into action:

> *Thursday 3 May 1796*: At around ten in the evening, the alarm sounded & everyone went immediately to their posts. I rode to town, consulted the Governor, & returned here at two in the morning. I then went to Vazon, la Mare de Carteret, &c., and came back home at four. At five, I left again for town, & returned via le Houmet where I gave the order to stand down the militiamen who had been under arms all night. Mr Gosselin (the Colonel) & Anthony Priaulx then came here for breakfast.

On this occasion, the alarm turned out to be false. On Friday 4 May, Mollet wrote: 'we learned that yesterday's alarm was raised in response to a signal from Jersey which had been made accidentally & without any cause.' However, he added, 'I think I must have covered 50 or 60 miles on horseback last night.'

Mollet's impromptu intervention notwithstanding, Dalrymple later appointed Jean Guille and André Cohu as his military co-ordinators in the Castel parish, and Charles Mollet was to perform this role no more.[99] Whether or not this came as a disappointment to Mollet is not recorded in the diaries. At all events, Mollet remained on a friendly footing with

---

[96] For a modern account of this action, see D. Shayer, What path did the Crescent follow? Sir James Saumarez's escape, June 8th 1794', *Transactions of la Société Guernesiaise*, 24 (1997), pp. 290–9.
[97] Diary, 21.3.1796.
[98] Diary, 7.4.1796. See Plate 11 for a contemporary painting of Dalrymple.
[99] See *Almanach Journalier à l'Usage de l'Ile de Guernesey pour l'Année 1797*, which states that the appointments were made on 22 July 1796.

Dalrymple until his departure from the island six years later.[100] Mollet also resumed his former practice of attending militia reviews at Vazon and les Mielles, and – just as he had done previously – he invited the Lieutenant-Governor and his party to refreshments at his home before or after these reviews.[101]

Throughout the French Revolutionary and Napoleonic Wars, Mollet was rostered to take his turn at watch-duty. Initially, he seems to have performed this duty in person, but when he reached his sixties and seventies, he paid substitutes to do it for him, usually one of his farm servants or labourers.[102] The going rate for this service seems to have been 2s 6d per night.[103]

From 1791 onwards, Charles Mollet became heavily involved with French *émigrés*.[104] This brought him into contact with Captain Philippe D'Auvergne (1754–1816). D'Auvergne, a Jerseyman, was responsible for administering British government grants to *émigrés* in the Islands, for assisting these *émigrés* to organise militarily, and for co-ordinating the collection of intelligence from France. He was promoted Rear-Admiral in 1808.[105] Mollet recorded meeting D'Auvergne, both in Jersey and in Guernsey, at least four times.[106] He also recorded writing to him on several occasions. It is most unlikely that Mollet was part of D'Auvergne's intelligence-gathering network, but one of his letters, preserved in the National Archives at Kew, imparted intelligence about the state of affairs in Cherbourg which Mollet had learned from a Frenchman with whom he had spoken in Guernsey.[107]

After Hew Dalrymple's departure, Charles Mollet's dealings with Lieutenant-Governors ceased. But, while he never got to know John Doyle, he had frequent contacts with officers serving under him. Towards the end of the Napoleonic Wars, one particular officer often featured in his journal. This was thirty-five-year-old Lieutenant-Colonel Hercules Scott of the 103rd

---

[100] In 1802, Dalrymple was promoted General Officer Commanding Northern District, and from this point absented himself permanently from Guernsey. Major-General John Doyle, who replaced him as commander of the garrison and militia in 1802, officially became Lieutenant-Governor in 1803.
[101] Diary, 4.9.1796, 31.7.1796, 5.6.1797, 25.3.1799, 25.5.1801, 24.6.1802.
[102] Diary, 15.12.1809, 7.4.1810, 29.4.1810, 25.5.1810, 24.8.1811.
[103] Diary, 29.4.1810.
[104] Mollet's involvement with *émigrés* will be discussed in greater detail in Chapter 7.
[105] G.R. Balleine, *The Tragedy of Philippe D'Auvergne* (Chichester, 1973).
[106] Diary, 26.5.1795, 19.6.1796, 10.10.1796, 22.11.1808.
[107] Mollet to D'Auvergne, 16.3.1796 (PC 1/117A/134, National Archives).

Regiment.[108] Soldiers from Scott's regiment built the new road connecting town with Vazon in the summer of 1810, and Scott was in charge of them.[109] This road cut through the edge of Mollet's property in the Castel. As a landowner, Mollet might potentially have raised difficulties concerning the road, and Colonel Scott wisely chose to forestall any problems by befriending him. Mollet had always enjoyed the company of military men and readily became friendly with Scott. This was just as well, as the problems Scott had anticipated soon materialised. These will be recounted in detail in the next chapter. Suffice it to say here that Scott's diplomacy ensured that the road was built without too many hitches, and his friendship with Mollet survived.

It was, indeed, through his connection with Scott that Charles Mollet's last involvement with military affairs came about. In the autumn of 1811, it was reported that French troops were massing at Cherbourg in preparation for an attack on the Islands. The military authorities decided to respond by erecting fascines along the west coast.[110] Mollet's property was in easy carting distance of the coast, and it was to him that Scott and his colleague Colonel Augustus De Butts turned to provide a proportion of the materials. Between 7 and 15 October that year, Mollet's farm was a hive of activity. Soldiers came in number to fell trees, lop branches and cut brushwood, and a fleet of carts arrived to convey the materials away.[111]

Six months later Colonel Scott was posted to Canada, whence he never returned.[112] The volume of Mollet's journal covering the end of the Napoleonic War is missing, and when the last surviving volume opened in 1815, all military activity had ceased. In the remaining three and a half years of his life, Mollet had nothing further to do with parish, militia or garrison. Now in his seventies, he was probably glad of the peace.

---

[108] Scott (1775–1814) was from Brotherton in Kincardineshire.
[109] For more on the new road, whose construction was instigated by Lieutenant-Governor Doyle for military reasons, see Chapter 6.
[110] Diary, 5.10.1811. Fascines were temporary barriers made of tree branches and brushwood.
[111] Diary, 7.10.1811, 8.10.1811, 9.10.1811, 11.10.18111, 14.10.1811, 15.10.1811.
[112] Diary, 20.4.1812. The 103rd regiment was sent to Canada to fight in the War of 1812. Hercules Scott was killed at the Battle of Erie.

6

Domestic Life

The focus of this chapter will be Charles Mollet's domestic economy. The chapter will look in detail at the nature of Mollet's home; how it was furnished; how it was heated and lighted; how and by whom it was cleaned. It will look at the food Charles Mollet and his household consumed; who cooked their meals; what they ate and when they ate it. It will also look at the clothes Mollet and his household wore; how they were made; how they were mended; and how they were laundered. Finally, it will look at Charles Mollet's personal transport; how and by what means he and his contemporaries moved around; how this was conditioned by the local environment; and how this changed as the local infrastructure changed.

The Gardner map of 1787 showed Mollet's house as set back a few metres from a lane or cart-track on its eastern side which is now known as Les Vallées.[1] The house (which still exists, though much extended) was accessed from this lane by a short drive. It was built out of local granite, with thick exterior walls.[2] As noted in Chapter 3, a modern expert on vernacular houses has estimated the original dwelling to have been built around 1540.[3] It was represented on the 1787 map as a single north-facing block with a small wing projecting forward from the front on the side nearest the lane. We know from Chapter 3 that there were several outbuildings adjacent to the house, and, further out, a large area of garden and orchard. Mollet's diaries also mention a paved courtyard directly under his bedroom windows, as well as some sort of greenhouse (which he also called an orangery) close by or attached to the house. This greenhouse was originally thatched, and later tiled.[4] Mollet's own dwelling retained its thatched roof throughout his residence. In 1791, Mollet insured the property for £300 with the Phoenix Insurance Company.[5]

---

[1] See Map 4 and back cover.
[2] Plate 17 depicts the house as it was about two decades after Mollet's death. Plate 19 shows it as it stood in the 1950s.
[3] J. McCormack, *Channel Island Houses* (Guernsey, 2015), pp. 792–3.
[4] See Chapter 3, n. 196.
[5] Diary, 24.11.1791. The Phoenix Company's local agent at the time was future Bailiff Robert Le Marchant.

F.B. Tupper, writing about Guernsey in the 1770s, said that most local houses 'were small and mean, with low and dark rooms'. He added that 'the furniture, even in the best, was poor and deficient, and many a gentleman's parlour was uncarpeted, having only a sanded floor.'[6] The rooms in Mollet's house certainly had low ceilings, with the average ground floor height perhaps as little as six feet. The main rooms on this floor were Mollet's kitchen and parlour. From his journals, we know that the kitchen contained a large open hearth and enough space for a long table flanked by two forms. It had its own water supply, in the form of a well sunk into the floor. Light was admitted through small-paned windows, which Mollet had replaced with more modern windows in 1778.[7] The floor of this kitchen consisted of flagstones which were probably sanded in order to absorb dirt.[8]

Mollet's parlour floor might also have been sanded, at least for most of his residence. Only in 1809 did he mention acquiring a parlour carpet.[9] From 1780, however, the parlour was equipped with what Mollet called a 'Blowing Stove', which he later replaced with a 'Bath Stove'.[10] These were cast-iron hob grates set into an existing fireplace. In 1799, Mollet ordered some fashionable black bamboo chairs for his parlour.[11] An auction of Mollet's effects after his death in 1819 further listed armchairs, occasional tables, chimney ornaments, a clock, a barometer, several unspecified 'pictures' and a Hogarth print.[12]

The bedrooms in Mollet's house were located on the first floor and in the garret (reserved for servants). They were accessed by a *tourelle* – a circular stone staircase projecting from the back of the house. Mollet's post-death auction catalogue included a mahogany four-poster bed with curtains; seven ordinary bedsteads; several hair and wool mattresses; feather beds; pillows; blankets; quilts; one mahogany wardrobe; an oak press; and a chest of drawers. The best bedrooms were wallpapered, at least from 1771.[13] Aside from the well in the kitchen, the house appears to have had no indoor

---

[6] F.B. Tupper, *The History of Guernsey and its Bailiwick* (Guernsey, 1854), p. 365.
[7] Diary, 15.5.1778.
[8] For kitchen flagstones, see Diary, 30.12.1816. For sand fetched for domestic floors, see Diary, 25.2.1809.
[9] Diary, 11.12.1809.
[10] Diary, 1.5.1780, 25.10.1798.
[11] Diary, 7.5.1799.
[12] Auction Catalogue, n.d., Box 18, De Sausmarez Collection, Greffe.
[13] Diary, 30.4.1771, 2.5.1771.

plumbing or sanitation. The auction catalogue showed that Mollet possessed several chamber pots.

Many of Guernsey's granite farmhouses acquired stucco facades during Mollet's lifetime.[14] Mollet never beautified his house in this way, but he kept the interior well maintained. His kitchen was regularly whitewashed and occasionally re-plastered.[15] Other rooms, including the parlour, were regularly re-painted.[16]

There were two forms of lighting in Mollet's house: oil lamps and candles. He regularly bought lamp oil in town, such as the three gallons he purchased at 6s per gallon in 1817.[17] The auction catalogue showed that he owned several brass lamps. The catalogue also listed a number of candle-holders and candlesticks. Mollet bought his candles by weight, as, for example, the 24 lb he had of Captain Denis in 1811.[18] Interestingly, Mollet never mentioned buying rushlights, which would have been a cheaper option than either candles or lamps.

The kitchen, where a fire would have burned all year round for cooking purposes, was probably the warmest room in Mollet's house. Most of the other rooms in the sixteenth-century building were probably permanently cold and damp. Mollet's post-death auction catalogue listed three foot-warmers and several foot rugs.[19] In the last decade or so of his life, Charles Mollet recorded the dates between which he had fires lit in his parlour and bedroom. In his bedroom, he would generally have a blaze between late September and mid-May. In his parlour, the dates were slightly later and earlier.[20] Coal was expensive in Guernsey, particularly during wartime. Mollet bought it only occasionally, at a price which varied from 7s 6d per quarter in 1772 to 29s per quarter in 1810.[21] He probably kept it for use in the parlour. As a supplement to coal, Mollet also used a large variety of other materials: logs and faggots from his trees; trimmings from his hedges;

---

[14] R. Hocart, *The Country People of Guernsey and their Agriculture, 1640–1840* (Guernsey, 2016), p. 156.
[15] Diary, 5.3.1771, 12.6.1778, 22.5.1780, 28.5.1810.
[16] Diary, 23.4.1778, 26.6.1803, 10.7.1817.
[17] Diary, 19.12.1817.
[18] Diary, 21.11.1811. These cost 11d per pound.
[19] Auction Catalogue, Box 18, De Sausmarez Collection, Greffe.
[20] Diary, 28.9.1808, 14.10.1810, 21.10.1810, 9.5.1809, 17.5.1811.
[21] Diary, 28.7.1772, 23.3.1810. For quarter, see Chapter 2, n. 12.

wood-shavings from processed timber; old roots and cabbage stumps; dried cowpats; *torve* and *gorban*.[22]

Housekeeping was female work. To begin with, Mollet's mother, who was sixty-three when the diaries began, was in charge of the housekeeping, although most of the actual work was done by female servants, of whom the Mollet household usually employed one or two. Sometimes female servants engaged by Mollet during his mother's absences were dismissed by her on her return, as, for instance, Elizabeth Le Roi, engaged by Mollet while his mother was away, but dismissed on her return a few weeks later on the ground that she 'was not clean'.[23] At this point, in the early 1770s, the recently widowed Mrs Mollet was travelling at least once a year to her native Jersey, where she spent time with her own mother and siblings as well as with her elder daughter. The last time Mollet recorded his mother on a visit to Jersey was in 1780/1. Thereafter, Mrs Mollet confined herself to stays with her younger daughter at Candie in St Peter Port. By the mid-1780s, she was spending entire winters at Candie and had effectively withdrawn from her housekeeping duties. In November 1787, Mollet's mother moved permanently to Candie, where she died, aged eighty-three, some four years later.[24]

The majority of the thirty-six female servants whom Mollet mentioned by name in his journals served from the 1780s onwards, from which time Mollet lived largely alone. Most appear to have been in their late teens or early twenties when they started work in his house, although some were as young as twelve.[25] They were typically the daughters of Mollet's less well-off Castel neighbours, and many of them were related, either to one another or to Mollet's labourers and farm servants. Susanne Collenette and Elizabeth Le Ray, who worked for Mollet at the turn of the century, shared a common grandmother.[26] Marie Ferbrache, who replaced Susanne Collenette, was the sister of Mollet's farm servant Daniel Ferbrache.[27] Mollet paid these servants

---

[22] *Torve* was a form of combustible sward composed of dry mosses and other vegetation (G. Metivier, *Dictionnaire Franco-Normand ou Recueil des Mots particuliers au Dialecte de Guernesey* (London, 1870), p. 471). *Gorban* was the local name for peat dug out from under the sands at Vazon (*The Guernsey and Jersey Magazine*, 2 (1836), pp. 379–80).
[23] Diary, 29.1.1771.
[24] Diary, 19.2.1792.
[25] Such as Elizabeth Letocq, who began working for Mollet in 1800 (Diary, 5.2.1800).
[26] Diary, 10.8.1801.
[27] Diary, 25.12.1801, 16.12.1805, 21.8.1806. On the relatedness on Mollet's servants, see Appendix 6.

according to their age. In the first decade of the nineteenth century, youngsters like fourteen-year-old Marie Le Page received £4 a year.[28] More mature women received £6.[29] Wages were paid annually in arrears. At certain points Mollet recorded supplementing them with a share in the returns from produce sold by the farm.[30]

Short periods of service were the norm: nineteen of Mollet's female servants stayed with him for less than a year, and only five stayed for longer than four years. Mollet's longest-serving domestic servants were Elizabeth Le Ray and Susanne Ozanne. Elizabeth Le Ray (to whom Mollet usually referred as Lisabo) started working for him in 1793 and – after marrying his farm servant Abraham Machon – remained with Mollet for the rest of his life.[31] Susanne Ozanne (whom he always called Suzon) was taken in by Mollet at the age of six, and started working for wages at the end of 1811, when she was fourteen.[32] She too stayed with Mollet for the remainder of his life. It was fortunate for Mollet, who never married, that his declining years were also his longest period of domestic stability.

Charles Mollet's female servants performed a great variety of work, and this included work about the farm as well as the house. Sleeping in the attic, they usually came downstairs at five in the morning.[33] Their indoor duties included lighting and tending fires, cleaning floors, dusting furniture, preparing and cooking food, serving at table, washing dishes, changing beds, and doing the household's laundry. Outdoors, they milked the cows, made butter and curds, cut bracken, gathered seaweed, cocked hay, and bought and sold produce at market. Last but not least, they also acted as nurses to Mollet when he was ill.

Food preparation was probably the most time-consuming duty of Mollet's female servants. They cooked not only for Mollet and his guests, but also for his workmen, who might number six or seven on any given day. Most

---

[28] Diary, 19.7.1809.
[29] Diary, 7.5.1809. We might compare this with the £15 Mollet paid his (male) farm servant in 1811 (Diary, 6.5.1811).
[30] Diary, 1.4.1809.
[31] Diary, 30.5.1793, 22.3.1798. Elizabeth Le Ray (1775–1850) was the daughter of Nicolas Le Ray of le Clos au Comte in the Castel parish.
[32] Diary, 9.1.1803, 5.6.1811. Susanne Ozanne (1795–1884) was the daughter of Jacques Ozanne, Mollet's tenant at the 'upper' house.
[33] Diary, 26.10.1809.

cooking was done on the open hearth.[34] Pots and kettles were boiled on three-legged iron stands (*terpids*) placed over the fire.[35] Meat was roasted on a spit or in a Dutch oven.[36] Bread and cakes were baked in a furze oven.[37] Among other kitchen equipment, Mollet's post-death auction catalogue listed iron and copper saucepans, a kettle, pitchers, bowls, jugs, ramekins, a colander, and a mortar and pestle.

The diet of Mollet's servants and labourers was very high in salt. As noted in Chapter 3, Mollet kept his own pigs, from which he produced a large quantity of salt pork, used to flavour the cabbage, potatoes and dried peas in farmhands' daily soups and stews. The household also consumed substantial amounts of salt fish. During the early summer, Mollet regularly bought 200 or 300 mackerel at a time from local fishermen.[38] Later in the summer, he would buy local conger, usually in quantities in excess of 100 lb.[39] Both were salted on his premises and packed away in barrels. Sometimes, home-caught mackerel and conger alternated with imported salt herrings or dried cod purchased by his servants in town.[40] Bread, made with barley flour and spread with pork fat or butter, was a ubiquitous accompaniment to servants' meals. To relieve the monotony, Mollet might now and again regale his household with the offal he sometimes reserved for himself when selling animals at the market. Tripe seems to have been a particular favourite.[41] On Sundays and holidays towards the end of his life, he occasionally shared a roast fowl or suckling pig with his servants.[42]

---

[34] Plate 21 depicts a typical eighteenth- or nineteenth-century kitchen hearth. Cooking ranges had existed since the 1790s, but Charles Mollet never owned one.

[35] Mollet's post-death auction catalogue listed five *terpids*.

[36] Dutch ovens (of which one was listed in the auction catalogue) were lidded iron cooking-vessels which could be pre-heated to high temperatures with coals placed beneath and upon the lid.

[37] Furze ovens were usually built into the thickness of the wall beside the hearth. They were pre-heated with furze set alight and then raked out before food was put in. Mollet had one in his wash-house as well as his kitchen.

[38] In the early nineteenth century, these typically cost him 14s or 15s per hundred (see Diary, 15.7.1809, 15.6.1812).

[39] This cost 1d or 1½d per pound (Diary, 12.9.1811, 4.8.1817, 23.8.1817).

[40] For herrings, see Diary, 5.4.1802. For dried cod, see 21.12.1807, 2.2.1809. Herrings sold for about 15s a barrel, dried cod for c.20s per 100 lb.

[41] Diary, 11.12.1816, 28.12.1815.

[42] Diary, 8.9.1811, 8.6.1817.

The fare served to parlour guests was more varied.[43] As well as poultry and pork, the meat on offer included lamb, steak and veal.[44] There was also fresh fish, such as hake, seabass and sardines.[45] Fresh green vegetables were also more in evidence: lettuce, celery, asparagus, artichokes, green peas, French beans and broad beans.[46] Desserts of seasonal fruits – strawberries, raspberries, melons, plums, figs, apples and pears – were also eaten, often complemented by home-produced cream or curds. In addition to fresh fare, Mollet's guests were treated to biscuits and cakes. Baking seems to have been a particular accomplishment of Lisabo Machon. Mollet, who clearly appreciated her efforts, frequently recorded her production of *merveilles*, *galettes* and lemon cake.[47] Lisabo also made jams and preserves: redcurrant jelly, plum jelly, gooseberry preserve, raspberry preserve, and raspberry vinegar, typically thirty or forty pints every summer.[48]

The principal beverages of Mollet's household were cider and tea. His workmen consumed cider both at mealtimes and in the fields, and Mollet drank it too. In this, he was largely self-sufficient, but tea he had of course to buy. When tea first reached Guernsey in 1715, its consumption was regarded as the prerogative of the better-off.[49] By Mollet's day, however, it had become an article of universal usage, and people of all ranks partook of it under his roof. Typically, Mollet might purchase hyson tea for parlour guests, and cheaper souchong tea for use in the kitchen.[50] Charles Mollet did not

---

[43] Mollet entertained guests to meals in his parlour. He does not seem to have had a dedicated dining room.

[44] See, for instance, Diary, 8.5.88, 5.4.1817, 31.5.1817.

[45] Diary, 17.12.1808, 3.10.1810, 26.8.1816.

[46] Fresh broad beans seem to have been especially appreciated by Mollet. Latterly, he always recorded the first time they were served each year (for example, Diary, 30.6.1817).

[47] *Merveilles* is translated as 'wonders'. In the twentieth century, this term referred to a local sweetmeat better known as 'Jersey wonders', which were a type of ring doughnut. *Galettes* were soft rolls made with butter and white flour. Marie De Garis gives the English term for *galettes* as 'Guernsey biscuits' (M. De Garis, *Dictiounnaire Angllais-Guernesiais* (1967; Chichester, 1982 edn), p. 252.) Lisabo made her lemon cake with lemon essence she distilled herself from the rinds of imported lemons (see Diary, 6.12.1808, Notes relating to 1808, 1.4.1817).

[48] Mollet recorded the household's output of preserves and vinegar in the notes relating to each year from 1800 onwards.

[49] Hocart, *Country People*, p. 124; R.-M. Crossan, *Poverty and Welfare in Guernsey, 1560–2015* (Woodbridge, 2015), p. 218.

[50] Such purchases are recorded among Charles Mollet's Correspondence and Memoranda (Priaulx Library).

mention coffee at all for the first twenty-five years of his diary. He only took to buying it when he started entertaining French *émigrés* in the 1790s. The first time he recorded serving coffee to guests was on Sunday 17 January 1796, when four *émigrés* paid him an afternoon visit. By the time of Mollet's death in 1819, however, coffee had also become popular with his native parlour guests (though less so with visitors to his kitchen).

With guests in mind, Mollet kept a well-stocked cellar. Notes at the beginning of Mollet's first volume contain an inventory taken on 20 May 1775. His wines included Port (forty-eight bottles), French and Spanish red (thirty-one bottles), Montagne (twenty-four bottles), Madeira (nine bottles) and Frontignan (seven bottles). He would regularly top up his supplies with barrels of red and white wine which he bottled at home.[51] The price of a barrel varied with size and quality. The highest price he recorded was £5 5s for a barrel of Bordeaux; the lowest was 54s for an unspecified table wine.[52] Mollet also purchased beer by the barrel (both small beer and strong beer).[53] The price he usually paid for a barrel of small beer in the early nineteenth century was 15s.[54] Among the spirits consumed by Charles Mollet and his guests were brandy, rum and gin. In the early years, Mollet bought substantial quantities of brandy from Peter Mourant.[55] In later years, he recorded sending his servants to town to purchase brandy, rum and gin from various merchants in three-gallon flagons. Brandy was by this point selling for 6s a gallon, and gin for 4s 8d a gallon.[56] Tobacco, which gentlemen were wont to consume with their spirits, Mollet mentioned buying only once – and this was in the form of 'a cartload of old tobacco and snuff'.[57] He did not record what the old tobacco and snuff were for, but they could hardly have been for offering to his guests.

Mollet and his household ate three main meals a day: breakfast, dinner and supper. For his workmen, breakfast was an early affair, usually taken before dawn. This was followed by dinner (the main meal of the day) at

---

[51] Diary, 27.11.1778, 7.12.1780, 15.12.1785. Mollet's wines were often purchased from his brother-in-law Peter Mourant, with whom he ran an account.
[52] Diary, 24.11.1780, 7.12.1780.
[53] Diary, 1.5.1772, 6.7.1772, 18.1.1809, 19.6.1811, 22.5.1812, 10.3.1817.
[54] Diary, 18.1.1809, 10.3.1817. Mollet noted on one occasion that such a barrel had yielded seventy-two bottles (Diary, Notes relating to 1810).
[55] Diary, 14.11.1772.
[56] Diary, 20.12.1816, Notes relating to 1816.
[57] Diary, 27.7.1802.

midday, and supper when the day's work was done. When Mollet was not entertaining, he would often take these meals in the kitchen with his household. When he had parlour guests, he followed an alternative timetable. Breakfast (to which he frequently invited company) would be served at 9.00 or 10.00, with guests often staying the rest of the morning.[58] Dinner would be served any time between 1.00 and 3.00, followed by tea (and later coffee) at 4.00 or 5.00. Supper, often substantial, was taken at 8.00 or 9.00. In later life, Mollet issued fewer dinner and supper invitations, and correspondingly more to breakfast or tea. This may partly have been because the fashionable dinner-hour was advancing (by the time Mollet reached his sixties, his peers often dined at 6.00 or 7.00) and this was a habit which does not seem to have suited him.

No portrait of Charles Mollet appears to have survived, and his journals contain very little about his personal appearance.[59] From his journals we know that, while in his twenties, he wore a wig, as did most of his peers at this time. In November 1771, he noted that his barber had brought him a new 'cut wig'.[60] Cut wigs were about the plainest available and were often worn by farmers. Within twenty years of the receipt of this wig, natural hair had displaced horsehair wigs as the fashion for men. Mollet, however, never mentioned any changes in his own wig-wearing habits. Hair powder, which could be used to whiten either wigs or natural hair, featured among the effects listed in his post-death auction catalogue.

Charles Mollet regularly mentioned being shaved, by barbers successively named Peaty, Deacon, Frecker and Caire. These men (or their apprentices) came to shave Mollet in his own home several times a week, a service for which he paid them 2 guineas or 2½ guineas per year. At one point, Mollet also paid for his farm servant to be shaved once weekly, an extra which cost him 10s.[61]

In the 1770s, a typical gentleman's outfit consisted of a full-skirted knee-length coat open at the front, a thigh-length waistcoat, a linen shirt with decorative cuffs and frills, a cravat or neck-cloth, knee-breeches, stockings,

---

[58] See, for instance, 30.6.1811, 9.4.1817. Mollet's term for this meal was *le déjeuner*, which did not mean lunch, as it does in French today.

[59] It is in some ways surprising that no portrait of Mollet exists, particularly since his god-daughter Marie De Ste Croix was the wife of the Jersey-born miniaturist Philippe Jean (Diary, 17.6.1791, 22.6.1796, 24.7.1818).

[60] Diary, 1.11.1771.

[61] Diary, 3.1.1810, 7.1.1810, 31.12.1816.

buckled shoes, and a tricorn hat. Mollet would have attired himself in a variant of this for at least the first forty years of his life. Towards the end of the eighteenth century, shorter coats and waistcoats replaced long ones, ankle-length trousers replaced knee-breeches, and flat-crowned hats replaced tricorns. It seems doubtful that Mollet would have adopted these new fashions very quickly, since he seems generally to have been of a conservative temperament.

In the early years, Mollet availed himself of occasional visits to England to have clothes, wigs and footwear made for him.[62] The last such visit was recorded in 1793. After this, he had his clothing made in Guernsey, often in his own home by local tailors whom he paid by the day. Peripatetic tailors appear to have been fairly common in the country parishes at this time. Mollet named Jean Torode of les Grands Moullins; Daniel le Prevost; and Mr and Mrs Daniel De Mouilpied, who worked as a team.[63] These tailors made Mollet clothes from fabrics he purchased himself (such as, for instance, the 35 yards of blue beaver he bought from a St Peter Port draper in 1799).[64] Mollet also had old garments of his own adapted to suit new tastes (such as the brown cloak originally purchased in London from which he had a jacket made in 1817).[65]

On some occasions, Mollet would employ a tailor only to measure and cut his cloth, having it sewn up by his seamstress, whose services were considerably cheaper. Mollet's end-of-year notes almost always included payments to a regular seamstress, who spent between twenty and thirty days annually working at his house. In 1811, he recorded paying her 1s per day.[66] Her main work was to maintain the household's stock of linen – patching sheets, mending tablecloths, darning stockings, replacing buttons, running up shirts. These seamstresses were usually mature women, often widows trying to eke out a living in the absence of a male wage. Olympe Girard, who worked as a domestic servant for Mollet in the 1770s, returned as his seamstress more than thirty years later.[67]

Keeping the household's clothes and linen clean was the work of Mollet's house servants, usually helped by a washerwoman. Mollet first began

[62] Diary, 3.11.1788.
[63] Diary, 28.4.1795, 18.4.1799, 29.10.1817.
[64] Diary, 4.4.1799. Beaver was a heavy woollen cloth with a napped surface.
[65] Diary, 27.2.1817.
[66] Diary, Notes relating to 1811.
[67] Diary, 18.11.1816.

recording wash-days in 1785.[68] To begin with, they came round only once a month, typically the first or second Monday. After the turn of the century, linen was washed once a fortnight. Towards the end of Mollet's life, Judith Machon, an unmarried sister of his farm servant Abraham, usually performed the office of washerwoman. Judith typically worked some eighty days for Mollet every year, for a daily wage of 1s. Like other workers and tradespeople, she was fed at the house. She usually also slept there the night before a wash-day in order to make the necessary preparations.[69] In the absence of mechanical aids, washing the laundry was a long and complex process. It involved bringing water to the wash-house from the pump in the yard; soaking items overnight; boiling them next morning in a copper together with a piece of soap or some lye;[70] rubbing them on a washboard; rinsing them in clean water; wringing them out; putting them outdoors to dry; starching them; and – last but not least – ironing them. In Guernsey's damp climate, the drying operation often stretched out over many days, especially in winter. On a December Sunday in 1810, Mollet remarked: 'the weather has lately been so wet that the linen we washed 4 weeks ago did not dry until Thursday, when we finished drying it in front of the fire (not even the sheets, despite being put out several times).'[71] One cannot imagine that dealing with the laundry was Mollet's servants' favourite chore.

Washerwomen and seamstresses probably made their way to Mollet's house on foot. Indeed, most of Mollet's less well-off neighbours lacked horses, so that all their journeys would have been on foot.[72] Mollet himself usually kept a complement of two or three horses. As noted in Chapter 3, he favoured imported mares as saddle horses, and used Guernsey horses to pull carts and farm implements. Mollet recorded himself riding on horseback until nearly the end of his life.[73] But, like his compeers, he was also no stranger to walking, and regularly went to town or other parishes on foot. On a single winter's day in 1816, he walked to town in the morning, returned

[68] Diary, 21.11.1785.
[69] Diary, 21.8.1815, Notes relating to 1816, 1817, 1818.
[70] Lye was an alkaline liquor, sometimes made from the ashes of burnt seaweed, which had grease-dissolving properties For seaweed brought to the wash-house, see Diary, 30.3.1816.
[71] Diary, 23.12.1810. Washed laundry was usually left immersed in water if it could not immediately be put out to dry (Diary, 2.1.1809, 25.1.1817).
[72] In 1817, only 55 per cent of households in the Castel parish owned a horse (Relevé des Propriétaires du Castel, May 1817, SG 23/43, Island Archives).
[73] The last time he specifically mentioned riding a horse was in June 1818, when he was nearly seventy-six (Diary, 3.6.1818).

home on foot for dinner, then walked to St Andrews' Rectory and back in the afternoon.[74] Mollet was seventy-four at the time, and these journeys would have covered about twelve miles.

Until the early nineteenth century, Guernsey's roads were primitive. A report compiled for the States in 1810 noted that they were seldom more than 4½ feet wide; that heavy use had caused many to be eroded to a level below adjacent fields; and that they were riddled with ruts and potholes filled with earth and rocks which moved when horses stepped on them and caused them to stumble.[75] 'Carriages', observed a nineteenth-century writer, 'were almost useless [...] and the few which existed were gigs, substantially constructed without springs.'[76] In 1771, Mollet recorded that he had been lent *une chaise* to convey him home on return from a trip to Jersey where he had fallen ill.[77] He also recorded having purchased *une chaise* from Thomas Le Marchant in 1779.[78] These might have been horse-drawn gigs, but they could equally have been sedan chairs. The *chaise* Mollet bought in 1779 may well have been intended for his elderly mother, who, given road conditions, would have found it hard to get around. Strangely, however, Mollet never mentioned this *chaise* again.

Problems of the elderly aside, the necessity of moving around on horseback or on foot could seriously hamper social intercourse. On many a wet day, guests Mollet was expecting to breakfast or dinner simply never turned up, as doing so would have ruined their attire as well risking their health.[79] In an era without telephones, Mollet was happy to put non-appearances down to the weather, and indeed he did the same thing himself. In 1797, Mollet invested in four umbrellas, which may have been as much for guests departing in the rain as for his own use.[80]

Mollet's diaries contained many complaints about the roads: 'never so bad'; 'filthy'; 'very muddy'; 'full of mud'.[81] Nevertheless, when, in June 1810, he heard of a plan to build two new roads from town to the west coast, he

---

[74] Diary, 4.12.1816.
[75] G.E. Lee (ed.), *Actes des Etats de l'Ile de Guernesey, 1780–1815* (Guernsey, 1910), pp. 249–54.
[76] *The Guernsey and Jersey Magazine*, 3 (1837), p. 234. Gigs were open two-wheeled carriages with a single bench seat for the driver and passenger(s).
[77] Diary, 3.4.1771.
[78] Diary, 3.4.1779.
[79] See, for instance, 20.2.1777, 20.10.1797.
[80] Diary, Notes relating to 1797.
[81] Diary, 17.2.1798, 19.2.1799, 7.11.1807, 17.11.1809, 8.12.1809.

seemed apprehensive.[82] The plan had been instigated by Lieutenant-Governor John Doyle, who was worried that the state of existing roads would impede the timely dispatch of troops to the coast in case of invasion. He was not the first Lieutenant-Governor to have entertained this concern. In 1779, Mollet had recorded a similar – though still-born – plan on the part of Lieutenant-Governor Paulus Aemilius Irving.[83] However, Doyle was a more proactive character than Irving, and in 1806, he had already organised the construction of a military road over the reclaimed Braye du Valle.[84] One of the roads Doyle planned for 1810 was to run between town and L'Erée, the other between town and Vazon. Our diarist's chief motive for unease lay in the fact that the road between town and Vazon was projected to run along a 68-metre stretch of his own land just south of the old road at les Eturs.[85]

Mollet's interest in John Doyle's new road was intense, and his journal provides a vivid account of its construction. As noted in the previous chapter, this thoroughfare was built by men of the 103rd Regiment.[86] On 26 June 1810, Mollet recorded seeing soldiers at work on the road leading from the bottom of les Rohais to the Castel church. On 2 July, he noted that some 200 men of the 103rd were camping in the Fair Field (about 20 minutes from his farm) and that an advance party was already removing old earthbanks along le Préel (a road which fed into les Eturs). Just two weeks later, on 17 July, Mollet recorded that the States surveyor Matthew Goodwin had come to measure up his own land.[87] The prospect of imminent interference with his property seems to have disquieted Mollet, who was now in his late sixties, and on the morning of 18 July he recorded going to remonstrate with the Lieutenant-Governor and Bailiff 'that no work should be started before compensation had been fixed.' Mollet reported that this intervention had produced 'a firm guarantee of full and ample compensation', although no

---

[82] Diary, 25.6.1810.
[83] Diary, 28.6.1779.
[84] See Chapter 1, n. 2. The British government had funded the original costs of reclamation and construction which were then recouped by selling the reclaimed land to private buyers (Hocart, *Country People*, p. 81).
[85] This measurement was given (in perches and feet) in text associated with an Ordinance of 8.8.1812.
[86] The British government had agreed to split the cost of the new roads with the States, and the government's contribution chiefly took the form of military labour.
[87] Matthew Pitton Goodwin (1785–1842) was the States' first official surveyor, architect and superintendent of works (G. Bramall, 'The architects and builders of Guernsey', *The Review of the Guernsey Society* (Winter 1993/4), p. 84).

precise sum was promised.[88] He added that, as he did not wish 'to be seen to hold up the works,' he had later given his consent to their continuation.[89] On the day immediately following, Thursday 19 July, the soldiers of the 103rd started in earnest along Mollet's stretch of les Eturs.

Mollet's seeming acquiescence notwithstanding, his fears regarding encroachment were not entirely allayed, and he kept a wary eye on the soldiers, objecting variously to edges cut off a wheat crop; a patch of parsnips destroyed; turf removed without leave, and so on.[90] All this the emollient Hercules Scott showed himself adept at managing, such that by August, Mollet had given his blessing to a military encampment in one of his fields and had even made friends with some of the soldiers (particularly with a Corporal Peggy, whom he persuaded Colonel Scott to promote to Sergeant).[91] He also gave casual farm work to a number of men from Scott's regiment.

Charles Mollet had also sufficiently softened his attitude to allow stone for the new road to be dug out of his field at les Tuzets, and to provide a cart and driver to transport it. Mollet charged nothing for the stone, on the proviso that the soldiers should dig the entire field to a depth of 6 or 8 feet, take only stone suitable for road-making, and return the surface to a level condition.[92] For the carting, Mollet was paid a total of £10 15s, as it was part of a general invitation to parishioners to assist with the project (at 11s a day for a cart drawn by three animals and 9s a day for a cart drawn by two animals).[93] This was a task performed largely by Mollet's farm servant Abraham Machon. By mid-September, work on the road itself was largely over, with only the footpaths to finish.[94] By mid-October, with the footpaths done, Mollet recorded that work on the new road was complete.[95]

However, Mollet was not quite done with road-related aggravations. Unwilling to accept paper money for Abraham's carting work, he became embroiled in a long dispute with Matthew Goodwin, who refused to pay him

---

[88] In due course, it was decided that individuals ceding property for the road (land, earthbanks, walls and buildings) would be compensated at the rate of £9 per quarter of the property's value (Ordinance of 8.8.1812).
[89] Diary, 18.7.1810.
[90] Diary, 30.7.1810, 6.8.1810, 7.8.1810.
[91] Diary, 2.9.1810, 4.9.1810.
[92] Diary, 3.8.1810, 19.9.1810.
[93] Diary 21.8.1810, 14.9.1810.
[94] Diary, 4.9.1810, 14.9.1810, 19.9.1810.
[95] Diary, 5.10.1810, 13.10.1810.

in coin.⁹⁶ Ultimately, Mollet only received full payment after actioning Goodwin in Court.⁹⁷ Mollet was similarly displeased with the £80 10s he was offered as compensation for land lost to the new road. Disputing the assessment, he initially declined to accept the money.⁹⁸ Whether he eventually did take it is not apparent, as the diary volume covering 1812 to 1815 is missing. On balance, however, it is likely that he did, as his income was dwindling and there was little to be gained by standing out against the States. In 1817, when States representatives attempted to sell him back part of the old roadway at les Eturs (now disused), he took some satisfaction in refusing them point blank.⁹⁹

As regarded the new roads themselves, Mollet seemed fairly pleased with the outcome. The Manxman Thomas Quayle, who visited Guernsey in 1812, described the new thoroughfares as 'substantial and excellent', made of broken stone a foot deep, with carriageways 18 feet in breadth and raised footpaths between 3 and 4 feet wide.¹⁰⁰ In the year of Quayle's visit, the States (evidently also impressed with the new roads) instituted a road-building programme of their own, commissioning three more, with a view to further expansion over future years.¹⁰¹

Frederick Lukis, who was thirty-two when Doyle's new road to Vazon was built, observed that, after this time, substantial close carriages, which had previously been almost unusable in the pitted old cart-tracks, began gradually to make their appearance in Guernsey's countryside, opening new possibilities and facilitating old ones.¹⁰² This was certainly reflected in Mollet's journal, which from this point onwards, made frequent references to carriages: on a summer Sunday in 1811, Mollet recorded that his farm servant had borrowed a carriage and taken two young women for an afternoon ride;¹⁰³ a little later, he reported that his widowed niece had hired a carriage

---

⁹⁶ Diary, 24.9.1810, 25.9.1810. Mollet did not like paper money because of the 5 per cent premium he was charged when he exchanged it for coin at the bank.
⁹⁷ Diary, 10.6.1811, 12.4.1812.
⁹⁸ Diary, 26.3.1811, 6.6.1811.
⁹⁹ Diary, 6.11.1817.
¹⁰⁰ T. Quayle, *A General View of the Agriculture and Present State of the Islands on the Coast of Normandy* (London, 1815), p. 286.
¹⁰¹ T.F. Priaulx, 'Guernsey's roads', *The Review of the Guernsey Society* (Winter 1974), p. 84.
¹⁰² F.C. Lukis, 'Reminiscences of Former Days in Connection with Guernsey' (unpub. MS, Priaulx Library).
¹⁰³ Diary, 11.8.1811.

and taken a spinster friend on a jaunt to St Peters.[104] Most importantly, perhaps, rain no longer impeded social gatherings. On 9 September 1816, Mollet noted:

> rain overnight, which became heavier towards morning & stopped at around 9 o'clock. This did not prevent my guests from coming to breakfast [...]. All of them came in carriages.[105]

This reference to breakfast and guests leads us conveniently to the subject of the next chapter: Charles Mollet's social life. Although – or, indeed, perhaps *because* – he was a confirmed bachelor, Mollet was eminently gregarious. The importance he set on hospitality will already have become apparent. In the following pages, we will explore in depth precisely whom he entertained and how he entertained them.

---

[104] Diary, 29.4.1816.
[105] See also Diary, 11.8.1817, 24.7.1818.

7

Social Life

It may be no coincidence that the only description I have found of Charles Mollet remembers him as a 'hospitable, facetious and inimitable Amphitryon'.[1] Hospitality featured heavily in Charles Mollet's journals. This was partly because he used the journals to keep track of whom he entertained and when, and partly because invitations, given and received, were so important to the class to which he belonged. Mollet and his peers had ample leisure time and could dispose of it much as they wished. Members of both sexes could – and did – come together at any time of the day on any day of the week. In the decade 1795–1805, Mollet entertained guests at his home on more than 1,000 occasions. Some 40 per cent of the invitations he issued were to afternoon tea, 33 per cent were to dinner, 19 per cent were to breakfast, and 8 per cent were to supper. Mollet was himself entertained at other people's homes some 250 times (mostly to dinner), in addition to which he paid innumerable informal visits to relatives, friends and acquaintances. During the 1790s and early 1800s, Mollet was at the peak of his sociability. In earlier and later periods, the nature of the hospitality he gave and received was slightly different, as was the identity of his guests and hosts. This chapter will examine the ebb and flow of Charles Mollet's sociability.

Family

Family gatherings of various kinds made frequent calls on Mollet's time, especially in the early years. As noted in Chapter 2, Mollet had many close relatives, spread between Guernsey and Jersey. From an earlier generation,

---

[1] 'Amphitryon' is used here in the sense of 'entertainer'. This description was written decades after Mollet's death by the poet and lexicographer George Metivier, who though fifty years Mollet's junior, grew up in Mollet's neighbourhood and met him many times (G. Metivier, 'Finucania ou Le tableau de Finucane', Edith Carey Scrapbook No. 2, Priaulx Library).
I thank Richard Hocart for drawing my attention to this passage.

there were his grandmother, his mother and some uncles and aunts.[2] From his own generation, there were two sisters and two brothers-in-law. From the next generation, there were eighteen nieces and nephews, all born between 1755 and 1770. Of these nieces and nephews, fifteen survived into adulthood and acquired spouses and children of their own. These children were Mollet's great-nieces and great-nephews.[3] Finally, there was a fifth generation – Mollet's great-great-nieces and great-great-nephews, of whom he recorded at least three, two boys and a girl, born when he was in his seventies.[4]

Slightly more distant but still an important part of the family were Mollet's Guernsey cousins, the Le Cheminants, offspring of his maternal aunt Rebecca Mollet and her husband Daniel Le Cheminant, who had married in 1710. In his early years, Mollet regularly mentioned James, Nicolas, Pierre and Daniel Le Cheminant, who were all of the smallholding and trading class.[5] James Le Cheminant (1714–96), a smallholding carpenter, was the cousin with whom Mollet had most to do. While James lived, he and his wife were regularly invited to Mollet's home for Sunday dinner (as were the others, albeit less frequently).[6] Any fellow guests at these Sunday dinners were, however, either family members or people of the Le Cheminants' own class. Sunday was Mollet's day for entertaining the lower ranks, and – while paying due respect to his kin – he always avoided mixing disparate social strata.

Although Charles Mollet never lost contact with the Jersey branch of his family, he perforce had more to do with the Guernsey branch. In the 1770s and 1780s, Mollet's interactions with his sister, Marthe Mourant, and her children Patty, Mary, Nancy and Peter, were at least weekly, and sometimes even daily. Mollet seems to have got on well with all four of Marthe's children, but Peter was probably the one with whom he was most involved, at least during Peter's youth. At the age of nineteen, Peter spent six weeks with Mollet in Alderney, where his uncle introduced him to the various

---

[2] Mollet's grandmother, Marie Le Vavasseur dit Durell, *née* Romeril, died at the age of eighty-eight in 1775 (Diary, 9.1.1776). All of his uncles and aunts seem to have died by the early 1790s (Diary, 19.5.1793).
[3] On these four generations of Mollet's family, see Appendices 2 and 3.
[4] Diary, 18.9.1816, 17.6.1818.
[5] Note that, while James, Nicolas and Pierre Le Cheminant were all first cousins of Mollet, Daniel was a first cousin once removed, the son of a deceased brother of James, Nicolas and Pierre who was also named Daniel.
[6] For examples of Sunday dinners with the various Le Cheminants, see Diary, 3.11.1771, 15.12.1771, 14.11.1779, 6.11.1780, 20.5.1787, 22.6.1794.

people with whom he socialised.⁷ A few months later, Mollet escorted his nephew to Caen, where they also engaged in a busy social round before the young man settled down to a two-year mercantile apprenticeship in the city.⁸

All of Mollet's Guernsey nieces and nephews married, but only Patty, who married Bonamy Dobrée, and Nancy, who married William Brock, had children. Of Patty's seven surviving offspring (a boy and six girls), Mollet again had most to do with the boy, Peter Dobrée (1784–1870), who followed in his father's footsteps as a merchant. This may chiefly have been because all the girls were educated at English boarding schools, and some of them never returned to the island.

Mollet's niece Nancy and her husband William Brock also moved to England in 1798, taking their children with them. The Brock child with whom Mollet eventually had most to do was their son William (1789–1869). This was because William, who trained as a doctor in England, returned to Guernsey to establish a medical practice in 1812.⁹ After his permanent return to the island, Mollet incorporated him fully into his social round.

Mollet's niece Mary and his nephew Peter were childless, but they both remained settled in Guernsey and played an important part in Mollet's life. Mary's husband Henry Brock (the brother of Nancy's husband William) died in 1812, leaving Mary a widow at the age of forty-four.¹⁰ Never remarrying, Mary continued living alone in her town house, and provided a measure of support to her uncle as he grew older. Her brother Peter married Sophia Carey in 1807. Although no children ensued, the couple took in the five youngest of Sophia's sister's children when the latter (Mary Le Marchant) died in childbirth in 1811.¹¹ These children included Mary's newborn baby (Thomas Le Marchant, who lived until 1873) and two little girls under ten. Initially, this arrangement was to last until such time as the wishes of their father, Major-General John Gaspard Le Marchant, could be known. Tragically, General Le Marchant himself died at the Battle of Salamanca in 1812, and the Mourants' care of the orphans became prolonged. The last time Mollet mentioned the Le Marchant children was in 1818, when the Mourants still had the three youngest living with them at Candie.¹² Peter,

---

⁷ Diary, 28.7.1788–5.9.1788.
⁸ Diary, 9.9.1790, 13.9.1790, 22.4.1792.
⁹ Diary, 6.5.1812.
¹⁰ Diary, 24.3.1812.
¹¹ Diary, 1.10.1811.
¹² Diary, 21.1.1818.

Sophia and their charges paid regular visits to Mollet in his last decade. To the Le Marchant orphans, Peter and Sophia must have been as good as parents, and Mollet must have seemed like a grandfather.

While Mollet's mother still lived at her Castel home, the house was very much a hub for the extended family. The Lerriers and their children would regularly come over from Jersey to stay for a few days.[13] The Mourants frequently ate at the house, and occasionally stayed overnight, sometimes accompanied by their children, and sometimes without them.[14] As Mollet's mother began spending more time with the Mourants, the family's centre of gravity gradually shifted to town, and after the Mourants acquired their new villa, Candie was confirmed as the family's focus. Visiting Lerriers now stayed there rather than at the Castel. Mollet very often took meals at Candie himself, and as noted in Chapter 4, he even lived there for two years.

In the early 1790s, the Mollet family suffered a double blow. An era came to an end with the death of Mollet's mother in 1792.[15] In 1794, his fifty-four-year-old sister Marthe suffered a stroke.[16] With Marthe now in fragile health and her daughters running homes of their own, Candie acquired a new long-term resident – thirty-seven-year-old Polly Lerrier.[17] Polly (1758–1834) was an unmarried niece of Mollet's from Jersey. She had stayed at Candie many times before, but was now entering upon a twelve-year residence there, serving as the Mourants' helpmeet and companion. Polly shared in all the family's social occasions and made frequent appearances in Mollet's journal throughout the next decade.

In 1798, the Mourants suffered further misfortunes. Marthe's daughter, Patty Dobrée, died in January at the age of thirty-two, and Marthe herself died in August at the age of fifty-eight.[18] The death of his sister permanently altered Mollet's interactions with Candie. While he continued to exchange regular visits with his nieces and nephews, he saw rather less of his brother-in-law, and his visits to Candie diminished in frequency. Mollet was never explicit on the nature of his relationship with Peter Mourant, senior, but it seems to have been a fairly distant one (Mollet invariably referred to him as 'Mr Mourant', whereas he called Philippe Lerrier 'my brother'). The diaries

---

[13] Diary, 21.7.1774, 7.9.1774, 20.5.1785.
[14] Diary, 22.5.1771, 7.1.1779, 14.7.1779, 13.8.1780.
[15] Diary, 19.2.1792.
[16] Diary, 23.11.1794.
[17] Diary, 15.1.1795.
[18] Diary, 2.1.1798, 18.8.1798.

convey the impression that Mourant wished to see Mollet improve his economic position and hoped that some of his own entrepreneurial zeal would rub off on him. When it did not, he rather lost interest in him.

'Mr Mourant', who had suffered recurrent bouts of what Mollet called 'gout', himself died at the age of sixty-seven in May 1807.[19] It was in the August of that year that his son Peter married Sophia Carey and installed her as the new mistress of Candie.[20] In September, Polly Lerrier left Guernsey for good.[21] From this point onwards, the family's centre of gravity shifted to Mollet's niece Mary, who was then living with her husband Henry Brock at le Vauquiédor on the outskirts of St Peter Port. In 1810, the couple began building a new house for themselves in the Grange, an up-and-coming suburb of town. Unfortunately, Henry died in March 1812, a short time before the house could be completed, and the widowed Mary was obliged to move in on her own.[22] It was this smart new house that then became the family hub. Whenever any relatives came to visit the island, it was with Mary that they stayed, and Mary who hosted important family get-togethers.[23] In some senses (and ironically, being childless herself), Mary had replaced her mother as family matriarch.[24]

Friends and acquaintances

Charles Mollet seems to have been on nodding terms with almost everyone who was anyone in eighteenth-century Guernsey,[25] but his social contacts fell into several distinct sub-sets. Some were family friends inherited from his parents. The oft-mentioned Condamine, Coutart, Roche and Chepmell families were all of this sort. The Mollets' primary link was with the Condamines: Jean-Jacques Condamine (1711–64) was married to the Jerseywoman Marie Néel (1732–1803), who was a relative of Mollet's

---

[19] Diary, 24.5.1807.
[20] Diary, 18.8.1807.
[21] Diary, 17.9.1807.
[22] Diary, 15.6.1812, 4.7.1812.
[23] See, for instance, 22.7.1816, 18.9.1816, 7.12.1816, 21.3.1818.
[24] For a portrait of Mary, see Plate 1.
[25] This is not so surprising as it might seem. In 1780, Guernsey had only c.14,000 inhabitants and perhaps 2,800 families. Out of these, only about fifty possessed anything like wealth or status.

mother.[26] This familial relationship then gave rise to all the others, as the Condamines, Coutarts, Roches and Chepmells were themselves all bound by ties of blood and marriage. Charles Mollet, his sisters and his nieces kept up contacts with these families for decades, regularly exchanging visits and sharing in social occasions. The spinster Anne Roche – 'Miss Roche', as Mollet called her – figured in his journal from its beginning to its end. Visiting Mollet with her parents in the early days, she later became a close friend of his niece Mary and often accompanied her to family gatherings during Mary's widowhood.[27] Mollet and his nieces also regularly socialised with the Bowden, Barlow, McCrea and Bell families, who married into the Condamines and Coutarts.[28]

Neighbours (at least those of similar standing to Mollet) comprised another sub-set of his social contacts. In his early days, Charles Mollet was friendly with the young Guilles from nearby St George, who were of a similar generation to himself. Not so much with the eldest, Jean, who was nearly ten years his senior and already married, but with Jean's younger brothers Thomas, Nicolas, Charles and Richard.[29] The first pages of Mollet's journal mentioned many interactions with Nicolas Guille (1742–1807) and Richard Guille (1745–1818) in particular. These interactions, typically informal in nature, ceased as the young Guilles focused on careers which took them away from the parish – Nicolas as a merchant and Richard as a surgeon. In later years, Mollet recorded sporadic visits from Nicolas, who settled in Spain, whenever he returned to Guernsey, but beyond the 1780s he made no mention of Richard until the latter's death.[30]

His immediate contemporaries having gone their various ways, Mollet then socialised chiefly with neighbours of a younger generation. Between 1774 and 1779, he recorded attending eighty-four sessions of what he variously called 'the Young Ladies' Club', 'the Castel Young Ladies' Club', or simply 'the Castel Club'. This consisted of a group of marriageable young

[26] Marie Néel was the sister of Françoise Néel who was married to Mollet's mother's cousin Charles De Ste Croix.
[27] Diary, 7.4.1771, 27.8.1817.
[28] Jean-Jacques Condamine's daughter Marie married John Bowden in 1780. Advocate Pierre Coutart's daughters Jane and Anne married Robert McCrea and John Barlow in 1786 and 1797 respectively. John Condamine's daughter Marie married George Bell in 1814.
[29] For the composition of the Guille family, see Appendix 4.
[30] Mollet's penultimate mention of Richard Guille came on 15.2.1785, when the latter was in Alderney. Mollet recorded Richard Guille's death on 20.1.1818. He had previously recorded Nicolas Guille's death on 11.2.1807.

people and their mothers, who met on Friday and Sunday afternoons to chat, play cards and take tea. The most frequent venues were the Le Marchant house at la Haye du Puits and the Ozanne house at la Houguette, although Mollet also recorded sessions at other peoples' homes, including his own.[31] At la Houguette resided two of the most marriageable young ladies in the parish, Marie Ozanne (1753–1834) and her younger sister Judith Ozanne (1756–1835), the only children and sole heiresses of the late Jurat Jean Ozanne. At la Haye du Puits resided the almost equally eligible Josias Le Marchant (1755–1831), Marie Le Marchant (1757–87), Carterette Le Marchant (1759–1800) and Pierre Le Marchant (1760–97).[32] Whether the Ozanne or Le Marchant girls considered the much older Charles Mollet an eligible marriage partner is a moot point. Whatever the case, Club meetings ceased once most of the young people had found spouses. Judith Ozanne married Josias Le Marchant in 1780. Her sister Marie Ozanne married future Bailiff Robert Le Marchant in 1782, and Josias's sister Marie Le Marchant married Robert's brother Hirzel Le Marchant in 1786.[33] This iteration of the Castel Club never appears to have been attended by Jean Guille of St George and his wife, who had already been married for two decades.

As it happened, the Castel Club was revived in a different incarnation some twenty years later, as a subsequent generation came of age to marry. This round of meetings ran between 1797 and 1801, although Mollet recorded his personal attendance at only nineteen. As previously, the Club met regularly for conversation, cards and refreshments. Among the venues were la Haye du Puits, where Josias's daughters Harriet and Caroline were now in their late teens and early twenties; les Beaucamps, where successful merchant Abraham Le Mesurier had offspring of similar ages; and St George, where Jean Guille's two surviving daughters, born in the 1760s, were also glad to participate.[34] Another regular attendee was Jean Guille's young niece Caroline, the daughter of his Barcelona-based brother Nicolas, who had come

---

[31] Some eight meetings of the Club took place at Mollet's house (Diary, 7.10.1774, 12.4.1776, 14.6.1776, 6.9.1776, 20.6.1777, 5.9.1777, 10.7.1778, 11.9.1778).
[32] These, together with two younger sisters, were the children of the late Josias Le Marchant, sen. and his wife Marie *née* Bonamy.
[33] We should note that Robert and Hirzel Le Marchant were only distantly related to the Le Marchants of la Haye du Puits.
[34] These were Carterette, *née* Guille, the wife of Nathaniel Le Cocq, and Esther, *née* Guille, the widow of Jean Metivier, who had moved back to her father's house after the death of her husband.

to spend a few years with her Guernsey family. Sadly, Caroline, whom Mollet described as 'dear sweet-natured Miss Guille', died suddenly at the age of twenty-three in 1801, after which Mollet recorded no more meetings of this Club.[35]

For Mollet, the resurgence of the Castel Club to an extent revitalised relations with the Guilles and Le Marchants, which had fallen somewhat into abeyance over the 1780s and early 1790s. For the remaining two decades of his life, Mollet was to maintain regular social contacts with both the St George and Haye du Puits families.

Another sub-group of Mollet's friends might be termed the 'breakfast set'. These breakfasts, which took place at Mollet's home on a Sunday and were usually followed by attendance at church, started properly in January 1794, when Mollet was fifty-two.[36] For many years, the breakfast guests generally numbered just three: former Jurat Jean Carey; future Bailiff Peter De Havilland; and Thomas De Sausmarez, who was HM Procureur and De Havilland's son-in-law.[37] Thomas De Sausmarez, once described by De Havilland as 'a gay, sensible and good-natured man',[38] turned out to be Mollet's most faithful Sunday morning guest. Jean Carey became less regular in 1808 and dropped out altogether on moving to France in 1816.[39] De Havilland himself dropped out for a few years between 1807 and 1811. From about 1807 onward, De Sausmarez was most often accompanied by his Royal Court colleague HM Prévôt Nicolas Lefebvre, though these two regulars might on occasion be joined by other friends of Mollet's, or bring members of their own families. These sociable Sunday breakfasts became markedly less regular as Mollet entered his seventies, but he kept them up until the very end of his life. Charles Mollet's last recorded formal Sunday breakfast took place in July 1818.[40]

It was noted in Chapter 5 that Charles Mollet maintained social relations with a number of Lieutenant-Governors. The first Lieutenant-Governor with

---

[35] Diary, 2.1.1801.
[36] Diary, 5.1.1794, 19.1.1794, 23.2.1794. There had also been a few isolated such breakfasts the previous year, e.g., 24.2.1793, 7.7.1793.
[37] There are portraits of these men in Plates 3,4, and 5. For the composition of the De Havilland, Carey and De Sausmarez families, see Appendix 4.
[38] R. Hocart, *Peter de Havilland: Bailiff of Guernsey: A History of his Life, 1747–1821* (Guernsey, 1997), p. 60.
[39] Diary, 25.8.1816.
[40] Diary, 26.7.1818.

whom Mollet recorded socialising was Lieutenant-Colonel Paulus Aemilius Irving (1714–96), who hailed from Bonshaw in Dumfriesshire. Mollet seems initially to have made Irving's acquaintance by chance, having found himself travelling from Southampton on the same boat, when Irving was on his way to take up his new post in 1771.[41] The two men established a rapport, exchanged invitations, and thereafter regularly dined at one another's homes (usually in company with other high-ranking Guernseymen) until Irving's term expired in 1784.[42] Irving was the first Lieutenant-Governor to take refreshments at Mollet's house following a military review at Vazon or les Mielles.[43]

In 1784, Paulus Aemilius Irving was replaced by fellow Scotsman Lieutenant-Colonel William Brown, who died while still in office in 1793. Mollet's relationship with Brown was personal as well as social, as the two men were friends long before Brown's arrival. As such, their relationship will be discussed in Chapter 9, which deals with Mollet's private life. Suffice it to say here that the post-review refreshments and formal dinners continued, while Mollet and Brown also had contacts of an informal nature.

The next Lieutenant-Governor with whom Mollet had a long-term social relationship was Major-General Sir Hew Dalrymple (1750–1830), a native of Ayr who was appointed in 1796.[44] Dalrymple brought with him his wife, Lady Frances, and their three young daughters, Charlotte aged nine, Frances aged six, and Arabella aged four.[45] As well as hosting the usual formal dinners and post-review refreshments, Mollet also socialised privately with the Dalrymples, inviting them and their children to afternoon tea and exchanging visits with them, much as he would with local friends and acquaintances.[46]

---

[41] Diary, 23.8.1771. Mollet himself was returning from a visit to London.
[42] See, for instance, Diary, 10.5.1772, 23.6.1772, 16.7.1773, 5.10.1774, 22.9.1777.
[43] Diary, 11.7.1779.
[44] Mollet had only brief contacts with Major-General Thomas Dundas and Lieutenant-Colonel James Craig, interim replacements for William Brown, both of whom were in Guernsey for brief periods in 1793 (Diary, 29.6.1793, 2.7.1793, 9.11.1793). As noted in Chapter 5, he had no social relations at all with Lieutenant-Governor Major-General John Small, who served between 1794 and 1796. It is interesting to note (though not particularly germane to our subject) that almost all of Guernsey's eighteenth-century Lieutenant-Governors were Scotsmen.
[45] The Dalrymples also had two sons at school in England: Adolphus aged twelve, and Leighton aged eleven.
[46] See, for instance, Diary, 14.9.1796, 19.8.1797, 6.6.1799, 17.6.1799, 28.8.1801.

Dalrymple was the last of the Lieutenant-Governors whom Charles Mollet knew socially. As well as enhancing Mollet's personal prestige, his association with Lieutenant-Governors also introduced him to many military men, whose company Mollet seems to have greatly enjoyed. Some of these soldiers were regular garrison officers, such as Major John Waugh, a Scotsman on the permanent staff whom Mollet knew socially from 1777 until Waugh's death in 1799.[47] Others were visiting VIPs, such as Major-General Sir William Green (Chief Military Engineer of Britain); Lieutenant-Colonel Arent Schuyler de Peyster (to whom Robert Burns once dedicated a poem); or Brigadier-General Napier Christie Burton (who was later to serve as Lieutenant-Governor of Upper Canada).[48]

The most illustrious person to whom Mollet was introduced by a Lieutenant-Governor was Charles Lennox (1735–1806), 3rd Duke of Richmond. The Duke visited Guernsey twice – in 1785 and again in 1786 while serving as Master-General of the Ordnance.[49] Mollet was introduced to him by his friend William Brown on the Duke's second visit to Guernsey.[50] He was also introduced to the Duchess of Richmond, Lady Mary Bruce (1740–96).[51] A military review was staged at Vazon expressly for the benefit of the ducal couple, followed by a formal dinner and reception at St Peter Port's Assembly Rooms. Mollet was invited to all three of these events, and was so taken by the interest the Duke and Duchess showed in him that he followed them to their next port of call in Jersey, where he attended a ball given in their honour by the inhabitants of that island.[52] During the Richmonds' stay in Guernsey, Mollet graciously presented the Duchess with a basket of fruit, carnations and roses from his garden.[53] In return, she sent him a note of thanks, which Mollet claimed was the only such note she had

---

[47] Diary, 25.9.1777, 27.1.1799. Waugh had married Guernseywoman Elizabeth Le Pelley in 1762.
[48] Diary, 13.7.1787, 6.6.1790, 6.7.1790, 4.9.1796.
[49] Diary, 12.5.1785, 15.5.1785, 22.7.1786, 26.7.1786.
[50] Diary, 22.7.1786.
[51] Diary, 24.7.1786.
[52] Diary, 25.7.1786, 31.7.1786.
[53] For a portrait of the Duchess of Richmond, see Plate 12.

penned while in Guernsey.⁵⁴ Mollet probably treasured it for the rest of his life.⁵⁵

One of the reasons Charles Mollet appreciated the company of military men was that most of them were from outside the island, and thus the source of fresh ideas and perspectives. It was probably for a similar reason that he liked to socialise with clergymen. Locally-born clergymen were thin on the ground in Mollet's day, chiefly on account of the paltriness of Guernsey livings.⁵⁶ As church services were conducted in French, most parish Rectors were therefore French or Swiss Protestants who had been specially ordained into the Anglican church. Not one of the local clergy was unknown to Mollet, but there were a select number with whom Mollet was particularly friendly. In his early days, he socialised extensively with the Reverends André Migault and Isaac Vallat, older men who may in some sense have been father figures to him. Migault, from Normandy, was Rector of Torteval between 1753 and 1758, of the Castel parish between 1758 and 1784, and of St Saviours between 1784 and 1798. In 1773, Migault moved permanently to Jersey and employed curates to serve his Guernsey parishes until his death twenty-five years later. Mollet called frequently at the Castel Rectory while Migault was in residence there. When Migault left the island, Mollet corresponded with him and regularly paid him visits in Jersey. Isaac Vallat, originally from Lausanne, served as Rector of St Peters from 1772 until his death in 1785 (having previously served in Alderney). Mollet seems first to have made Vallat's acquaintance in 1773, and thereafter the two men exchanged regular visits, dinners, and afternoon teas. Mollet remained in touch with Vallat's wife (the Guernseywoman Jeanne Allez) for many years after his death.⁵⁷

In his fifties, Charles Mollet became friendly with the Reverends Etienne Gibert and Edward Mourant. Gibert (1736–1817) was a Huguenot minister from the Cévennes who had been ordained an Anglican priest in London in 1771.⁵⁸ Mollet first met Gibert when the latter, then serving as Preacher to

---

⁵⁴ Diary, 25.7.1786.

⁵⁵ It is surprising that the Duchess's note does not form part of the collection of Mollet's correspondence and memoranda gifted to the Priaulx Library along with his journals. Perhaps it survives in some other bundle of Mollet records as yet undiscovered.

⁵⁶ J. Jacob, *Annals of some of the British Norman Isles constituting the Bailiwick of Guernsey* (Paris, 1830), p. 197.

⁵⁷ Diary, 6.4.1804.

⁵⁸ Etienne Gibert and his brother Louis form the subject of D. Benoît, *Les Frères Gibert: Deux Pasteurs du Désert et du Refuge* (Toulouse, 1889). Extracts from this book were published in Guernsey's *Magasin Méthodiste* between June and December 1890.

the French Chapel Royal, briefly visited Guernsey in 1785.[59] When, in 1794, Gibert took up permanent residence in Guernsey as the Rector of St Andrews, Mollet hastened to befriend him and remained in regular contact with him until Gibert's death in 1817. Edward Mourant (1768–1836) was a Jerseyman whom Mollet first recorded meeting when he arrived in Guernsey in 1793.[60] In 1794, twenty-six-year-old Mourant became Minister of Bethel Chapel in St Peter Port and curate of the Castel church.[61] In 1797 he was appointed Rector of the Forest and Torteval.[62] Until 1800, Mollet was frequently in Mourant's company, but, for reasons which are unclear, his association with the young clergyman (who remained in Guernsey for the rest of his life) ceased abruptly in 1801. Because Charles Mollet's relationships with both Edward Mourant and Etienne Gibert had a strong personal as well as social component, they will be further discussed in Chapter 9.

In the first two decades of the nineteenth century, Charles Mollet socialised extensively with yet another two young clergymen – Thomas Carey (1772–1849), Rector of St Saviours, and Thomas Brock (1777–1850), Rector of St Peters. These were both local men known to Mollet since their boyhood.[63] References to these gentlemen and their young families abound in the final years of Mollet's journal. People of their rank and education were rare in the country parishes, and Mollet was keen to foster good relations with all who were in easy reach of his home.

Another sub-set of Mollet's social circle was acquired through his nieces' husbands – Bonamy Dobrée who married Patty Mourant in 1783; Henry Brock who married Mary Mourant in 1784; and William Brock who married Nancy Mourant in 1786.[64] Mollet struck up friendships with all three of his young nephews by marriage, often referring to them simply as Bon, Harry and Billy. The Dobrée family fell into two main branches in the late

---

[59] Diary, 1.8.1785. A letter survives in the Kent History and Library Centre dated 22.6.1782 (U1350/C41/156) recommending Gibert – 'a worthy French clergyman' – to the patronage of the Guernsey Governor Jeffery Amherst. The appointment of Guernsey's Rectors lay with the Governor, and the purpose of Gibert's 1785 visit may have been to gauge the island's suitability for the future exercise of his ministry.

[60] Diary, 7.6.1793. The Reverend Mourant does not appear to have been related to Mollet's brother-in-law Peter Mourant.

[61] Diary, 19.9.1794.

[62] Diary, 8.3.1797.

[63] Thomas Carey was the son of Mollet's old breakfasting friend Jean Carey. Thomas Brock was Jean Carey's son-in-law.

[64] For the composition of the Brock and Dobrée families, see Appendix 4.

eighteenth century, based respectively at houses named 'Beauregard' and 'Bellevue' in St Peter Port. Mollet was long acquainted with the 'Bellevue' branch, but less so with the 'Beauregard' branch. The entry to his family circle of Bonamy Dobrée, who was from the 'Beauregard' branch, remedied this deficit, and Mollet began thereafter to socialise regularly with Bonamy's eight siblings and their spouses, a well-connected and influential set who included the diarist Elisha Dobrée.

William and Henry Brock were similarly well-connected. Their sisters Judith and Harriet were married to the brothers Captain Thomas Saumarez and Dr Jean [De] Sau[s]marez, which gave Mollet an *entrée* into this distinguished branch of the De Sausmarez family.[65] Dr Jean [De] Sau[s]marez (1755–1832) was the older brother of the naval hero Captain James Saumarez (1757–1832), whose exploits on the 'Crescent' were related in Chapter 5. Captain Thomas Saumarez (1760–1845) was their younger sibling.[66] Though less well-known than his naval brother, Captain Thomas Saumarez also achieved high rank.[67] A veteran of the American War of Independence, he was appointed Inspector and Brigade-Major of the Guernsey militia in 1793, knighted in 1799, and made a Major-General in 1811, after which he served for two years as commander-in-chief of New Brunswick. Owing to their connections with the Brocks, it was with Jean and Thomas Saumarez that Mollet socialised most. Mollet had only a distant relationship with the future Admiral and peer of the realm.[68]

William and Henry Brock also provided Mollet with an introduction to the many children of their uncle Jean Brock. These included the future Bailiff Daniel De Lisle Brock, Mary Brock, Savery Brock and Irving Brock, most of whom were between twenty and thirty years younger than Mollet. The age gap notwithstanding, Charles Mollet became particularly friendly with Savery Brock (1772–1844), a wine and spirits merchant who was a regular visitor to Mollet's house in the last decade of the diarist's life.[69] In a further ramification, Mollet also struck up a friendship with Savery Brock's brother-

---

[65] See Appendix 4.
[66] It is said that Thomas and James altered their surname from 'De Sausmarez' to 'Saumarez' to make it more acceptable to the British forces in which they served. The alteration was sometimes applied by analogy to other family members.
[67] For a contemporary portrait of Captain Thomas Saumarez, see Plate 7.
[68] James Saumarez was made an Admiral in 1801 and created Baron de Saumarez in 1831.
[69] This man's name was John Savery Brock, but Mollet and most of his contemporaries knew him simply as Savery. For a portrait, see Plate 8.

in-law, Thomas Potenger, a clergyman without cure from Berkshire who was married to Savery's sister Mary Brock. The Potenger family lived at les Vauxbelets in St Andrews, within walking distance of Mollet's home. Proximity fostered social contact, and the Potengers featured frequently in Mollet's turn-of-the-century journal, which charted the family's tragic course: Mary Brock died aged twenty-seven in 1798; Thomas Potenger then remarried, but himself died aged thirty-eight in 1805, leaving four children from his first wife and another four from his second.[70] Even after Potenger's death, Mollet maintained contact with his children, one of whom, Richard Potenger (1792–1860), later became Rector of St Martins.

As noted above, Mollet always showed an interest in meeting people from outside the island. Possibly educated in Normandy himself, he had a particular fascination with France and the French (his journal documented four visits to France, and his book collection, as recorded in the journal, comprised more French than English books).[71] The French Revolution, which began just before Mollet turned forty-seven, afforded him an unanticipated opportunity to make new contacts with Frenchmen. *Emigrés* from the Revolution first began arriving in the Channel Islands in the spring of 1791, when the French aristocracy felt threatened by the growing radicalism of the revolutionaries.[72] On 9 April that year, Mollet recorded dining with le Comte du Parc, le Comte de Kernel and le Chevalier de Médic at his friend the Lieutenant-Governor's house. Between that time and the end of the Napoleonic War, Mollet went on to record contacts with at least 111 named *émigrés* at his home in the Castel, some of whom came just once, and others on scores of occasions.[73] Many of these came by invitation – to dinner or to coffee – many others spontaneously beat a path to Mollet's door as knowledge of his hospitality spread through the *émigré* community. One *émigré*, whom Mollet identified as 'Monsieur de la Roche Vernay', even lodged for a few months at his Castel property.[74]

---

[70] Diary, 4.8.1798, 23.5.1801, 31.12.1805.
[71] Appendix 11 lists some of the books in Mollet's collection.
[72] R.J.W. Mills, ' "L'île des bannis": Jersey, Britain and the French emigration, 1789–1815', *European Review of History*, 28 (2021), p. 107.
[73] These *émigrés* are listed, together with the dates of their first appearance in the journal, in Appendix 10.
[74] Diary, 27.7.1796. This is likely to have been Henri Delaroche-Vernay, a Royalist army officer from Touraine, who briefly occupied one of the rooms in Mollet's 'upper' house.

The majority of Mollet's *émigré* guests were minor nobles from Normandy and Brittany. There were particularly large numbers of these in Guernsey in 1794–5, when a corps of Royalist fighters in the pay of the British government was formed in the Channel Islands in preparation for an expedition to the Quiberon peninsula. Once landed at Quiberon, the Royalist forces were intending to link up with counter-revolutionary *Chouans* and contribute to the rebellion which was already under way in la Vendée.[75] The expedition launched from Jersey in July 1795 with around 3,500 *émigré* troops.[76] It ended in catastrophe as the troops were wiped out by their revolutionary adversaries, who knew of their coming and were waiting for them. Mollet recorded the unfortunate outcome of the expedition in his journal, as also his fears that a number of his French friends had perished.[77]

Mollet also entertained many *émigré* ecclesiastics, who started arriving in number in the late summer of 1792. Their exodus from France was prompted by a decree originally issued in 1790 requiring them to swear *le serment constitutionnel*, designed to free the French church from the papacy. Losing patience at the slow pace of response, the French National Convention ordered in August 1792 that all remaining non-juring priests should either take the oath or go abroad within two weeks – at which point large numbers left Normandy and Brittany for the Islands.[78] Mollet first recorded entertaining French priests on 26 September 1792, when he invited two *curés* to dinner.[79] Thereafter, he entertained at least twenty named ecclesiastics, including Claude Coulon, the former chaplain to Marie Antoinette.[80] Some of these ecclesiastics had fled with few possessions and found it hard to make ends meet, as did also many lay *émigrés*. Despite differences of religion, Guernsey people seem to have been helpful and supportive towards the

---

[75] C. Hettier, *Relations de la Normandie et de la Bretagne avec les Iles de la Manche pendant l'Emigration* (Caen, 1885), pp. 238–71.

[76] Diary, 19.7.1795; Mills, 'Jersey, Britain and the French emigration', p. 121.

[77] Diary, 3.8.1795.

[78] On the 1792 exodus, see Mills, 'Jersey, Britain and the French emigration', p. 108; D.A. Bellenger, *The French Exiled Clergy in the British Isles after 1789* (Bath, 1986), p. 2.

[79] Diary, 26.9.1792.

[80] Diary, 26.4.96, 2.5.96, 2.6.96, 27.6.96. Claude-Antoine Coulon (1746–1820) had also been vicar-general of Nevers (S. Clapp, 'Catholic priests exiled in Guernsey after escaping la terreur of the French Revolution', *The Review of the Guernsey Society* (Spring 2015), pp. 20–1).

refugees.[81] In 1795, Charles Mollet's friend the Reverend Edward Mourant, who occupied the Castel Rectory as a curate, was sharing his accommodation with two French priests, Monsieur Paris and Monsieur Morvan.[82] In 1796, Mollet himself served on a committee which raised £225 in aid of the island's destitute *émigrés*.[83]

In July 1796, the British government ordered that all non-fighting *émigrés* in the Channel Islands should be relocated to England, and some 128 French priests were transferred from Guernsey to Southampton.[84] The following month, two companies of Royalist soldiers who had replaced the Quiberon contingent were also withdrawn from Guernsey. On 26 August 1796, Mollet remarked: 'there are only a few *émigrés* left here.'[85]

Nevertheless, this was only a temporary situation and very far from the end of the story. Over the next few months, some of the priests, who had evidently felt comfortable in Guernsey, started to drift back.[86] There were also fresh arrivals, both clerical and lay. From 1797, Mollet began entertaining *émigrés* again and became acquainted with a whole new cohort of French refugees. These included the Capuchin friar Frère François Marie, already encountered in Chapter 4. According to F.C. Lukis, Frère Marie was a herbalist and naturopath as well as a maker of cordials, and he 'devoted much of his time to the care of incurable cases and accidents'.[87] Aside from becoming a valued member of the local community, Frère Marie also became one of Mollet's most faithful visitors in the years after 1799.

Charles Mollet also took an interest in French prisoners-of-war, particularly those of gentlemanly rank. Captured Revolutionary soldiers were detained at what was known as the 'French prison' at St Jacques on the

---

[81] According to Robin Mills, this was not the case in Jersey, where *émigré* numbers were so high as to cause resentment (Mills, 'Jersey, Britain and the French emigration', pp. 112–13).
[82] Diary, 22.10.1795.
[83] Diary, 11.1.1796, 13.1.1796, 15.1.1796, 16.1.1796, 4.2.1796, 6.2.1796, 10.2.1796, 22.2.1796. Mollet identified the other committee members as Sir Thomas Saumarez, Peter De Jersey, Matthew De Sausmarez, HM Greffier Joshua Gosselin and HM Comptroller John Condamine.
[84] Diary, 28.7.1796. The priests are listed by name in an annexe to a letter from Sir Hew Dalrymple to the Duke of Portland dated 28.7.1796 which is preserved at the National Archives (HO 98/25).
[85] Diary, 26.8.1796.
[86] Diary, 14.11.1796, 13.2.1797, 7.3.1797.
[87] F.C. Lukis, 'Reminiscences of Former Days in Connection with Guernsey' (unpub. MS, Priaulx Library).

outskirts of St Peter Port. Mollet was on friendly terms with Nicolas Dobrée, the British government agent for prisoners-of-war, and it was comparatively easy for him to obtain permission for such prisoners to go out. He was therefore able to entertain several prisoners-of-war at his Castel home, and sometimes even invited mixed groups of Revolutionary soldiers and Royalist *émigrés* to the same occasions.[88]

The Peace of Amiens, combined with Napoleon's 1801 *Concordat* with Rome, altered the complexion of Mollet's *émigré* guest list, as many former Royalist fighters and almost all ecclesiastical *émigrés* departed permanently.[89] Although the resumption of hostilities in 1803 brought in a small influx of new refugees, this meant that Mollet was by and large reduced during the Napoleonic period to 'intransigents' and 'the old', as the historian Robin Mills described those left in Jersey.[90] Mollet's hospitality towards such people, however, continued unfailing. One of the last *émigrés* with whom he struck up an acquaintance was a Monsieur de Vauxlandry, who came unexpectedly to Mollet's house in 1811. As Mollet noted with some surprise, this gentleman had been in Guernsey for several years, but Mollet had never yet met him.[91] The *émigré* in question was eighty-one-year-old Louis-Joseph-Guy Landry de Vauxlandry, who died in Guernsey two years later.

Aside from French *émigrés*, the Revolutionary and Napoleonic Wars also brought contingents of allied foreign troops to Guernsey. Characteristically, Mollet was also keen to meet these. Between November 1799 and June 1800, some 6,000 Russian soldiers were temporarily accommodated in Guernsey.[92] On 20 December 1799, amid the heaviest snowfall for years, Mollet picked his way to Fort Hommet on the west coast expressly to introduce himself to the Russian soldiers quartered there while barracks were being erected for them at Delancey.[93] Several breakfasts, dinners and suppers with Tsarist

---

[88] Diary, 19.7.1796, 17.10.1800, 22.10.1800, 16.11.1800.
[89] For departures of some known to Mollet, see Diary, 10.4.1801, 21.6.1802.
[90] Mills, 'Jersey, Britain and the French emigration', p. 120.
[91] Diary, 26.7.1811.
[92] Jersey also took around 7,000 of these soldiers, who had fought with the British in Europe but could neither be sent home before the Baltic ports became ice-bound, nor quartered in Britain, since the Bill of Rights prohibited the introduction of foreign troops to the kingdom (A. Day, 'A Russian army on Guernsey and Jersey', *The Review of the Guernsey Society* (Summer 1997), pp. 40–5; J. Duncan, *The History of Guernsey* (London, 1841), pp. 175–6).
[93] Diary, 20.12.1799.

officers ensued.[94] These cordial affairs were largely unhampered by communication problems, as most Russian officers spoke French.[95] Nevertheless, on a few occasions Mollet also invited a fellow Castel parishioner who could speak good Russian (as well as Polish and German).[96] Mollet clearly enjoyed the company of these Russian officers, and – though he had less to do with other ranks – he seemed genuinely impressed with the Russian soldiers as a body. At the end of their sojourn in Guernsey, Mollet remarked:

> It would scarcely be possible to have been better behaved, or more honest & peaceable than these 6 or 7 thousand soldiers during their sojourn here, both officers & men. Those who were in Jersey (an even greater number) were equally well behaved.[97]

In 1801 and 1802, soldiers of the King's Dutch Brigade were also stationed in Guernsey. This was a British army unit composed of defectors from Dutch forces, commissioned in 1799. Mollet was pleased to make the acquaintance of several Dutch Brigade officers, whom he entertained at his home on a number of occasions.[98]

One contingent of foreign troops with whom Mollet conspicuously did not socialise were the Black Brunswickers (Brunswick Ducal Field Corps), who spent a few months in Guernsey in 1809–10, after their evacuation from the Continent following a failed campaign to re-take Brunswick from the French.[99] Mollet recorded in his diary that Lieutenant-Governor John Doyle 'mistrusted' the Brunswickers, although he did not give the reasons for

---

[94] Diary, 28.12.1799, 31.12.1799, 1.1.1800, 3.1.1800, 27.1.1800, 15.4.1800, 16.4.1800, 20.4.1800, 27.4.1800, 1.5.1800, 13.6.1800, 16.6.1800.
[95] French, the international language of culture and diplomacy, was widely adopted as a second language by the Russian upper classes.
[96] Diary, 1.1.1800, 3.1.1800, 4.1.1800, 13.6.1800, 16.6.1800. The polyglot parishioner was Richard Ozanne (1765–1836) of les Mourains, who had married Catherine Zukowska in Warsaw in 1799.
[97] Diary, 3.6.1800. Records of criminal proceedings contain only one reference to a Russian soldier during the troops' stay in Guernsey. The soldier was accused of rape in January 1800, but the case against him was dropped the following June for lack of evidence, and he was allowed to leave the island with the rest of the Russian contingent (23.1.1800, 7.6.1800, Livres en Crime, Greffe).
[98] Diary, 20.10.1801, 24.6.1802.
[99] Duncan, *History of Guernsey*, p. 179.

Doyle's wariness.[100] The Lieutenant-Governor ordered the local militia to keep a close watch on these Germans, and Mollet recorded several night-watches in which his men took part.[101] In light of these circumstances, it would clearly have been inappropriate for Mollet to invite the Brunswickers to his home.

In the final years of the Napoleonic War, Mollet found an opportunity to renew contacts with ordinary French civilians, when Guernsey developed a role as an entrepôt in the so-called 'licence trade' between Britain and France.[102] The merchant Harry Dobrée (1771–1851), of the 'Bellevue' branch of the family, was a leading participant in this trade, and through him, Mollet gained introductions to a number of visiting French sea captains and merchants. Dobrée, who often accompanied these traders to entertainments at Mollet's home,[103] kept up relations with Mollet after the War, and became a regular guest of Mollet's in his last decade.

It was noted above that Charles Mollet was on nodding terms with almost every member of Guernsey's elite. Throughout his life, however, he also socialised with people from Guernsey's middling orders, whom, in a sort of parallel social life, he entertained separately from their social superiors. In his early years, his guests were often drawn from a stratum of Castel farmers who were less well-off than himself, though still better-off than many of their co-parishioners – Moullins, Cohus, Doreys, Dumaresqs – whom he would invite to spend convivial evenings with him at his home (typically while his mother was away).[104] In the late 1770s and early 1780s, Mollet developed a particular association with the four Le Pelley brothers – Jean, Denis, Nicolas and Thomas – whose farm was about half a mile from his.[105] Beginning on a purely social level, the Le Pelleys' relationship with Mollet increasingly metamorphosed into one revolving around agricultural assistance. Once this relationship was fully in train, occasional socialising seems to have ossified into an expectation on Mollet's part of regular client-patron visits. From the turn of the century, these became routinised into an annual obligation upon Thomas Le Pelley to spend *la longue veille* (Guernsey's main Christmas

---

[100] Diary, 14.12.1809.
[101] Diary, 14.12.1809, 15.12.1809, 7.4.1810, 29.4.1810.
[102] See Chapter 1, n. 23.
[103] Diary, 21.9.1809, 10.9.1809, 31.12.1809.
[104] See, for instance, Diary, 23.1.1778, 20.1.1779.
[105] For more on these men, see Chapter 3, n. 78.

celebration) with Charles Mollet.[106] Mollet's servants would celebrate it in the kitchen with festive food and drink, while Mollet and Le Pelley did likewise (but perhaps more sedately) in the parlour.[107] When the Le Pelleys' mother died in 1815, it is perhaps significant that her sons neither told Charles Mollet nor invited him to the funeral.[108]

In his last two decades, Charles Mollet's 'middling' social circle expanded to encompass a number of local retailers and tradesmen. They included the master carpenter Daniel Torode, the draper Jean Goguet, and – in particular – the grocers Joseph Davy and Thomas Bowls, with whom Mollet became acquainted through Frère Marie, who sold his herbal remedies and cordials in their High Street shop. Between 1801 and 1817, Davy and Bowls came regularly to Mollet's home for tea or coffee on a Sunday afternoon.[109] This was perhaps another client-patron relationship, as Charles Mollet never reciprocated their visits. However, the arrangement seems to have suited Mollet at a time when his elite circle was becoming depleted and he himself felt less inclined to go out.

Social activities

Much of Mollet's routine social activity took the form of casual visits – unannounced calls on friends or neighbours to catch up on the latest news. He also met his friends informally in public venues. Inns and taverns were a frequent resort of Mollet's when he was in his twenties and thirties. In the 1770s and 1780s, he specifically mentioned frequenting hostelries at les Houmets, les Grands Moulins, les Cauvins and la Mare de Carteret.[110] While the first three were ordinary public houses, the hostelry at la Mare de Carteret appears to have been an establishment patronised exclusively by the upper

---

[106] This was usually held on the night of 23 December, although Mollet also recorded holding it on 22 and 24 December. For more on *la longue veille*, see E.F. Carey (ed.), *Guernsey Folk Lore from MSS by the late Sir Edgar MacCulloch* (London, 1903), p. 32. The duty fell upon Thomas Le Pelley as Denis and Nicolas were at sea and Jean had died in 1797.
[107] Diary, 23.12.1806, 24.12.1807, 23.12.1808, 23.12.1809, 22.12.1810, 23.12.1811.
[108] Diary, 1.9.1815.
[109] See Diary, 24.5.1801 and 29.12.1817 for Messrs Davy and Bowls' first and last visits to Mollet's home.
[110] Diary, 16.1.1771, 24.6.1772, 25.12.1772, 23.11.1774, 25.8.1778, 16.7.1780, 4.3.1785. These visits were unrelated to his inspections as Constable.

ranks, somewhat akin to a members-only club. In 1786, William and Henry Brock took out a lease on the whole establishment and lived there for four years.[111] In 1792, Bonamy Dobrée and his family occupied it for the summer season.[112]

Mollet's friendship with Dobrée also gained him access to another well-appointed 'clubhouse' overlooking the cliffs at Fermain. This house was co-owned by Dobrée and a number of other wealthy gentlemen. In 1798, it was described in the following terms by William Money, an Englishman who was himself entertained there by Bonamy Dobrée:

> Once a month they all meet and spend the day [there], and in rotation each has the use of the house for his family and friends, for which purpose a constant establishment is maintained for the use of the society.[113]

Mollet recorded dining at Fermain with Dobrée and other gentlemen from Guernsey's top set on several occasions.[114] Bonamy Dobrée's brother the diarist Elisha Dobrée frequently mentioned 'hard drinking' in relation to evenings spent with Bonamy and his friends.[115] F.B. Tupper, writing retrospectively about the late eighteenth century, observed that 'the convivial meetings of the gentlemen, who had few amusements or intellectual resources, were often stained by hard drinking'.[116] 'Hard drinking' was never a phrase used by Charles Mollet, but he often mentioned 'merry' evenings in masculine company.[117]

For mixed social groups, there were always tearooms. Mollet regularly mentioned taking tea at le Bourg after visits to the south cliffs at Petit Bôt or la Corbière.[118] Tourtel's in St Martins was a favourite stopping-place after excursions to the eastern cliffs.[119] St Peter Port also hosted several luncheon-rooms and coffee-houses frequented by both sexes: Vining's, Grayman's,

---

[111] Diary, 13.6.1786.
[112] Diary, 22.6.1792, 16.8.1792.
[113] E.F. Carey (ed.), 'A trip to Guernsey in 1798 by W.T. Money', *Transactions of la Société Guernesiaise*, 11 (1931), p. 244. William Money was a Director of the East India Company.
[114] See, for instance, Diary, 28.6.1773, 5.8.1790, 10.7.1794.
[115] 9.9.1785, 2.6.1787, 29.10.1788, Diary of Elisha Dobrée, vols 1 and 2, AQ 1572/03, AQ 1572/04, Island Archives.
[116] F.B. Tupper, *The History of Guernsey and its Bailiwick* (Guernsey, 1854), p. 367.
[117] See for instance, Diary, 23.1.1778, 15.2.1788.
[118] Diary, 6.6.1773, 6.8.1776.
[119] Diary, 19.7.1786.

Lovick's, Sebire's and Gullick's were among those mentioned by Charles Mollet.[120]

Horse-racing was another entertainment which could be enjoyed in mixed parties. Mollet recorded attending several race meetings over the years, either at Vazon or L'Ancresse.[121] From the late 1790s, Mollet also went on picnics with ladies and gentlemen of his acquaintance. Picnics were newly fashionable in the British Isles at this time, having been popularised by the Romantic poets.[122] Mollet recorded participating in eighteen picnics between 1797 and 1811, but there were probably more in the gaps between diaries. The locations chosen were variously Pleinmont, Herm, le Creux Mahié, la Corbière, Petit Bôt, Port Soif, Lihou Island, les Sommeilleuses, and Mont Cuet. Like the picnic at Box Hill described by Jane Austen in *Emma*, these picnics were elaborate affairs. This is how Mollet described one in 1811:

> *Tuesday 9 July 1811*: I spent the day at Plein Mont, where I laid on dinner & tea for my guests, who breakfasted here, set off for Plein Mont at eleven & departed from Plein Mont at seven in the evening. The party consisted of Mr & Mrs Robt Le Marchant, Mr & Mrs Jean Le Marchant, Miss Henriette Le Marchant, Mrs MacGregor & her sister Miss Sophie Le Marchant, Colonel Scott, Peter Mourant & his wife. We were attended by Colonel Scott's batman, Ab. & Lisabo, Jean, Suzon, young Isac & little Pierre. We borrowed a horse from Eleazar, as also one from le Clos au Comte & one from the Messrs le Pelley. Ab. took most of our necessaries in the small cart, & the other horses carried some in panniers. The horses had difficulty coming back at night & did not arrive here until after eleven o'clock.

On other occasions, Mollet recorded bringing 'plates, glasses and teacups' for his picnic guests, as also having potatoes cooked for them by women occupying houses near the chosen location.[123]

Theatre-going was another activity relished by Mollet, especially in his younger days. During the 1770s and 1780s, he recorded several theatre visits. Some of these took place during trips away from the island,[124] but he also attended theatrical performances in St Peter Port, where, according to a later magazine article, 'a theatre was fitted up in a store near the hospital, and a

---

[120] Diary, 20.6.1772, 5.7.1779, 9.12.1779, 24.6.1791, 10.4.1795.
[121] Diary, 12.7.1780, 5.10.1786, 20.10.1786.
[122] A. Hubbell, 'How Wordsworth invented picnicking', *Romanticism*, 12 (2006), p. 44.
[123] Diary, 18.1.1807, 17.8.1808.
[124] Mollet noted attending performances in London, Jersey, Bath, Southampton and Cherbourg (Diary, 9.8.1771, 14.3.1776, 3.3.1788, 23.8.1789).

small company of actors came over every three or four years to perform in it.'[125] Between November 1774 and February 1775, Mollet recorded seeing twenty-three plays put on by a visiting English troupe, typically in the company of male friends of his.[126] These plays included *The Fop's Fortune* by Colley Cibber, *The Stratagem* by George Farquhar, and *The Jubilee* by David Garrick.[127] In October and November 1787, it was the turn of a French troupe.[128] Mollet and his friends saw eight of their plays, including Denis Diderot's *Le Père de Famille*, Jean-François Regnard's *Le Joueur*, and Molière's *Le Médecin Malgré Lui*.[129]

Mollet also attended a variety of other shows and spectacles. Among these were music concerts, such as those given in May and June 1791 by the diminutive Polish musician Jósef Boruwlaski (1739–1837).[130] Boruwlaski recorded his visit to Guernsey in a volume of *Memoirs* published the following year, to which Mollet was one of the subscribers.[131] He mentioned having on his arrival delivered 'letters of recommendation addressed to some of the principal inhabitants'.[132] Charles Mollet was himself a recipient of one of these letters, and entertained Boruwlaski and his travelling companion at his home during their stay, as well as escorting them on excursions around the island.[133]

Another celebrated visitor to Guernsey was the showman and pioneer balloonist Jean-Pierre-François Blanchard (1753–1809), who brought his 'automata' to the island in 1802. Mollet attended several performances by Blanchard and seemed fascinated by the way he was able to make his

---

[125] *The Guernsey and Jersey Magazine*, 3 (1837), p. 233. This was replaced by a purpose-built theatre at the corner of Lefebvre Street in the mid-1790s (G. Stevens Cox, *Social Life in Georgian Guernsey* (Guernsey, 2014), pp. 2,3, 31).

[126] Diary, 23.11.1774–13.2.1775.

[127] Diary, 23.11.1774, 28.11.1774, 25.1.1775.

[128] Diary, 29.10.1787–24.11.1787.

[129] Diary, 29.10.1787, 17.11.1787, 24.11.1787.

[130] Diary, 27.5.1791–17.6.1791. For an image of Boruwlaski, who was only 3 ft 3 in tall, see Plate 13.

[131] J. Boruwlaski, *Memoirs of the Celebrated Dwarf, Joseph Boruwlaski, A Polish Gentleman* (Birmingham, 1792), pp. 123–5.

[132] Boruwlaski, *Memoirs*, p. 123.

[133] Diary, 30.5.1791, 6.6.1791, 13.6.1791.

dummies speak.[134] Mollet also attended shows by the visiting conjurors Hermann Boaz and Mr Maggioretti.[135]

We will conclude this chapter by looking at gift-giving, which played a pivotal role in Charles Mollet's social life. Historians have shown how eighteenth-century gentlefolk bestowed gifts on one another in order to establish and maintain social bonds.[136] This was certainly also true of Mollet and his friends. As noted in Chapter 3, fruit – greatly valued in an age when other sweet treats were few and expensive – was often given away by the diarist. The quantities involved could be quite surprising. A list survives among Mollet's correspondence and memoranda showing that he gave away 323 lb of strawberries to twenty-nine individuals in 1799.[137] Mollet was also constantly exchanging plants and cuttings with his peers, many of whom shared his interest in herbaceous novelties.[138] To his inner circle, he sometimes gave more substantial gifts, such as the six piglets he distributed to Sir Thomas Saumarez, Mrs Coutart, the Reverend Thomas Brock, Monsieur de Vossey, Bonamy Dobrée and Peter Mourant in 1804.[139]

When friends were overseas, gift-giving (along with letter-writing) became even more vital to the maintenance of a relationship. Mollet regularly sent gifts to friends and relatives in Jersey, such as the peacocks he dispatched to Charles Lemprière and Jean Durell in 1786.[140] On his return from Alderney to Guernsey, he kept up contacts there by occasionally sending over delicacies such as artichokes and gooseberries.[141] In interludes between wars, Mollet sent produce to his old friends in France, and they reciprocated with gifts such as game, which was in short supply in Guernsey.[142] To his friends in England, Mollet never failed to send annual gifts of Chaumontel pears,

---

[134] Diary, 10.7.1802, 17.7.1802, 22.7.1802. Blanchard, who died in 1809 after falling from a balloon, is depicted in Plate 14.
[135] Diary, 3.2.1777, 6.1.1816. Maggioretti has not been traced. Hermann Boaz (c.1736–1820) was an Englishman whose real name was James (or Thomas) Bowes. He was otherwise known as 'the Wizard of the North'.
[136] L. Zionkowski and C. Klekar (eds), *The Culture of the Gift in Eighteenth-Century England* (New York, 2009).
[137] Charles Mollet's Correspondence and Memoranda, Priaulx Library.
[138] For instance, Diary, 18.8.1774, 16.12.1780, 15.6.1794, 3.5.1800, 12.1.1807, 15.9.1809.
[139] Diary, Notes relating to 1804.
[140] Diary, 1.2.1786.
[141] Diary, 15.6.1794.
[142] Diary, 2.3.1791, 1.3.1801, 26.8.1815.

Guernsey lilies and, later, hampers full of his home-made cordials.[143] There are examples of Mollet's largesse on almost every page of his journal, and the instances given here cannot do it justice. So extensive was his gift-giving that it must have accounted for a sizeable proportion of his farm output.

In sum, Charles Mollet's social life was important to him, and he put a great deal of time, resources and effort into it. Partly, this arose from obligations imposed by eighteenth-century codes of 'politeness', and partly also from a need to surround himself with company. What is termed 'social life' can often be superficial, however. There are entries in Mollet's journal which seem to indicate that his many relationships did not compensate for a lack of meaningful relationships. There are also signs that loneliness marked his later years. The next two chapters will look at Charles Mollet's private life. Chapter 8 will investigate his tastes, beliefs, pursuits and interests. Chapter 9 will probe his inter-personal relationships more deeply.

---

[143] Diary, 4.9.1806, 23.10.1810, 30.10.1815.

8

Private Life, Part 1: Health, Interests, Opinions

Health

In reaching his mid-seventies without falling victim to serious accident or disease Charles Mollet was fortunate among his contemporaries. For if anything did go wrong in the eighteenth and nineteenth centuries, it could rarely be properly diagnosed, let alone effectively treated. His journal offers us a sobering reminder that, for people living two centuries ago, death was ever-present. Mollet recorded more than 200 funerals in his diary, many of which he attended himself. They were not, as today, chiefly of the elderly, but of children, teenagers, young adults, and people in the prime of life. Before focusing specifically on Mollet's own health, it is worth summarising the general situation which pertained in his lifetime.

Health perils started with the beginning of life itself. It was not unusual for newborns to succumb in short order to the effects of prematurity or birth trauma, or, later down the line, to pneumonia or diarrhoea. Mollet recorded many such infant deaths.[1] Those who survived beyond infancy were often later claimed by endemic childhood illnesses such as whooping cough, measles, chickenpox, scarlet fever, and their complications. In 1796, Mollet recorded the deaths on consecutive days of his niece Nancy's two-year-old daughter Harriet and four-year-old son Beauvoir.[2] He did not identify the cause, but it must surely have been some sort of infectious illness.

For young adults, tuberculosis was a major cause of death. This affected all social classes and certain families were decimated by it. Mollet's labourer Etienne Lihou lost three adult sons – Thomas, Jean and Etienne junior – to tuberculosis (or consumption as Mollet called it).[3] His wealthy neighbour Jean Guille was even worse hit. Within the space of a decade, Guille lost his

---

[1] See, for instance, Diary, 10.10.1798.
[2] Diary, 30.12.1796, 31.12.1796.
[3] Diary, 15.3.1810.

son William, his daughter-in-law Rachel and his grand-daughter Caroline – all, as Mollet stated, to consumption.[4] In the next few years, Guille lost a further two sons-in-law (Jean Metivier and Nathaniel Le Cocq) and another daughter (Carterette) while they were all in their prime.[5] Although Mollet did not record the cause of these deaths, it too may have been tuberculosis. In all, Mollet attributed a score of deaths specifically to consumption, but there were probably many more tuberculosis victims among the deaths he left unattributed.

For women of child-bearing age, pregnancy was another significant risk. In the absence of artificial contraception, a woman might easily give birth every twelve to eighteen months during her fertile years. Mollet's sister Marie Lerrier bore thirteen children over two decades. His niece Nancy Brock produced at least seventeen over a similar period. These were evidently strong women, able to withstand the strain of constant pregnancy. The younger of Mollet's two sisters, Marthe Mourant, was less resilient. As well as four live children, her repeated pregnancies resulted in five stillbirths during the course of Mollet's journals.[6] These may have seriously undermined Marthe's health and perhaps contributed to her death at the age of fifty-eight.[7] Marthe Mourant's daughter, Patty Dobrée, died a few months before her mother, at the age of thirty-two. Patty had suffered from fragile health since girlhood, and her nine pregnancies in the nine years following her marriage cannot have done much to improve it.[8]

Many women of Mollet's acquaintance did not survive pregnancy at all, succumbing to haemorrhage or puerperal fever shortly after parturition. Childbirth was the second commonest cause of death for all women aged between twenty-five and thirty-five until as late as the 1930s.[9] Again, all classes were affected. In 1798, Mary Potenger (*née* Brock) died in childbirth leaving five children.[10] In 1799, Marie Gavet (*née* Nicolle) died in childbirth

---

[4] Diary, 8.8.1792, 8.3.1797, 12.8.1801.

[5] For the composition of the Guille family, see Appendix 4. For a portrait of the much-bereaved Jean Guille, see Plate 6.

[6] Diary, 5.10.1771, 20.5.1773, 23.3.1774, 29.1.1776, 10.7.1778.

[7] Diary, 18.8.1798. In the two decades following her last stillbirth, Marthe suffered almost constant ill-health.

[8] Patty had experienced a long spell of ill-health during childhood (Diary, 24.10.1776). For her death, see 1.1.1798, 2.1.1798.

[9] I. Loudon, *Death in Childbirth: An International Study of Maternal Care and Maternal Mortality, 1800-1950* (Oxford, 1992), p. 163. Tuberculosis was the most common cause.

[10] Diary, 4.8.1798.

leaving six children.[11] In 1811, Mary Le Marchant (*née* Carey) died in childbirth leaving nine children.[12]

Many men of Mollet's acquaintance also died prematurely, for causes which remained essentially obscure. Thomas Potenger's death at the age of thirty-eight was attributed to 'gout'.[13] Henry Brock's death at the age of fifty-one was ascribed to 'an abscess on the lungs or the liver'.[14] In 1810, Mollet introduced his nephew Dr William Brock to master plasterer James Le Page of le Mont Durand, who had 'a very large swelling in his neck & throat'.[15] Brock could do nothing, however, and within weeks Le Page was dead.[16]

What, then, of Charles Mollet's own health? We know nothing of it at all in the three decades before the opening of his first surviving diary, but not long after the diary opened, Mollet recorded a bout of scarlet fever, contracted while he was in Jersey. This began on 20 March 1771 with cold symptoms and soon progressed to severe ulceration of the throat. He took to his bed on 22 March, and had himself repatriated to Guernsey on 3 April. It then took him a further fortnight to get back on his feet, making about a month of illness in all. When, some years later, the Castel parish suffered an outbreak of what was likely also scarlet fever, Mollet was fortunately immune.[17]

In 1775, Mollet had another protracted bout of illness. He never put a name to his complaint, but it was sufficiently serious to keep him in bed between 6 October and 16 November, as also to justify his spending six weeks convalescing in Bath.[18] Two months after his return from Bath, Mollet had himself 'electrified' in Jersey.[19] Later in life, Mollet suffered from regular attacks of what he called 'rheumatism', for which he self-prescribed bed rest.[20]

---

[11] Diary, 20.12.1799.
[12] Diary, 1.10.1811.
[13] Diary, 31.12.1805.
[14] Diary, 24.3.1812.
[15] Diary, 23.9.1810.
[16] Diary, 11.11.1810.
[17] Diary, 14.9.1780, 16.9.1780, 17.9.1780, 21.9.1780. The first of these entries reported twelve deaths in the parish within the previous fortnight.
[18] Diary, 1.10.1775, 6.10.1775, 25.10.1775, 7.11.1775, 16.11.1775, 26.11.1775, 9.1.1776.
[19] Diary, 27.3.1776. On the therapeutic use of electricity, which began in the 1740s, see P. Bertucci, 'Therapeutic attractions: early applications of electricity to the art of healing', in H. Whitaker, C.U.M. Smith and S. Finger (eds), *Brain, Mind and Medicine: Neuroscience in the Eighteenth Century* (New York, 2007), pp. 274, 276–7.
[20] For two such bouts, see Diary, 10.7.1795, 26.7.1795, 31.7.1795, 2.2.1803, 28.2.1803, 15.3.1803.

In his seventies, he suffered from winter illnesses which may have started as colds and progressed into chest infections. Again, bed rest was the self-prescribed remedy, and this largely proved effective.[21]

Mollet also suffered at least four fairly serious falls from his horse. The first, which occurred on one of his debt-collecting trips to England, caused a fracture of his right collar-bone. This was bound up by a doctor when Mollet returned to Guernsey, and seems to have healed well.[22] Mollet's next two falls both occurred when his horse stumbled and threw him when out riding near Petit Bôt. On the first occasion, Mollet's face was badly lacerated. His doctor irrigated the wounds with mineral water, and then bled him.[23] On the second occasion, Mollet was trampled underfoot and recovered from extensive bruising by spending two weeks in bed .[24] Mollet's last documented fall took place outside a timber-yard in St Peter Port when he was seventy-four, again as a result of a stumble. Mollet was helped to his feet by the son of a neighbouring blacksmith and, despite his age, rode home apparently unharmed.[25]

The one episode which seems to have most endangered Charles Mollet's life was an infection he suffered in the early months of 1809, when he was in his mid-sixties. It arose when one of his cockerels attacked him, piercing his right foot with a filthy spur.[26] Within hours, Mollet developed a violent infection, which produced a high fever, great pain, and swelling the length of his right leg. For days, he was unable to leave his bed, nor even to eat or drink. His only treatment consisted in bathing the injured foot, applying poultices to it, and, later, softening it with olive oil.[27] A full five weeks elapsed before Mollet was able to spend an entire day out of bed, and a further few weeks until the swelling and pain in his right leg abated and he was able to walk properly again.[28] Extraordinarily, Mollet kept his diary throughout this period, though the severity of his illness caused a marked deterioration in his handwriting.

---

[21] See, for instance, Diary, 26.1.1816–17.2.1816.
[22] Diary, 24.12.1792.
[23] Diary, 21.8.01.
[24] The fall took place in 1813 (a year for which no diary survives), but Mollet recorded it retrospectively on 2.9.1816.
[25] Diary, 16.9.1816.
[26] Diary, 16.1.1809.
[27] Diary, 21.1.1809, 10.2.1809.
[28] Diary, 16.2.1809, 19.2.1809, 3.3.1809.

Mollet survived the encounter with the cockerel, but his illness may have undermined his native vigour. In his final decade, Mollet would spend days in bed at a stretch, sometimes from a minor indisposition, and sometimes (as he put it himself) from *paresse*, or indolence.[29] Given that the last few pages of his diary have been torn out, it is impossible to know what Charles Mollet died of. There are, however, hints that, latterly at least, what he called 'rheumatism' might possibly have been heart disease. In November 1808, he wrote that his 'rheumatism' had spread to his stomach and was accompanied by a cough and a feeling of oppression.[30] In March 1817, he described 'a sort of cramp or rheumatism' in his lower neck, which had spread into his shoulders and was accompanied by pain in the head and stomach.[31] He might thus have died of a heart attack. On the other hand, perhaps one of his winter colds turned into pneumonia, and that carried him off. Whatever the ultimate cause of Mollet's death, in having reached the age of seventy-six still comparatively hale and hearty, Mollet had done far better than his siblings and, indeed, the majority of his contemporaries.[32]

Interests and pursuits

Charles Mollet may have suffered from *paresse* in old age, but for the greater part of his life, he was active and full of curiosity about people and places. Travel was one obvious way he satisfied his curiosity. In the quarter-century between 1771 and 1796, his diaries chronicled twenty-one sojourns outside the Bailiwick.[33] Numerically, most of the voyages Mollet undertook were to Jersey. He made ten trips to this island, sometimes alone, sometimes accompanied by a servant or a friend.[34] Unsurprisingly, given Mollet's Jersey connections, these were chiefly to see relatives, visit friends, and transact

---

[29] Diary, 15.12.1810.
[30] Diary, 28.11.1808.
[31] Diary, 14.3.1817, 16.4.1817.
[32] Mollet's Jersey-based sister Marie Lerrier died at the age of seventy-three, but she had spent many years debilitated by what appears to have been dropsy (Diary, 29.5.1808, 29.8.1809).
[33] Mollet also recorded travelling to all the islands within the Bailiwick on at least one occasion (with the sole exception of Brecqhou).
[34] Diary, 6.3.71–3.4.71, 12.6.71–4.7.71, 12.10.73–17.11.73, 11.3.76–2.4.76, 3.3.80–24.3.80, 27.7.86–4.8.86, 26.10.90–28.10.90, 20.5.95–28.5.95, 17.6.96–23.6.96, 2.10.96–14.10.96.

family business. His earlier sojourns in Jersey averaged about a month in length; his later ones decreased to a week or ten days.

Mollet also recorded seven visits to England.[35] All except the first two were made during or shortly after his Alderney years, and their ostensible purpose was to collect money owed him by the purchasers of his wines and spirits. These trips have been covered in Chapter 4. Mollet's two earliest stays in England, in 1771 and 1775, were essentially leisure trips – part of the education of a young man who could not afford the 'grand tour'. His very first trip, a six-week sojourn in London in June and July 1771, was in some sense a coming-of-age journey, undertaken not long after he had entered into his inheritance. Here, he joined a group of other Channel Islanders, which included his Jersey-based sister and brother-in-law, his friend William Chepmell, Peter Le Mesurier of Alderney, and newly-weds Peter and Carterette De Havilland. The young Charles Mollet did all the conventional things a middle-class provincial visiting London might do. He saw the Tower of London, Sadler's Wells Theatre, the Chelsea Physic Garden, the British Museum, Astley's Amphitheatre (an early circus), Bagnigge Wells and Ranelagh pleasure gardens.[36] In company with five others, including his sister and brother-in-law, he also made a longer excursion to Kew, Richmond, Windsor Castle and Hampton Court.[37]

Charles Mollet's visit to Bath was undertaken four years later. Although the pretext was his health, his sojourn had essentially the same 'tourist' character as his London visit. Taking his servant Pierre Gavet with him, Mollet stayed at Mrs Viel's on Abbey Green.[38] He took the water in the Pump Room and had eleven therapeutic bathes in the Hot Bath.[39] He also visited most of the usual tourist sights, including Sir Bevil Grenville's monument on Lansdown Hill, Ralph Allen's stone quarries, Dash's Riding School, and Prior Park.[40] In addition to this, he made two journeys to nearby Bristol, where he

---

[35] Diary, 6.7.71–19.8.71, 30.11.75–4.1.76, 31.10.88–15.11.80, 21.4.89–20.5.89, 17.2.90–28.4.90, 11.10.92–23.12.92, 6.10.93–7.11.93.
[36] Diary, 18.7.1771, 23.7.1771, 15.8.1771, 29.7.1771, 30.7.1771, 2.8.1771, 7.8.1771, 16.8.1771.
[37] Diary, 4.8.1771–6.8.1771.
[38] Diary, 30.11.1775. Mrs Viel may have been the wife of the Guernsey-born cooper John Viel who had opened a wine-shop in Bath in 1761 (T. Fawcett, *Bath Commercialis'd: Shops, Trades and Market at the 18th-Century Spa* (Bath, 2002), p. 128).
[39] Pierre, too, had a beneficent thermal soak (Diary, 3.1.1776).
[40] Diary, 3.12.1775, 4.12.1775, 19.12.1775, 20.12.1775.

stayed overnight and visited Hotwells and Clifton.[41] He did not record attending any balls, concerts or other *soirées* in Bath, but this would perhaps have been more than his farmer's purse could bear.

Four of the journeys Mollet recorded in his diaries – and arguably the most interesting – were to France.[42] The first of these French trips took place over six days in June 1786 and was perhaps the most historically significant of all Mollet's travels. The trip was deliberately timed to coincide with a visit to Cherbourg by King Louis XVI, the purpose of which was to witness the sinking of a 'cone' forming part of the projected new naval basin. The outer wall of the basin, hailed as a marvel of modern civil engineering, was to comprise ninety wooden cones 60 feet tall, sunk in a line and filled with stone.[43] Mollet, then approaching his forty-fourth birthday, travelled to Cherbourg with sixteen other well-to-do Guernseymen, including the diarist Elisha Dobrée, Hellier Gosselin, John Condamine, Daniel De Lisle Brock, Peter Mourant (senior) and his sons-in-law Bonamy Dobrée and Henry Brock.[44] They divided themselves into two parties, one group travelling on the 'Liberty' (a pleasure yacht co-owned by Elisha Dobrée and some of the other participants), and the other group (which included Mollet) on a second vessel hired expressly for the trip. Mollet, who spent every night but one on board ship with his fellow voyagers, greatly enjoyed the masculine comradeship and reported at the end of his sojourn that the six days had been spent 'very merrily'.[45] One of the highlights of the trip was the sight of a cone being sunk:

> *Friday 23 June 1786*: this morning I witnessed the floating out to sea of the finished cone we saw yesterday. Borne up by a large number of empty barrels, it was manoeuvred into the position where it was to be sunk, close to one of the cones which was already in place, & on which the king & his retinue were standing. We were sufficiently close to see the piercing of the cone, which was accomplished with perfect success.[46]

Another highlight was a brief 'communication' with Louis XVI:

---

[41] Diary, 12.12.1775, 13.12.1775, 28.12.1775, 29.12.1775.
[42] Diary, 21.6.86–26.6.86, 15.10.88–20.10.88, 21.8.89–26.8.89, 11.9.90–25.10.90.
[43] These cones proved unstable, and the project was ultimately abandoned.
[44] Diary, 21.6.1786.
[45] Diary, 26.6.1786.
[46] This event is depicted in Plate 25.

> *Sunday 25 June 1786*: the King sailed almost as far as Querqueville in the morning, then made a wide circuit so as to pass alongside us. We saluted him in the English fashion. He looked at each of us attentively & instructed one of his retinue to enquire whether we were from Jersey or Guernsey. He was accompanied by 20 or 25 notables. The one who questioned us spoke in English. Billy Marchant answered him.

Mollet's next trip to France was a leisure trip to the Cotentin peninsula made with his Alderney friend Tom Williams in October 1788. This five-day trip consisted mainly of sightseeing and social calls, and was relatively uneventful. The same cannot however be said of his next two journeys to France, which were both undertaken while the Revolution was in train. The first, made just six weeks after the storming of the Bastille, has already been described in Chapter 5. Historically significant in its own right, it allowed Mollet to witness and record the ceremony pledging 'fidelity to the Nation and King' held in Cherbourg. Charles Mollet's fourth and final French trip was made while he was living at Candie.[47] Beginning in mid-September 1790, the trip lasted six weeks. Its initial purpose was to conduct his twenty-year-old nephew Peter Mourant to Caen, where Peter was to serve a commercial apprenticeship with Michel-Louis Lamy des Vallées (1728–1800), a prominent Protestant merchant and local politician.[48] During the trip, Mollet socialised with many old acquaintances and made many new ones. Having left Peter Mourant with his host, he took the opportunity to travel around Normandy and Brittany and spent time in Cherbourg, Caen, Valognes, Bayeux, Saint-Lô, Coutances, Granville, le Mont Saint-Michel, Fougères, Avranches, Dol and Saint-Malo.

The very last journey outside the Bailiwick recorded by Charles Mollet took place in the autumn of 1796. This was a twelve-day visit to Jersey, made when he had reached the age of fifty-four.[49] For the next twenty-two years of his life, Mollet does not appear to have gone any further than Herm.[50] This may partly have been due to the special hazards of sea journeys during wartime. However, in the eighteenth and nineteenth centuries, all sea journeys could be dangerous, and Mollet does not seem to have been a confident sailor. Even in his twenties and thirties, it is possible to detect a

---

[47] This trip has also been touched on in Chapter 5.
[48] Diary, 9.9.1790, 1.10.1790, 22.4.1792.
[49] Diary, 2.10.1796 – 14.10.1796.
[50] For Mollet's last trip to Herm (which also took in Jethou), see Diary, 22.8.1808. Mollet also went to Lihou several times on picnics.

certain unease in his journals when he was contemplating a sea voyage. Typically, Mollet would spend the night before such a voyage in town, ready to embark when word was sent up, as departure depended on tide, wind and weather. Sometimes, one night's waiting might turn into three, as in the stormy spring of 1771, when Mollet took up residence in town on a Saturday, but was unable to leave until the following Wednesday.[51] Sometimes, weather delays were so long that he lost heart, returned to his house and abandoned his travel plans.[52] On other occasions, his ship left port, only to put back after a few hours of struggling against adverse winds and waves. On one such abortive voyage from Alderney, Mollet recorded that his ship and all its passengers 'had been close to perishing'.[53] Shipwreck was a very real possibility in Mollet's day, and he recorded no fewer than fourteen local instances between 1771 and 1818.[54] One particular incident which occurred in 1800 must powerfully have reinforced his sense of maritime danger, as it claimed the life of a valued farm servant:

> *Tuesday 29 April 1800*: Mr Ebdon came to tell me that it is likely young James Radford perished (together with a youth whom he was bringing us as a servant) on the night of 18/19 April. A vessel left Beer on Friday 18 April & has not been heard of since. A ship's rowing boat & other flotsam have been found washed up at Chidiock. The vessel had on board a crew of 7 men & two young passengers, one of whom answered young James's description & the other that of the youth travelling with him. James was such a good young fellow that we are all much afflicted. I had never found any fault with him & I am grieved by his loss.

This incident left a deep impression on Mollet, who was still writing to James Radford's mother eleven years later.[55] Given the stressful nature of sea travel, and having seen what he wished of the world, it is understandable that Mollet preferred in later life to stay at home.

---

[51] Diary, 2.3.1771, 6.3.1771.
[52] Diary, 26.2.1779, 23.12.1788.
[53] Diary, 18.10.1787. Mollet's voyages between Guernsey and Alderney could take anything between two and a half and twenty-two hours depending on weather and tidal conditions (Diary, 1.1.1788, 10.2.1790).
[54] Diary, 11.10.1771, 28.11.1772, 25.10.1778, 16.11.1779, 25.1.1789, 29.1.1798, 29.1.1800, 3.11.1806, 18.2.1807, 30.11.1807, 12.2.1808, 10.12.1816, 13.12.1816, 9.3.1818. These are far from representing the sum total of shipwrecks off Guernsey's coast during this time, as Elisha Dobrée's diaries recorded others which Mollet did not mention.
[55] Diary, 7.12.1811.

There were, of course, other ways Charles Mollet could satisfy his curiosity about people and places. One of these was books and newspapers. Mollet subscribed regularly to Guernsey's first newspaper, *la Gazette de Guernesey*, which began publication in 1791. English newspapers only began to reach Guernsey with any regularity after 1794, when Guernsey and Jersey were incorporated into the British postal system and a weekly packet service from Weymouth was introduced.[56] When in Alderney in the late 1780s, Mollet seems to have received a newspaper directly from England, to which Alderney was closer than Guernsey.[57] Once the packet connection with Weymouth had been established, Mollet subscribed consistently to at least one English newspaper. In the last decade of his life, he was receiving his papers via newsagents Chevalier and Mauger, to whom he noted paying 24s 3d in 1815 for nine months' supply of the *St James's Chronicle*, published in London by Henry Baldwin.[58] These newspapers were comparatively expensive, and Mollet recorded passing them around among his friends and neighbours.[59]

Charles Mollet was also an avid reader of books, which he recorded purchasing on multiple occasions. In the spring of 1771, he bought a dozen volumes from the library of the recently deceased Bailiff, Samuel Bonamy.[60] Later that year, he bought more books while visiting London.[61] While in France in 1790, he purchased yet another selection of books.[62] On other occasions, he ordered books by mail, sometimes by the boxful.[63] In addition to such purchases, Mollet also noted subscribing to several of Guernsey's circulating libraries, notably Whitley's, Chevalier's, Hicks's and Seager's.[64]

Charles Mollet must have been known for his well-stocked bookshelves. Joseph Renouf, who later became schoolmaster at the Town Hospital, visited Mollet several times in 1810 and 1811 specifically to borrow books.[65] Mollet

---

[56] J.M.Y. Trotter, 'Early Guernsey postal history', *Transactions of la Société Guernesiaise*, 15 (1950), p. 30–1; F.B. Tupper, *The History of Guernsey and its Bailiwick* (Guernsey, 1854), pp. 398–9.
[57] Diary, 9.8.1789, 11.8.1789.
[58] Diary, Notes relating to 1815.
[59] Diary, 3.7.1808, 24.11.1815.
[60] Diary, 5.3.1771.
[61] Diary, 25.7.1771.
[62] Diary, 9.10.1790.
[63] Diary, 29.1.1793, 18.12.1797, 21.12.1809.
[64] Diary, Notes relating to 1799, 1804, 1806, 1809; 22.11.1802, 22.12.1817.
[65] Diary, 24.10.1810, 1.11.1810, 14.11.1811. Joseph Renouf (1790–1879) was the father of Victorian Egyptologist Sir Peter Le Page Renouf, and a keen scholar in his own right.

also lent out books to his friends. Between 1772 and 1807, he recorded in his year-end notes which books he had lent and to whom. This affords us a valuable insight into the breadth of his taste and the diversity of his interests.[66] Mollet owned Enlightenment classics such as Voltaire's *Œuvres Complètes* and Marmontel's *Contes Moraux*. He owned English classics such as Defoe's *Robinson Crusoe* and Boswell's *Life of Samuel Johnson*. He also owned books on plants and gardening such as Mallet's *Dissertation sur la Manière de Cultiver des Plantes Choisies* and Martyn's *Language of Botany*; history books such as Audra's *Histoire Générale* and Falle's *Account of Jersey*; poetry books such as Delille's *Homme des Champs* and Akenside's *Pleasures of Imagination*. And last but not least, he owned several volumes on medicine and herbalism, including Tissot's *Avis au Peuple sur sa Santé*, Lind's *Essay on Diseases*, and Meyrick's *New Family Herbal*.[67] For an obscure farmer on a small island, Charles Mollet was well abreast of contemporary European science and culture.

Before turning to Mollet's opinions and beliefs, we will briefly survey some of his hobbies. Hunting was a popular pursuit among eighteenth-century gentlemen. Many of Mollet's local contemporaries were keen ferreters and shooters notwithstanding that their prey was limited to rabbits and birds. Exceptionally, Mollet's neighbour the elder Jean Guille (1712–78) kept a few deer for sporting purposes, which Mollet was invited to hunt with a party of other guests in 1774.[68] Although he joined in, Mollet's personal enjoyment of the chase comes across as lukewarm. Like Guille, he invited hunting friends to enjoy their sport on his land, but while he accompanied them in the 1770s and 1780s, he later dropped out of personal participation.[69] What Mollet could not abide was people hunting in his fields without permission. In 1812, on finding a party of army officers on his property with dogs and guns, Mollet peremptorily had one of their dogs shot.[70] Captain Thomas Andrews, to whom the dog belonged, later actioned

---

[66] Appendix 11 lists a selection of the books recorded in Mollet's year-end notes.
[67] It is not known whether Mollet's interest in herbalism pre-dated his friendship with Frère François Marie, but he seems to have taken the subject seriously. In 1812, he recorded making a circuit of Guernsey's coast scattering seeds of stramonium (also known as thorn apple), a herb used against arthritis and inflammation (Diary, 29.5.1812, 4.6.1812).
[68] Diary, 2.11.1774.
[69] Diary, 28.1.1773, 30.12.1774, 18.10.1780, 10.1.1798, 15.3.1809, 4.12.1811, 27.3.1816.
[70] Diary, 23.1.1812.

Mollet in Court.[71] Unfortunately for Mollet, the Court found his destruction of the dog unjustified, and he was sentenced to pay a fine and compensation.[72]

Mollet's own favourite leisure activities were more peaceful. Between his twenties and early forties, he enjoyed an occasional swim in the sea.[73] Sea-bathing, as then practised by the English upper classes, was associated with elaborate paraphernalia, such as horse-drawn bathing machines and bathing attendants. Mollet, who had probably been doing it since boyhood, seems to have taken simple 'dips' at nearby Vazon, perhaps as much to cool down as anything else. Mollet also enjoyed shore-gathering – looking for crabs and ormers on low spring tides.[74] This he engaged in with his farm servants and labourers.[75] He gave it up around the turn of the nineteenth century, finding, perhaps, that it exacerbated his rheumatism, but he continued to record his servants' shore-gathering expeditions, sometimes reporting hauls of 400–600 ormers from a single trip.[76]

Something which Mollet never gave up was samphire-gathering. This was another quiet pastime he engaged in with his servants. Every summer they would ride or walk to the south cliffs at Bon Repos (west of la Corbière), and spend several hours gathering the asparagus-like succulent, which seems to have grown in abundance on the rocky slopes. The last time Mollet recorded participating in such an excursion was in 1816, when, aged seventy-four, he gathered samphire at Bon Repos with his farm servant Abraham Machon.[77]

Opinions and beliefs

Mollet's journal gives away disappointingly little in respect of his political opinions. In general terms, he seems to have shared Enlightenment disapproval of autocracy and absolutism. His presumed distaste for some of George III's policies has already been noted in the account of the Alderney

---

[71] Diary, 1.2.1812.
[72] Diary, 15.2.1812.
[73] Diary, 15.7.1775, 17.7.1779, 27.7.1780, 16.8.1780, 9.7.1785.
[74] Ormers, edible molluscs elsewhere known as abalones, were (and still are) at the northern extreme of their range in the Channel Islands.
[75] Diary, 19.2.1772, 11.3.1773, 11.3.1785, 11.4.1785, 20.8.1785, 9.9.1786, 6.6.1792.
[76] Diary, 5.3.1806, 24.2.1807.
[77] Diary, 2.9.1816.

window-smashing episode in Chapter 4.[78] His ownership of such books as Voltaire's *Œuvres Complètes* suggests at least a knowledge of the critique of the French Court credited with contributing to France's pre-revolutionary ferment. His association with the Guernseymen who sailed to Cherbourg on the 'Liberty' indicates at least a passing dalliance with the pro-democratic ideas said to have been entertained by members of the so-called 'Liberty Club' to whom the yacht belonged.[79]

As regards the detail of insular politics, Mollet's journal is all but silent. The most that can be said is that, wishing to remain on good terms with all members of the local elite (who were sometimes at war with each other), Mollet avoided taking sides in the battles which beset the Royal Court in the 1770s and 1790s.[80] In 1777, at the height of a dispute between Bailiff William Le Marchant and Advocate Peter De Havilland (with both of whom he maintained social relations), Charles Mollet refused to join his fellow Constables when they went to make a formal representation to the Bailiff.[81] Following the meeting, Mollet reported that Le Marchant had given the Constables 'very short shrift', so he had perhaps adopted the wisest course.[82]

On matters of religion, Mollet's diaries provide more plentiful evidence, though he never recorded his beliefs outright. When his first extant diary opened in 1771, Guernsey was uniformly Anglican. Like almost everyone else, the young Mollet regularly attended his parish church on a Sunday, and went quarterly to Communion. For a few years, he also conscientiously noted the Biblical text on which the Minister had preached. After the departure to Jersey of the long-serving parish Rector André Migault in 1773, Mollet began to alternate services in his own parish church with services in other parishes, although this did not prevent him purchasing a new pew in the Castel church in 1785.[83]

---

[78] See Chapter 4, n. 95.

[79] A note appended to published excerpts from Elisha Dobrée's diary states that the 'Liberty Club' (of which Dobrée was a member but Mollet was not) had been 'founded by Captain Hellier Gosselin and others who were by way of admiring the English Tom Paine and the leaders of the French Revolution' (J.P. Warren, 'Extracts from the diary of Elisha Dobrée', *Transactions of la Société Guernesiaise*, 10 (1929) p. 525).

[80] For which see, R. Hocart, *Peter de Havilland: Bailiff of Guernsey, A History of his Life, 1747–1821* (Guernsey, 1997), pp. 16–23, 35–51.

[81] Mollet did not specify what the representation was about.

[82] Diary, 25.1.1777.

[83] Diary, 2.8.1785. He also purchased a pew in Bethel Chapel (a proprietary chapel in town) when it opened in 1794 (Diary, 19.9.1794).

From 1784, the incumbent at the Castel was Nicolas Dobrée (1755–1843), of the 'Bellevue' branch of the family. Mollet's relations with Dobrée were not of the most cordial, and this seems rather to have soured Mollet's relationship with his own parish church. Dobrée was a pluralist, with benefices at Wigginton in Oxfordshire and Furtho in Northamptonshire as well as in Guernsey. In 1794, he and his wife exchanged residence in Guernsey for residence in one of his English parishes.[84] In 1798, after Dobrée had been absent four years and showed no sign of returning, Mollet met with a group of other parishioners to instigate legal action aimed at forcing Dobrée to perform his parochial duties in person.[85] As it turned out, the action was never undertaken, but the threat seems to have sufficed to secure Dobrée's return, and the Rector reappeared in the Castel in the autumn.[86] Mollet's relationship with Nicolas Dobrée never quite recovered, however, and in ensuing years he attended other churches more often than he did his own – particularly St Saviours after his young friend Thomas Carey became Rector there in 1798, and St Peters after Thomas Brock became Rector of that parish in 1802.

Mollet's church attendance in any event declined perceptibly after the turn of the century. In the last five years of his life, he only attended church on a few summer Sundays each year.[87] One reason for his non-attendance was the cold. Guernsey's ancient churches lacked heating and were glacial in winter – on one occasion Mollet noted having to leave the church before the sermon as he felt so 'cold about the head'.[88] Mollet also had other reasons of a physical nature. In 1816, having turned out for the first sermon preached at the Castel by the newly ordained William Guille, Mollet commented somewhat sadly afterwards: 'I have become deaf & could not hear him.'[89] In 1818, the last year of his journal, Mollet did not record attending church at all.

Church attendance, of itself, tells us little about underlying attitudes. This was particularly the case for Mollet and his contemporaries, for whom attendance was so much a matter of convention. In the reigns of Elizabeth,

---

[84] Diary, 29.1.1795.
[85] Diary, 30.6.1798, 19.8.1798.
[86] Diary, 14.10.1798.
[87] Diary, 7.7.1811, 14.6.1812.
[88] Diary, 11.10.1801.
[89] Diary, 7.7.1816. William Guille (1792–1869) was the grandson of the younger Jean Guille of St George. He was to marry Mollet's great-niece Judith Brock in 1818.

James and Charles I, Guernsey had been an austere Calvinistic theocracy.[90] This austerity had however largely worn off by the mid-eighteenth century, and most members of Mollet's own class evinced a fairly easy-going latitudinarianism, such as prevailed in England. A local Methodist later remarked of the period (not, perhaps, without slight exaggeration):

> All the Anglican ministers were wordly and unconverted. Some were of doubtful morality, to say the least. Others made a game of religion and mocked it.[91]

After Mollet's death, Guernsey underwent great changes under the influence of Methodism and Evangelicalism, and some of his attitudes might have surprised islanders born in the Victorian era. For one thing, Mollet always demonstrated a lively interest in other denominations. While in Bath, he took the opportunity to attend several non-Anglican chapels and meeting-houses: Lady Huntingdon's chapel, the Moravian meeting, the Quaker meeting, and the Roman Catholic chapel.[92] During his French travels in 1790, Mollet freely associated with Roman Catholic ecclesiastics.[93] From 1792, he entertained many *émigré* priests at his home. In 1796, he rode to town on four successive Sundays to hear sermons preached by the former French royal chaplain Claude Coulon.[94] From 1799, he formed an enduring friendship with Frère François Marie. For Mollet, religious curiosity always trumped religious bias. But he was not alone among his contemporaries. Many of his peers also attended l'Abbé Coulon's sermons. The Anglican curate Edward Mourant sheltered *émigré* priests at the Castel Rectory.[95] Even Etienne Gibert, renowned for his Protestant zeal, openly received Frère Marie at his home.[96]

When it came to matters of morality, Mollet's attitudes were pragmatic and (in his diaries at least) he passed no judgments. A case in point is that of his friend, the Lieutenant-Governor William Brown. Mollet was aware that Brown, who never married, had natural children, but he treated this as a mere

---

[90] See D.M. Ogier, *Reformation and Society in Guernsey* (Woodbridge, 1996), especially chapters 5 and 6.
[91] 'Biographies du Révérend Etienne Gibert', *Magasin Méthodiste* (November 1890), p. 366 (translated from the original French).
[92] Diary, 17.12.1775, 25.12.1775, 31.12.1775.
[93] Diary, 7.10.1790, 14.10.1790, 16.10.1790.
[94] Diary, 13.3.1796, 20.3.1796, 25.3.1796, 3.4.1796. For more on l'Abbé Coulon, see Chapter 7, n. 76.
[95] Chapter 7, n. 78.
[96] Diary, 14.5.1812.

matter of fact.[97] Before coming to Guernsey, Brown had a son named William and a daughter named Mary. During his tenure as Lieutenant-Governor, he had two further sons: George, born in 1786, and Richard, born in 1792. Both boys were born to Brown's servant Mary Skinner, and their baptisms (at St Andrews) were registered under her surname. William Brown was present as godfather at both christenings and acknowledged his children in his will.[98]

Charles Mollet adopted a similarly businesslike attitude when one of his own servants, Nanon Le Page, became pregnant by another of his servants, Nico Martel, during Mollet's Alderney sojourn.[99] Perhaps valuing Nanon's services more than Nico's, Mollet dismissed Nico, but sent Nanon back to his house in Guernsey, where she stayed with his tenants Pierre Gavet and Eleazar Ingrouille.[100] After an absence of just over five weeks, Nanon returned to Alderney and resumed working for Mollet as if nothing had happened.[101] She had only been four months pregnant on her departure, but was no longer pregnant on her return. What had transpired during her absence in Guernsey is unclear.

Charles Mollet's obituary in *L'Indépendance* made much of his practical philanthropy. 'The poor, whom he never ceased to help,' it asserted, 'will bemoan the loss of a liberal hand, always open to relieve them.'[102] There was no shortage of poor people in Guernsey's country parishes. Many families led a hand-to-mouth existence, piecing together a living from growing and selling vegetables, fishing, labouring, practising crafts. Without a margin in reserve, any of life's vicissitudes – illness, injury, loss of a spouse – could plunge them into difficulties overnight. In the earlier volumes of Mollet's journal, there are very few mentions of philanthropic deeds. In the last two volumes, however, they abound.

Mollet's philanthropy took many forms. On several occasions, he took the initiative in organising subscriptions among his better-off friends in order to help someone in misfortune, (as he did in 1817 on behalf of Jean Torode of les Moullins who had injured his foot with a spade, or in 1818 on behalf of

---

[97] Diary, 8.8.1792.
[98] The baptisms were registered on 18.6.1786 and 2.9.1792. For William Brown's will, see PROB 11/1248/217, National Archives.
[99] Diary, 5.5.1788.
[100] Diary, 20.5.1788, 17.6.1788.
[101] Diary, 31.7.1788.
[102] *L'Indépendance*, 6.3.1819 (translated from the original French).

Nico Roussel of les Roussiaux who had lost two horses to sickness).[103] On other occasions, he supplied poor parishioners with free timber to help them build their cottages (as he did in 1808 to Pierre Le Page who was building a cottage at le Guet, and to Thomas Collenette who was building one at le Crocq).[104] Less formally but more frequently, Mollet might invite retired former servants to Sunday dinner in his kitchen (as, in 1806, he invited Marie Robin and Marie Le Ray, who had worked for his parents four decades previously).[105] Or else he might pay for an elderly ex-labourer to be shaved (as he did in 1816 for the septuagenarian Charles Nicolle).[106] Or yet again he might take the strain off a hard-pressed family by temporarily accommodating one of their youngsters (as in 1810 he did the apprentice boy Jean Guilbert).[107] More frequently still, he might simply supply needy parishioners with hand-outs of basics such as straw, faggots, peat, bracken and potatoes, which he gave away on a regular basis.[108]

One branch of Mollet's philanthropy which dovetailed neatly with his curiosity about the outside world was the help he gave to people who emigrated from Guernsey. The island's first substantial wave of emigration occurred between 1806 and 1810 in the wake of St Peter Port's demise as an entrepôt. The two main destinations were Prince Edward Island in the Gulf of St Lawrence, and Cambridge, Ohio.[109] Charles Mollet's interest was initially awakened by the personal connections he had with some of the emigrants, notably Daniel Machon, the elder brother of his farm servant Abraham Machon, and Henry Ingrouille, the younger brother of his occasional labourer Eleazar Ingrouille. Daniel Machon and his family were among a group of Guernsey people who sailed to North America in the spring of 1806 in order to take up land offered for sale by the wife of Prince Edward

---

[103] Diary, 8.4.1817, 4.7.1818.
[104] Diary, 28.10.1808, 17.11.1808, 6.12.1808.
[105] Diary, 17.8.1806.
[106] Diary, 12.5.1816.
[107] Diary, 26.11.1810.
[108] Diary, 6.10.1809, 12.3.1816. Mollet also helped many 'respectable' poor people in this way, among them town-based widows such as Mrs Amiraux, Mrs Reynolds and Mrs Mitchell. Deliveries to such people, locally termed *pauvres honteux*, were tactfully made under cover of darkness (see, for instance, Diary, 20.9.1816).
[109] For accounts of local emigration to these places, see M.G. Turk, *The Quiet Adventurers in Canada* (Detroit, 1979), pp. 71–5; Anon., *Portrait and Biographical Record of Guernsey County, Ohio* (Chicago, 1895), p. 516.

Island's Lieutenant-Governor.[110] Henry Ingrouille, who also travelled to North America at this time, seems to have settled in New York,[111] as did another acquaintance, James Jehan, a little later.[112] Among other emigrants Charles Mollet knew personally were Elizée Le Page, the former bandmaster of the Town militia regiment, who settled at Prince Edward Island;[113] Nicolas Cohu of the Castel, who left for Norfolk, Virginia in 1807 with seventy other Guernsey people;[114] Nicolas Le Huray, a watchmaker, who departed for Baltimore in 1807;[115] Jean Brehaut of St Saviours, who settled at Prince Edward Island;[116] Thomas Lenfestey, who settled in Cambridge, Ohio;[117] Charles Marquand of le Bouet, who settled at Prince Edward Island;[118] and Jean Brehaut of les Moullins, who made his home in Canso, Nova Scotia.[119]

Mollet was a great letter-writer, and corresponded with many of these emigrants, sometimes acting as an intermediary between them and relatives who had difficulty reading and writing.[120] He also took to providing departing migrants with a sea-stock for their voyage – baskets of cabbages and kale, sacks of potatoes, hampers full of his home-made cordials and raspberry vinegar.[121] Later, he took it upon himself to send out packages of useful goods to those beginning a life in the New World. These packages, which he sent on trading vessels departing from Guernsey, contained such things as vegetable seeds, sewing thread, ready-made shoes, gin, rum and brandy.[122]

One very personal form of assistance which Mollet frequently noted was sitting with the sick and dying. Whilst Mollet doubtless concurred in this service (and perhaps even suggested it), it was actually performed by his servant Lisabo Machon. Mollet's last two volumes record countless nights

---

[110] See advertisement in *la Gazette de Guernesey* of 8.4.1806 for 'tracts of rich, fertile forest land' to be sold at between 10s and 20s per acre. Buyers of this land were offered a passage to Prince Edward Island for £6 10s each.
[111] Diary, 12.5.1807, 16.6.1807, 4.8.1807.
[112] Diary, 19.8.1810.
[113] Diary, 28.8.1806, 6.7.1812.
[114] Diary, 26.4.1807, 26.1.1817.
[115] Diary, 4.8.1807, 8.8.1807.
[116] Diary, 3.10.1808.
[117] Diary, 14.1.1809.
[118] Diary, 18.4.1816.
[119] Diary, 4.4.1818.
[120] See, for instance, Diary, 7.9.1807, 13.12.1807, 3.10.1808.
[121] Diary, 9.5.1807, 11.5.1807, 8.8.1807.
[122] Diary, 9.7.1809, 6.7.1812, 4.4.1818, 6.4.1818.

spent by Lisabo at the bedsides of dying neighbours: that, for example, of Thomas Dorey, who died leaving ten children and a pregnant wife in 1807;[123] that of seventeen-year-old Marie Breton who died of consumption in 1809;[124] that of twenty-eight-year-old Elizabeth Priaulx who died after giving birth in 1817.[125] The neighbours who received this help seemed truly grateful, and Lisabo often found herself called for when families were in trouble.[126]

Another contribution made by Lisabo was the care of Mollet's fosterlings. In the first decade of the nineteenth century, Mollet took three young children into his household on a long-term basis. The first was Susanne Ozanne, whom Mollet took in at the age of five or six around 1800.[127] She was the eldest daughter of his tenant Jacques Ozanne, who eventually brought twelve children into the world. For the first few years of her residence in his house, Mollet sent Suzon (as he called her) to school, and paid her school fees.[128] When she left school at the age of thirteen, she became a full-time servant in his household.[129] Mollet's interest in the Ozannes also extended to the younger children (Judith, Elizabeth, Caroline, Jean, Marthe, Margueritte, Esther and William), whom he regularly invited to stay at his home, or else to dine with Suzon in his kitchen.[130] By 1817, Suzon's ten-year-old sister Margueritte was also spending all her weekends at Mollet's house.[131] Suzon herself remained with Mollet until the end of his life.

Isaac Marquand was the second of Mollet's fosterlings. Born in July 1798, he was the son of Lisabo Machon's sister Marie and her husband Abraham Marquand. With Abraham in poor health and Marie burdened with many children, Isaac made frequent stays at the farm from the age of three.[132] In 1810, when his father's health deteriorated sharply, he took up permanent residence at Mollet's.[133] Mollet sent Isaac, who was eleven, to school, and

---

[123] Diary, 4.7.1807, 17.3.1807.
[124] Diary, 3.12.1809, 11.12.1809.
[125] Diary, 16.4.1817.
[126] Diary, 11.12.1809.
[127] Diary, 9.1.1803.
[128] Diary, 7.4.1807, Notes relating to 1809.
[129] Diary, 5.6.1811.
[130] Diary, 25.5.1807, 25.3.1809, 22.4.1809, 26.12.1815, 5.5.1816, 9.2.1817, 28.12.1817.
[131] Diary, 31.8.1817, 28.12.1817.
[132] Diary, 26.7.1801, 20.12.1801, 6.2.1803, 27.6.1807, 15.8.1808, 4.3.1810.
[133] Diary, 4.3.10. Abraham Marquand died the following year, leaving Marie with nine children (Diary, 28.4.11).

again paid his school fees.[134] In 1812, when Isaac reached the age of thirteen, Mollet negotiated an apprenticeship for him (as a plasterer), after which he moved out of Mollet's house and into lodgings, for the first year of which Mollet paid.[135] In subsequent years, Isaac maintained the connection with Mollet, often dining at the farm on a Sunday, or when working in the neighbourhood.[136] Mollet's last mention of a visit from Isaac came three weeks before his diaries ended.[137]

Charles Mollet's third and last fosterling was Pierre Nicolle (born in 1805). Pierre's father Isaac Nicolle and grandfather Charles Nicolle had both worked for Mollet in previous decades. His mother Rachel, *née* Ferbrache, was a sister of Mollet's former farm servant Daniel Ferbrache.[138] It was when Rachel died prematurely of consumption that Mollet took her five-year-old son into his care.[139]

As he had done with Suzon and Isaac, Mollet paid for Pierre's schooling. He sent him first to St Andrews parish school,[140] and then, when he was eleven, to a school, or rather two schools, in town.[141] Pierre remained at school until the summer of 1818, when he reached the age of thirteen.[142] Thereafter, he became a full-time worker on Mollet's farm, and was still present in this role when the diaries broke off. As well as being the youngest of Mollet's fosterlings, Pierre Nicolle was perhaps also his favourite. When Mollet sold the 'upper' house to Abraham and Lisabo Machon in 1815, he had a stipulation inserted into the conveyance to the effect that, if the Machons died without surviving heirs, the property should devolve to Pierre.[143]

Pierre, Isaac and Suzon were not the only children whose voices were heard around Mollet's farm in his last two decades. Little Judith Collenette

---

[134] Diary, 12.3.1810, 17.9.1810, Notes relating to 1810, 6.5.1811.
[135] Diary, 29.3.1812.
[136] For example, Diary, 14.1.1816, 10.3.1816, 5.4.1816, 28.7.1816, 23.3.1817, 31.5.1818.
[137] Diary, 5.7.1818.
[138] See Appendix 4 for the connections between all these people.
[139] Diary, 27.7.1810, 30.8.1810.
[140] Diary, 6.5.1811.
[141] Between April and July 1816, Pierre attended a school in the Bordage run by a Mr Berry. Mollet then moved him to St Peter Port's National School, where the Master was Berry's brother (Diary, 22.4.1816, 8.7.1816). Mollet had previously also sent Suzon to a town school.
[142] Diary, 10.6.1818, 13.6.1818.
[143] Conveyance dated 18.5.1815 (AQ 1133/021, Island Archives).

(born in 1800) was also a regular guest, staying at the farm for a long succession of weekends and holidays between 1804 and 1812.[144] Isaac Marquand's younger brothers Abraham, Daniel and Henry were equally frequent visitors,[145] and so too were Pierre Nicolle's brothers Isaac and Hellier.[146] Finally, Charles Mollet also entertained disadvantaged children from town (some of them Town Hospital inmates), with youngsters such as John Hock, John Millman, Tom Marquis and Andrew Mitchell featuring regularly on his Sunday dinner list.[147]

This chapter has brought together many disparate elements of Charles Mollet's life. We have seen that Mollet was relatively privileged compared with most Guernseymen in that he enjoyed reasonable health; had a decent education; had access to books and culture; and had the opportunity to engage in leisure travel. It would probably also be fair to conclude that Mollet was towards the liberal end of the spectrum in respect of his religious and political views. What is most striking, however, is the extent of Mollet's private philanthropy. For all his privilege, Mollet lived out his life in close proximity to people of far fewer means than his, and this gave him a clear understanding of their hardships. Charles Mollet was no saint, and he certainly enjoyed the good things in life; however, it cannot but be to his credit that he genuinely tried to palliate the lot of his neighbours.

---

[144] Diary, 1.1.1804, 4.3.1804, 16.2.1806, 17.12.1807, 17.5.1807, 13.4.1811, 23.12.1811. This little girl was the daughter of Captain Abraham Collenette and Judith, *née* Nicolle. Her aunts Susanne Collenette and Marie Nicolle (who married Pierre Gavet) were both former servants of Mollet's.
[145] Diary, 1.9.1811, 8.12.1811, 19.1.1812, 24.5.1812, 13.9.1815.
[146] Diary, 8.3.12, 3.9.1815.
[147] Diary, 23.8.1807, 22.7.1810, 13.4.1817, 10.8.1817, 9.11.1817.

9
Private Life, Part 2: Relationships

Charles Mollet's diaries tell us much about externalities. They allow us to analyse his economic life, his civic life, his domestic life, his social life, and even his pursuits and interests. What the diaries tell us singularly little about are his personal relationships. This was primarily because Mollet was using the diaries to record matters of fact – when and how he had done what and with whom. He was not using them to discourse on matters which were already well known to him – his inner life and intimate feelings. There are nevertheless two qualifications to this general assessment. These concern the excisions to which Mollet's journal was later subject, and his use of symbols and codes. In the first instance, it is possible that the excisions were made precisely *because* of their personal content. In the second instance, Mollet may have used codes to cloak matters he did not care to spell out.[1]

This chapter resumes where the chapter on Mollet's social life left off, in an attempt to look behind the surface of his relationships. For this, however, it is necessary to adopt an indirect approach. The importance of any given relationship to Mollet may in part be measured by the bulk of entries concerning it. As regards the nature and substance of relationships, we must read between the lines. Taking this approach, it is possible to identify three main clusters of significant relationships in Charles Mollet's life: relationships with his family; relationships with a select group of friends; and relationships with members of his household. Each of these clusters will be examined in turn.

Charles Mollet was more explicit about his familial relationships than most of his other relationships. Of all his emotional bonds, the closest seem to have been with his mother and the younger of his two sisters. Mollet always referred to his mother as *ma Chère Mère*. She was sixty-three when the diaries opened, there are entries regarding her until she died at the age of eighty-three. As she grew older and more infirm, Mollet evinced increasing concern for her, especially when she suffered three serious falls in as many years. At the age of seventy-seven, Mollet's mother broke her left wrist in a

---

[1] For a sample of Mollet's codes and symbols, see Appendix 7.

fall down the *tourelle* staircase at her Castel home; the following year, she injured her thigh when she slipped on some flagstones at the back of the house; the year after that, she had another serious fall on flagstones at Candie.[2] This last fall prevented Mrs Mollet from walking unaided again and signalled the start of an inexorable decline. In January 1792, she became seriously ill and took to her bed. Mollet did not record what illness his mother was suffering from, and probably did not know himself. Following a few weeks of steady deterioration and an eventual lapse into unconsciousness, she died in mid-February 1792. Her death seems to have been a peaceful one, but, even at the age of eighty-three, it seems to have touched Mollet profoundly. 'Her tenderness & affection for me were such that my loss is inexpressible,' he wrote on the day she died.[3] Returning home alone after her funeral, he mused 'Ah, how sad I am when I think of my loss', adding that he would find his life 'unbearable', were it not for the 'affectionate friendship' shown him by other relatives.[4] For a seemingly gregarious man with a great number of social contacts, this remark comes as something of a surprise.

Aside from his mother, the relative Charles Mollet saw most frequently was his sister Marthe Mourant. Marthe was closer to Charles than his Jersey-based sister in terms of both age and geography, and she seems to have been an important emotional support to him. When, in 1794, Marthe suffered a stroke and seemed in danger of dying, Mollet wrote: 'I truly wish that my own hour had come & that God would take me instead.'[5] Again, this is rather a surprising remark for a man with as full and active a social life as Mollet's.

In the event, Marthe Mourant survived her stroke, and though plagued by constant ill-health, she lived for another four years. 'May God give her rest', Mollet wrote when she finally neared her end: 'I will feel her loss sorely.'[6] No such words accompanied Mollet's record of his other sister's death in 1809. Physical distance was a barrier to emotional closeness, and by the time his Jersey-based sister died, Mollet had not seen her for more than twenty years.[7]

The closeness Mollet had experienced with his mother and Marthe was never to be repeated. He actively kept up social contacts with his Guernsey-

---

[2] Diary, 16.5.1786, 9.5.1787, 19.6.1788.
[3] Diary, 19.2.1792.
[4] Diary, 25.2.1792.
[5] Diary, 23.11.1794.
[6] Diary, 12.8.1798, 18.8.1798.
[7] Diary, 29.8.1809.

based nieces and nephews, but they all had their own lives to lead and did not manifest any very strong attachment to him.[8] Mollet's widowed niece Mary Brock was the family member of whom he saw most in later years. It is difficult to tell if Mary was particularly close to her uncle, but having no children of her own to keep her busy, she at least had time for him in his old age.

There is nothing of a romantic or sexual nature in Charles Mollet's diaries.[9] In his twenties and thirties, he behaved as expected of a young bachelor and participated in outings and other social occasions with marriageable young ladies of his own class, such as Judith and Marie Ozanne of la Houguette and Rachel Guille of St George.[10] His diaries however contain no indication that he actively courted any of them (unless they are in the missing volume for 1781–5). In his earliest volume, two brief allusions to Judith Ozanne hint that he may possibly have considered her as a partner, but there was nothing by way of a sustained courtship, and Mollet expressed no resentment when Judith married Josias Le Marchant in 1780.[11] For all this, Charles Mollet was no misogynist, and ladies always played a part in his social life. In his mature years, these were the wives and daughters of male friends, regularly invited to tea or dinner along with their male relatives. On many occasions, too, Mollet hosted genteel parties composed entirely of ladies.[12]

It is clear, however, that Mollet's primary relationships were not with these ladies but their men. Since he rarely made his feelings explicit, it is hard to identify at a glance which of his male friends might have been of most importance to him. Frequency of mention is however a reasonable proxy, and it is possible to pick out four names which figure especially often in his diaries (albeit at different times of Mollet's life). These are William Brown, Etienne Gibert, Thomas Williams and Edward Mourant. We shall consider each of

---

[8] For these nieces and nephews, see Appendix 3.

[9] The only 'sexual' matter briefly alluded to was Nanon Le Page's unplanned pregnancy in Alderney (see Chapter 8).

[10] Diary, 8.1.1771, 8.6.1772, 25.4.1773, 6.6.1773. For Judith and Marie Ozanne, see Chapter 7. Rachel Guille, born in 1751, was the sister of Mollet's friends Nicolas and Richard Guille. She died unmarried in 1803.

[11] The hints – hardly anything in themselves – come in the summer of 1772, when Mollet, aged thirty, recorded escorting the sixteen-year-old Judith home from St Peter Port on her return from boarding school, and then, a few weeks later, spending an afternoon alone with her (Diary, 6.8.1772, 24.8.1772).

[12] For instance, Diary 8.8.1787, 10.6.1790, 29.8.1792, 9.8.1793, 28.8.1794.

these men more closely in an attempt to elicit what they might have meant to Charles Mollet.

Mollet's friendship with the Lieutenant-Governor William Brown was perhaps one of his most positive non-familial relationships. It pre-dated the beginning of the journal by about seven years. Brown, whom we already encountered in Chapters 7 and 8, was born into a Scottish gentry family in 1739.[13] In 1758, at the height of the Seven Years War, he joined the Black Watch as an Ensign. Promoted Lieutenant the following year, he served in North America under Jeffery Amherst, as also in the West Indies, where he was wounded in 1762. At the end of the Seven Years War, Brown became a Captain of Invalids, and while stationed in Jersey in 1764 or 1765, he met Charles Mollet.[14] After a term as Governor of Upnor Castle in Kent in the 1770s and early 1780s, William Brown was promoted to the rank of Lieutenant-Colonel and made Lieutenant-Governor of Guernsey in 1784. Brown had two nephews (sons of his older brother Richard) who spent time with their uncle in Guernsey and were also known to Charles Mollet. James Brown (born in 1768), who was an army officer, served as one of his uncle's aides-de-camp. William Brown (born in 1769) married local woman Anne Maingy in 1794 and settled in Guernsey as a wine and spirits merchant.[15]

Mollet, who typically referred to Lieutenant-Governor Brown as his 'dear friend' or 'good friend', frequently exchanged hospitality with him, not only in company with others, but also alone. In the spring and summer, Mollet would spend many hours with Brown at le Château des Marais, a dilapidated medieval fort on the east coast, where Brown had had a garden laid out and went to relax.[16] Mollet, three years Brown's junior, seems to have prized the attention shown him by Brown, and Brown, for his part, had an accurate grasp of his friend's character. As already noted in Chapter 4, Brown actively attempted to deter Mollet from going to Alderney.[17] When Mollet nevertheless insisted on carrying out his plan, Brown generously

---

[13] He was a grandson of Sir George Broun, 3rd Baronet of Colstoun, Haddingtonshire.
[14] Diary, 17.5.1793.
[15] I am grateful to the archivist of Blair Castle in Perthshire, and to the archives department of the Black Watch Museum in Perth for their assistance in piecing together William Brown's biography.
[16] Diary, 15.8.1787, 15.6.1789, 12.9.1789, 15.5.1790, 28.7.1791. Mollet recorded supplying Brown with trees for this garden (Diary, 21.1.1787). For an image of le Château des Marais (also known as Ivy Castle), see Plate 23.
[17] Chapter 4, n. 73.

accommodated him at his own home during one of Mollet's returns to Guernsey.[18] And when everything eventually fell through, Brown appointed Mollet a supernumerary aide-de-camp.[19] Mollet never recorded assistance of this nature on the part of anyone else. It is little wonder that his friend's sudden death at the age of fifty-four came as a considerable shock to Mollet.[20] Brown was buried in Guernsey's Town Church. Charles Mollet, who attended the funeral, wrote that it left him feeling 'very sad'.[21]

Mollet's relations with Etienne Gibert were more ambivalent. As noted in Chapter 7, Mollet first met Gibert on a visit to Guernsey in 1785, and struck up a long-lasting relationship with him after he was appointed Rector of St Andrews in 1794. Gibert's French origin no doubt attracted Mollet, as did his reputation as a scholar and a writer.[22] Etienne Gibert was already fifty-eight when he took up his appointment in Guernsey. He brought with him his second wife (and former housekeeper), fifty-five-year-old Elizabeth (*née* Berry), whom he had married in London in 1776.[23] As the years went by, Mollet's diaries evinced a growing measure of exasperation at the clergyman's relations with his wife. The chief reason for this was that, for all Gibert's erudition, he was very much under Elizabeth's thumb. On one occasion in 1807, Mollet personally took Mrs Gibert to task for her behaviour and (in his own words) 'almost quarrelled with her'.[24] A few weeks later, when the dust had settled, Mollet invited Etienne Gibert to dinner without his wife. Having initially accepted the invitation, Gibert subsequently cried off, alleging illness. Mollet went to see him the following day, and to his surprise, he found Gibert hard at work in his garden. 'I believe Mrs Gibert prevented him from coming,' Mollet wrote; 'she is angry with me for intervening in their disagreement.'[25] Whether for this reason or some other cause, Gibert, who was by now seventy-one, never visited Mollet's home again. Mollet

---

[18] Diary, 29.12.1788.
[19] Diary, 2.6.1790.
[20] Diary, 17.5.1793. The diarist Elisha Dobrée reported that Brown had succumbed to 'an apoplexy' (17.5.1783, Diary of Elisha Dobrée, vol. 1, AQ 1572/03, Island Archives).
[21] Diary, 20.5.1795.
[22] Gibert published fourteen books between 1788 and 1811, including *Observations sur les Ecrits de M. de Voltaire* (1788), a copy of which Mollet owned; *Réflections sur l'Apocalypse* (1796); and three volumes of collected sermons, to which Mollet himself subscribed (Diary, Notes relating to 1806).
[23] 'Biographie du Révérend Etienne Gibert', *Magasin Méthodiste* (December 1890), p. 401.
[24] Diary, 6.3.1807.
[25] Diary, 24.4.1807. See Plate 9 for a contemporary image of Gibert.

nevertheless continued his own regular visits to the Rectory, often finding Gibert 'despondent' at his domestic situation.[26]

Whatever the state of their marriage, when Elizabeth died in 1815, seventy-nine-year-old Etienne Gibert felt himself unable to continue as Rector and resigned his living. Charles Mollet, who had been apprised of the resignation in August, waited patiently for Gibert to tell him face to face.[27] Doubtless from a feeling of pride – and despite repeated visits from Mollet – Gibert did not let on for several weeks. Only in mid-October did Charles Mollet finally report: 'Mr Gibert at last told me today that he had resigned his parish.' 'I made no comment,' Mollet added.[28] The fact was that Gibert had been forced to tell Mollet, since the new Rector, Thomas Grut, was about to move in with his wife and children.[29] Their arrival did not however entail Gibert's expulsion from the Rectory. Gibert had no local family of his own, and by arrangement with Mr and Mrs Grut, he continued living at St Andrews for the next eighteen months, again with regular visits from Mollet. Etienne Gibert eventually died at St Andrews Rectory on 14 February 1817, Charles Mollet having last visited him on the 8th.

Following Gibert's death, Mollet recorded that the elderly clergyman had left all his books, furniture and effects to the Reverend Grut and an individual named Nicolas De Mouilpied. He also noted that Gibert had bequeathed £1,350 in government securities to the Moravian Church 'for the propagation of the faith'.[30] Mollet's plain language notwithstanding, we can detect something of a raised eyebrow at both the refugee clergyman's wealth, and his choice of legatees.[31]

Charles Mollet's friendships with Thomas Williams and Edward Mourant were very different from his friendships with William Brown and Etienne Gibert, not least because both Williams and Mourant were more than twenty-five years younger than Mollet.[32] The diaries themselves contain little of a substantive nature on these two relationships, but the relationships

---

[26] See, for instance, Diary, 12.10.1808.
[27] Diary, 31.8.1815.
[28] Diary, 9.10.1815.
[29] The Gruts were in residence by 24 October (Diary, 24.10.1815).
[30] Diary, 20.2.1817.
[31] A nephew of Gibert's from France later visited Guernsey, and De Mouilpied and Grut relinquished part of their share in the clergyman's estate to Gibert's blood relatives ('Biographie du Révérend Etienne Gibert', pp. 405–6).
[32] Thomas Williams was born in 1769 and Edward Mourant in 1768.

nevertheless attract attention because of the unusual number of entries concerning them. Thomas Williams has already been mentioned in a previous chapter. His father, whom Mollet also knew, was the Alderney Greffier and Procureur.[33] Mollet recorded ferreting with Tom Williams; visiting the Casquets lighthouse with Tom Williams; rowing to the island of Burhou with Tom Williams;[34] breakfasting, dining, taking tea and supping with Tom Williams.[35] He even spent a few days in Normandy with Tom Williams.[36] On his trips back to Guernsey and debt-collecting journeys to England, Mollet also wrote to Tom Williams (and *vice versa*).[37] In the months after Mollet's permanent departure from Alderney, Williams came twice to see him in Guernsey.[38] Early in 1791, however, Tom Williams seems to have left the Channel Islands for good. Mollet's last-ever reference to the young man came in September that year, when he recorded sending a letter to Williams in Madras.[39] An elusive relationship indeed, but seemingly an important one.

Between 1793 and 1801, Mollet's journal was similarly peppered with references to the Jerseyman Edward Mourant. As noted in Chapter 7, Mourant served as curate of the Castel parish in the mid-1790s, during which time he resided at the Castel Rectory.[40] This placed him within easy distance of Mollet's home, and the two exchanged frequent visits, both *tête-à-tête* and in company with others. In a detail that might seem quaint to the modern reader, Mollet recorded that, in 1795 and 1796, they spent many a summer's evening by a gate between Mollet's property and les Eturs road, chatting and watching the world go by.[41]

In 1796, twenty-eight-year-old Mourant married the Englishwoman Catherine Whiskin. The following year he was appointed Rector of the Forest and Torteval. At first, the marriage and promotion did not appear to affect Edward Mourant's relationship with Mollet, with whom he continued to socialise, sometimes with his wife and sometimes alone. In the autumn of

---

[33] See Chapter 4, n. 84.
[34] Diary, 29.3.1788, 5.3.1788, 17.1.1788.
[35] On 15.2.1788, Mollet recorded that Williams had 'taken tea & supped with me every day since the 8th.'
[36] Diary, 15.10.1788–20.10.1788.
[37] See, for instance, Diary, 9.11.1788, 25.4.1789, 11.5.1789, 2.6.1789.
[38] Diary, 22.7.1790, 28.10.1790.
[39] Diary, 24.9.1791.
[40] Diary, 29.1.1795 records Mourant's removal to the Rectory.
[41] Diary, 16.8.1795, 30.8.1795, 21.8.1796.

1798, however, Mollet recorded that Mourant had had 'a bad dinner' at his house, after which the clergyman had departed abruptly.[42] Over the next few months, the two men saw each other less often. Finally (perhaps seeking to clarify matters), Charles Mollet called in person at the Forest Rectory on 27 January 1801.[43] Though the outcome of this visit is not noted in the diary, it does not seem to have gone well, and on a loose sheet preserved among his correspondence and memoranda, Mollet recorded that, on this precise date, he had seen Mr Mourant at the Forest *pour la dernière fois*.[44] Mollet never gave a reason for the rupture in his journal. Perhaps scruples as to the propriety of recording clashes with social peers prevented him. When it came to frictions with plebeians, however, Mollet was more explicit.

Charles Mollet's relationships with his employees are the best documented of all his relationships. This is perhaps just as well, since they represent a class of islanders about whose lives relatively little is known. In the following section, we will look in detail at Mollet's relations with six of his workmen.[45] These were all either farm servants or day labourers.[46] Before investigating individuals, however, it is necessary to examine Mollet's treatment of his workers in more general terms. Mollet lived in close physical proximity to his employees. His house servants and farm servants slept on the upper floors of the main house, under the same roof as him, and when not entertaining higher-class guests, Mollet usually ate with them in the kitchen. As F.B. Tupper correctly remarked of this period, 'the gentlemen who cultivated their own small estates usually dined in the kitchen with their farm servants, who sat below the salt'.[47]

Mollet's relations with his staff had both positive and negative aspects. On the positive side, he could be generous. In several instances, Mollet recorded having had smart clothes made for his farm servants. In 1799, for example, he had a brown velvet suit made for Daniel Ferbrache and a spencer made for James Radford.[48] He also paid for some of his farm servants to be taught reading and writing. In 1805, for instance, he noted paying Nicolas Brouard

---

[42] Diary, 11.11.1798.
[43] Diary, 27.1.1801.
[44] Correspondence and Memoranda, Priaulx Library.
[45] Mollet's diaries did not discourse on his female servants to any great length.
[46] Short biographical details for all of these men are given in Appendix 5.
[47] F.B. Tupper, *The History of Guernsey and its Bailiwick* (1854; Guernsey, 1876 edn), p. 407.
[48] Diary, 18.4.1799, 3.12.1799. Spencers were waist-length double-breasted jackets.

8s for five months' evening tuition to Daniel Ferbrache and James Torode.[49] Mollet also allowed his farm servants occasional time off to perform family labour. In 1796, as in most years, he released them for the week devoted to *vraic à la poche* (when the poor had exclusive rights to cut seaweed) so that they could help their families gather as much of this valuable commodity as possible.[50]

On the negative side, Charles Mollet could strike a hard bargain in matters of remuneration. In 1796, 1798 and 1809, Mollet recorded having dismissed labourers peremptorily when they requested an increase in their daily rate.[51] He could also be possessive of his workmen's time. When, for instance, his farm servant Thomas Blondel attended a plough supper without leave after helping with a neighbour's ploughing, Mollet threatened to dock his pay.[52] When Blondel – and all of Mollet's other farm servants – attended militia exercises and reviews, Mollet would systematically record the time at which they left, the time at which the exercise or review ended, and the time at which they returned home. If they spent a few extra hours socialising with fellow militiamen after proceedings were over, Mollet was not pleased. 'Ab. & Thos were under arms at l'Hyvreuse from eight in the morning,' Mollet noted in 1812; 'Ab. returned here at 4 o'clock. Thos did not come back until 9 o'clock […]. The men had nevertheless been dismissed just after midday.'[53] Mollet particularly disapproved of his servants staying out late at night, and when they did so, he would sometimes lock his doors against them. In 1793, he recorded that his servant Nanon Heaume had walked out on him 'because she found the door locked against her when she returned from a party at three in the morning.'[54] Nanon, exasperated at such treatment, never resumed work for Mollet.

Mollet could also sometimes be hypocritical *vis-à-vis* his employees. One Monday morning in 1800, he recorded dismissing his farm servant Pierre Machon because Pierre had missed church the previous day, gone out socialising in the evening, and not returned until one in the morning.[55] Mollet's journal however showed that Charles Mollet himself had not

---

[49] Diary, Notes relating to 1805.
[50] Diary, 4.7.1796. On this week, see Chapter 3, n. 30.
[51] Diary, 3.9.1798, 27.7.1809. See also 1.8.1818.
[52] Diary, 17.2.1818.
[53] Diary, 4.6.1812.
[54] Diary, 27.9.1793.
[55] Diary, 20.1.1800.

attended church that Sunday and had also been socialising till one in the morning. It was a very asymmetrical relationship.

Pierre Gavet (1752–1818) moved into Mollet's house as a farm servant in 1775, when he was twenty-three.[56] Gavet seems to have been particularly versatile: as well as working on the farm, he served Mollet as a valet on trips to Jersey and Bath. He also waited at table, on one notable occasion at the Lieutenant-Governor's house when Brown was entertaining Prince William Henry.[57] Mollet himself wrote that he was 'much attached' to Gavet,[58] but their relationship – like Mollet's relationships with most of his farm servants – had many ups and downs. On two occasions, in 1776 and 1780, Pierre walked out on Mollet after a disagreement, only to return a few days later.[59]

In 1786, Pierre Gavet married Mollet's house servant Marie Nicolle, and (as noted in Chapter 4) Mollet accommodated them in his 'upper' house in return for their continuing to work for him.[60] Just over a year later, the newly-weds, wishing to forge an independent life for themselves, terminated their arrangement with Mollet and moved out. Mollet was clearly hurt:

> He left me without any expression of gratitude, only 'Thank you & Goodbye'. He did not even come in to see my Dear Mother [...]. I would have liked him to stay on, as I am much attached to him & appreciate his hard work & good qualities. However, his proud temperament makes him impatient of dependence.[61]

As it was, Pierre's association with Mollet was far from at an end, though his 'proud temperament' would continue to raise problems. In partnership with Eleazar Ingrouille, Pierre rented Mollet's farmhouse and gardens for four years after Mollet left for Alderney in 1787. This was perhaps a mistake on Pierre's part, since Charles Mollet seems to have taken his two ex-employees shamelessly for granted. Mollet reserved the use of a bedroom at the farm for himself, and repeatedly descended on Pierre and Eleazar during visits to Guernsey.[62] He had them send him regular supplies of fruit, vegetables and

---

[56] Diary, 8.5.1775.
[57] Diary, 6.6.1786. Prince William Henry was the future William IV, then a twenty-one-year-old naval officer.
[58] Diary, 30.9.1787.
[59] Diary, 10.9.1776, 12.9.1776, 20.10.1780, 23.10.1780.
[60] Diary, 23.8.1786.
[61] Diary, 30.9.1787.
[62] For instance, Diary, 6.4.1788–8.4.1788, 10.4.1788–12.4.1788, 4.1.89, 9.9.89.

meat, such as the 'wheat & flour, [...] 4 hams, 4 large pigs' cheeks, [...] apples, [...] pears & walnuts, [...] beef & a cake' they shipped to him in October 1788.[63] He also continued to treat them as servants, summoning them several times to Alderney when he had work for them to do.[64] Once Mollet was permanently back in Guernsey – and with at least two years still to run on the lease – Mollet's intrusions became even worse. Though nominally living at Candie, he visited the farm several times a week, planted flowers and shrubs in the gardens, and freely entertained friends and family in the house.[65]

In September 1791, Charles Mollet gave Pierre and Eleazar three months' notice of his intention to re-occupy his property; but Pierre, perhaps resenting his treatment at Mollet's hands, pre-empted him and moved out in October.[66] His contacts with Mollet during the remainder of the lease were minimal, and when, in the spring of 1792, he came to retrieve some peat which he had left at the farm, he cut his former employer dead. Mollet was again clearly hurt: 'he came three times with two carts, but he did not speak to me, nor even acknowledge my presence'.[67]

Pierre Gavet did eventually forge an independent life as a smallholder, buying a property at la Masse in the Castel and, later, one at les Truchots in St Andrews.[68] But fate was not kind to him. In 1799, his wife Marie died and left him with six young children.[69] This bereavement, painful as it was for Pierre, seems to have been seized by Charles Mollet as an opportunity for rebuilding bridges. He recorded paying Pierre a visit two days after Marie's death and arranging for his youngest children to be looked after at his home on the day of the funeral.[70] Thereafter, he continued inviting the children for occasional meals, and now and then gave them light work. He also seems to have given Pierre a heifer when his own cow died in 1802.[71]

For all Mollet's kindness, however, Pierre Gavet himself remained an infrequent visitor to Mollet's house. He was evidently of an unforgiving

---

[63] Diary, 22.10.1788.
[64] For Pierre and Eleazar's stays in Alderney, see Diary, 6.1.1788–11.1.1788, 13.3.1788–6.4.1788, 7.10.1789– 15.10.1789, 13.12.1789–20.12.1789.
[65] For instance, Diary, 1.6.1790, 9.7.1790, 16.7.1790, 1.2.1791, 17.3.1791, 13.7.1791.
[66] Diary, 14.9.1791, 23.10.1791.
[67] Diary, 10.5.1792.
[68] Diary, 4.1.1809, 19.2.1818.
[69] Diary, 20.12.1799. Pierre married again in 1804. His second wife was Judith Tostevin.
[70] Diary, 22.12.1799, 23.12.1799.
[71] Diary, 10.5.1802.

temperament. At the age of sixty-five, after a life distinctly more marked by hardship than Mollet's own, Pierre fell seriously ill. He took to his bed and died within weeks, but in a last poignant detail which typified their lopsided relationship, Charles Mollet recorded coming to sit by Pierre's bedside just two days before he died.[72]

Eleazar Ingrouille (1766–1832) was the second son of the miller Paul Ingrouille, tenant of le Grand Moulin du Roi. He came to work for Mollet as a day labourer in the early 1780s while still in his teens.[73] In some respects, Eleazar's relationship with Charles Mollet was similar to Pierre Gavet's. In other respects, owing to character differences, it was very dissimilar. In his early days, Eleazar also had his clashes with Mollet, as in 1786 when he disobeyed his employer's injunction against acting as a *pion* in the *Chevauchée de St Michel*;[74] or again in 1788 when he repeatedly stayed out late in Alderney, twice obliging Mollet to fetch him from a party.[75]

After his marriage in 1789, however, Eleazar became more circumspect.[76] In the months after Mollet returned to Guernsey from Alderney, he obligingly vacated the main bedroom at Mollet's house so that Mollet could re-occupy it.[77] Unlike Pierre, he took Mollet's notice to quit the farm calmly, leaving it on Christmas Eve 1790 without apparent resentment.[78] Also unlike Pierre, his departure from the property was not accompanied by any break in relations. In fact, Eleazar continued working on and off for Mollet for the rest of Mollet's life.

The continuance of relations was doubtless facilitated by the fact that Eleazar became a close neighbour of Mollet's. In 1799, he was able to purchase a farm from James Rouget, the elderly husband of his Aunt Judith. This was situated at la Contrée des Grands Brulins, bordering on Mollet's own property. The Greffe register described it as comprising a house, driveway, stables, barn, cartshed, garden and three fields.[79] The 1817

---

[72] Diary, 19.2.1818, 21.2.1818.

[73] Precisely when is unknown, as this is a period for which the volume is missing.

[74] Diary, 7.6.1786, 12.6.1786. The *Chevauchée* was a ceremonial inspection of the king's highway which involved *inter alia* Royal Court members riding around parts of the island accompanied by unmounted *pions*. For more on this tradition, see E.F. Carey (ed.), *Guernsey Folk Lore from MSS by the late Sir Edgar MacCulloch* (London, 1903), pp. 65–77.

[75] Diary, 23.3.1788, 24.3.1788, 25.3.1788, 30.3.1788.

[76] Eleazar Ingrouille married Elizabeth Robert (1761–1860) on 13 August 1789.

[77] Diary, 22.6.1790.

[78] Diary, 24.12.1790.

[79] 23.5.1799, Contrats pour la Date, Greffe.

agricultural census gave its extent as 12 acres, and showed that Eleazar owned two horses, one ox, five cows and seven pigs.[80] Having become a respectable farmer in his own right, Eleazar's association with Mollet deepened. He organised ploughing teams for Mollet and lent him equipment and animals.[81] He became a grafting specialist for Mollet, carrying out shield-budding whenever required.[82] He slaughtered animals for Mollet.[83] He attended Mollet and his guests as a servant when they went on their picnics.[84]

Socially, too, Eleazar's association with Mollet deepened. He became a frequent visitor to Mollet's house, dining at Mollet's on a Sunday, and spending many a winter evening in the kitchen, sometimes accompanied by his wife and other relatives.[85] On Mollet's side, though Eleazar's origins were too lowly to admit him as a friend on a level with the Brocks or Dobrées, he was arguably a more dependable ally. During a spell of illness and bed rest in 1816, Eleazar visited Mollet morning and evening every day for almost two weeks.[86] On many occasions in Mollet's last decade, he was Mollet's only visitor all day.[87] Mollet was undoubtedly fond of him. In an entry written when he was nearly seventy-five, Mollet described a solitary evening in his room:

> I did not go to bed until two in the morning. I had a fire in my room, bathed my feet, & re-read some of Eleazar's letters.[88]

Charles Mollet's relations with Eleazar Ingrouille probably owed much of their harmony and durability to Eleazar's own forbearance. Abraham Machon (1770–1835) was a man in a similar mould (perhaps unsurprisingly as he was a first cousin of Eleazar's).[89] Mollet first took Abraham on, aged nineteen, towards the end of his Alderney sojourn.[90] His employment on this occasion

---

[80] Relevé des Propriétaires du Castel, May 1817 (SG 23/43, Island Archives).
[81] See, for instance, Diary, 27.4.1804, 2.5.1804, Notes relating to 1805, 24.2.1816.
[82] Diary, 2.8.1816, 27.8.1816, 4.8.1817, 8.7.1818.
[83] Diary, 17.5.1816.
[84] Diary, 1.9.1806, 26.7.1808.
[85] Diary, 15.11.1815, 10.12.1815, 20.12.1815, 31.12.1815.
[86] Diary, 8.2.1816.
[87] Diary, 10.2.1816.
[88] Diary, 19.5.1817. These letters may have been written by Eleazar when Mollet was in Alderney.
[89] See Appendix 6 on the inter-relatedness of Mollet's employees.
[90] Diary, 7.8.1789.

lasted only five months, as Mollet soon moved to Candie, where he did not require servants.[91] When Mollet resumed residence on his farm, however, he re-engaged Abraham, and their association thereafter was lifelong.[92] Patient as he was, Abraham (like almost all of Mollet's farm servants) was not immune from conflicts with his employer, and he left him briefly at least four times.[93] Mollet hardly ever specified the substance of their disagreements, but this entry from 1812 provides a clue:

> I was vexed with Ab. this morning & I threatened to dismiss him. I even told him he could leave tomorrow if he refuses to do what I order. This was mainly on account of the ox, which I would like to keep permanently indoors, but which he insists on putting outside.[94]

Mollet did not record whose view prevailed. But, like all the other spats, this one blew over without any further consequence. At bottom, the two men respected one another.

As noted above, Abraham Machon married Mollet's house servant Elizabeth Le Ray in 1798. Lisabo, then aged twenty-three, had been working at Mollet's for five years. Reinstituting his earlier arrangement with Pierre and Marie Gavet, Mollet allocated the newly-weds two rooms and a portion of the garden at the 'upper' house.[95] This time, the arrangement was successful. Abraham became Mollet's *de facto* farm manager (though Mollet never described him so), and Lisabo the manager of his house, kitchen and dairy. The couple worked hard, and patiently saved money. They sold produce grown and raised in their portion of the 'upper' garden.[96] They ate at Mollet's table, so did not pay for their own food. They spent their evenings in his kitchen, so their outlay on heating and lighting was minimal. Though still in service, they worked single-mindedly towards independence, and by 1809, they had accumulated sufficient cash to begin investing in *rentes*.[97] The one thing that was conspicuously lacking in their lives were children to leave their acquisitions to. By 1811, they had spent fourteen years as man and wife,

---

[91] Diary, 24.1.1790.
[92] Diary, 22.3.1792.
[93] Diary, 13.9.1793, 25.3.1794, 31.8.1795, 14.9.1795, 1.8.1796, 16.8.1796, 3.7.1800, 21.7.1800.
[94] Diary, 5.7.1812.
[95] Diary, 22.3.1798.
[96] Diary, 17.1.1800, 22.10.1810.
[97] Diary, 7.1.1809, 11.2.1809.

but their union was blessed with no progeny. Amazingly, in the autumn of that year, Mollet recorded that Lisabo was about to give birth. It is a measure of the intermeshing of master and servants' lives that Mollet gave a detailed account of her labour and delivery.[98] The infant, who came into the world on 15 November 1811, was a girl, born when her mother was thirty-six and her father forty-one. Named Elizabeth (though Mollet always referred to her as Betsy), she was to be the Machons' only child. On 17 November, Mollet graciously postponed a breakfast and dinner he had organised previously to allow Lisabo time to recover.[99] Over the next few years, she performed her duties with Betsy close by in the kitchen and dairy.

By the spring of 1815, the Machons had sufficient means to make Mollet an offer on the 'upper' house. The conveyance shows that, in addition to the house itself, Mollet also sold the Machons the surrounding gardens, a furzebrake, a corner of his field at les Eturs, and part of a pew at the Castel church.[100] The 1817 agricultural census showed the land acquired by the Machons to have encompassed just under one acre in total.[101] Although this was insufficient to free Abraham entirely of the need to labour for others, he and his wife lived out the rest of their lives at the 'upper' house. Their daughter Betsy and her husband Thomas Sarre inherited the house after their deaths, and it passed down through Sarre hands until the twentieth century.

Daniel Ferbrache (1782–1851) was another long-term presence in Charles Mollet's life. He began working for Mollet as a fourteen-year-old day labourer in 1797 and took up residence in Mollet's house the following year.[102] From the beginning, however, Daniel (to whom Mollet sometimes referred as *mon Daniel*)'[103] seemed to be straining to get away. In 1799, aged sixteen, he tried on two occasions to hire himself out as a sailor, and was prevented from doing so by his father and Mollet.[104] In 1800, he tried again, and was once more prevented by Mollet.[105] Later that year, he apprenticed himself to a stonemason and left Mollet's service, only to return when the

---

[98] Diary, 15.11.1811.
[99] Diary, 17.11.1811.
[100] AQ 1133/021, Island Archives.
[101] SG 23/43, Island Archives.
[102] Diary, 7.8.1797, 28.6.1798. Daniel Ferbrache was related to both Eleazar Ingrouille and Abraham Machon through his maternal grandmother Margueritte Ingrouille. His father Jean Ferbrache had also worked for Mollet in the past. See Appendix 6.
[103] For instance, Diary, 20.8.1810.
[104] Diary, 16.2.1799, 24.2.1799, 25.2.1799.
[105] Diary, 21.1.1800.

work did not suit him.¹⁰⁶ In 1800, 1801, 1802 and 1803, Daniel again left Mollet for short periods, each time returning when necessity compelled him and each time finding Mollet willing to take him back.¹⁰⁷

Finally, at the age of twenty-three in 1805, Daniel managed to make his escape. His sailor brother Jean introduced him to a Captain Flère under whom he was serving as boatswain's mate, and Flère agreed to engage Daniel as a crewman. Daniel was by then no longer a minor, so there was little Charles Mollet could do. 'I will miss him greatly,' Mollet wrote.¹⁰⁸ There followed several round trips to Norfolk, Virginia, after each of which Daniel dutifully called at the farm to pay a visit to his former employer.¹⁰⁹

In 1809, after nearly four years at sea, Daniel Ferbrache suffered a misfortune. Injuring his left arm in an accident, he temporarily lost the use of it. As soon as Charles Mollet learned of this, he wrote to his great-nephew William Brock, then training as a surgeon in London, and asked Brock to have Daniel admitted to Guy's Hospital.¹¹⁰ Daniel's six-week stay at Guy's was almost certainly paid for by Mollet. On his discharge from hospital, the young seaman returned to Guernsey.¹¹¹ Mollet, who was clearly expecting some show of gratitude, took Daniel to task a few weeks later for being 'less than assiduous' in visiting him.¹¹² Mollet also seemed to be under the impression that the young man's disability was permanent and he would not be going back to sea. However, in a matter of months, Daniel was off once more, having joined the crew of a privateer.¹¹³ Again, there followed several voyages, after each of which Daniel dutifully paid Mollet a visit.¹¹⁴

Daniel's seafaring days finally came to an end in 1812, following a fateful voyage to the West Indies in a trading vessel captained by Thomas Moullin. In the course of this voyage, Moullin's vessel was captured by a French privateer off the Cuban coast and taken under escort to Spain.¹¹⁵ Daniel was

---

[106] Diary, 5.10.1800, 27.10.1800.
[107] Diary, 9.9.1801, 25.9.1801, 19.8.1802, 22.8.1802, 21.3.1803, 19.4.1803, 9.3.1804, 12.3.1804.
[108] Diary, 16.12.1805.
[109] Diary, 26.10.1806, 16.5.1807, 3.12.1807.
[110] Diary, 4.1.1809, 7.2.1809, 23.2.1809. See also 18.1.1809, Guy's Hospital Admissions Register (HO9/GY/B/01/015/001, London Metropolitan Archives).
[111] Diary, 10.3.1809.
[112] Diary, 28.5.1809.
[113] Diary, 19.11.1809.
[114] Diary, 23.12.1809, 3.2.1810, 6.4.1810, 24.5.1810, 3.9.1810.
[115] Diary, 27.1.1812.

eventually able to make his way back to Guernsey, but thereafter he went to sea no more. In 1813, aged thirty-one, he married Judith Trachy.

Between 1813 and 1816, Daniel appears to have worked a rented plot near the west coast on his own account, combining this with fishing (in a boat he owned with two of his brothers) and labouring a few days a week for Charles Mollet.[116] He came off Mollet's books as a day labourer in 1816, but Mollet nevertheless seems to have retained his soft spot for him. Daniel, for his part, knew how to reap the advantages. His wife sold Mollet fish;[117] he and his children sometimes dined in Mollet's kitchen;[118] he even undertook occasional piece-work for his former employer.[119] Daniel's economy of makeshifts eventually paid off. He was not listed as a landowner in the 1817 agricultural census, but a conveyance at the Greffe shows that, fifteen years later, he managed to purchase two houses, outbuildings, a field and dunes close to Vazon.[120] Nearly thirty years after Charles Mollet's death, Daniel Ferbrache himself died at the comparatively advanced age of sixty-nine. He and his wife Judith had a total of eleven children, of whom at least seven survived infancy. In an odd twist of fate, while Mollet's line died out with him, one of Daniel's descendants became Chief Minister of Guernsey.

Jean Cateline (1786–1812) replaced Daniel Ferbrache as Mollet's live-in farm servant when Daniel left him for a life at sea in 1805.[121] Jean was then aged nineteen and well known to Mollet. His father and two of his brothers had worked for Mollet in the past, and Jean, too, had laboured for Mollet prior to becoming his farm servant. Charles Mollet devoted more diary entries to Jean Cateline than to any of his other farm servants, but their relationship was unusually turbulent. This turbulence arose for two main reasons (which may have been related). The first was that Jean was a drinker. The second was that Jean had an illness which affected both his physical capacities and his mood.

Charles Mollet first mentioned Jean Cateline's drinking the year after he had engaged him, noting on one occasion that Jean had come home from

---

[116] Diary, 1.5.1816, 4.7.1816.
[117] Diary, 3.7.1816, 23.8.1817.
[118] Diary, 10.5.1818.
[119] On one occasion, Mollet evinced annoyance when he discovered that Daniel had sub-contracted weeding Mollet had arranged for him to do at 9d per perch to his brother-in-law for a lesser rate (Diary, 22.9.1816).
[120] 2.2.1832, Contrats pour la Date, Greffe.
[121] Diary, 16.5.1805.

town drunk after delivering a sea-stock to some emigrants.[122] He first recorded Jean's illness in 1808, when the young man became too ill to work around harvest-time.[123] Jean's complaint seems to have been arthritic in nature. Mollet identified it as 'a sort of rheumatism' which, among other things, prevented Jean from 'grasping slim things, such as spade- or fork-handles'.[124] It also seems to have made Jean irritable.[125] The illness took the form of acute flare-ups followed by periods of normal health.

Jean's intermittent drunkenness, bad temper and illness might have tempted many another employer to dismiss him. Not so Mollet. On two occasions in the winter of 1808/9, Jean (like Pierre, Abraham and Daniel before him) even briefly left Mollet after an argument. However (like the others) he found Mollet quite willing to take him back.[126] This, unfortunately, may only have encouraged his fractiousness, which became markedly worse in ensuing months. Late in 1809, there was a strange showdown between the two men:

> *Wednesday 25 Oct 1809*: I [was] alone in the kitchen with Jean. When Jean made as if to go to bed, I advised him to find himself a candle, & he suddenly flew into a rage, reminding me of what I had said to him in jest at supper (that he would become a drunkard if he left us & end up in the Hospital or worse). This had not seemed to bother him during the evening, when he came twice into my room (to ask for a pack of cards & fetch some cider for Eleazar). After his outburst, he went upstairs to his bedroom, & I followed him closely in order to light his way. When I later entered his room, he was already in bed. He shouted to me that he would indeed go to the Hospital, &c., so I said "go as soon as you like; go tomorrow; go tonight". He then sprang out of bed & hurriedly put on his clothes. I went into my own room, where he followed me still shouting. I tried to make him sit down & calm himself, but he marched off shoeless, stockingless, hatless & very dirty, exiting the house through the greenhouse.

Mollet, clearly worried about the young man, rose at 4 o'clock the next morning to go looking for him. It turned out that Jean had spent the night

---

[122] Diary, 11.5.1807.
[123] Diary, 13.6.1808, 14.6.1808, 15.6.1808, 2.7.1808, 4.7.1808, 19.7.1808, 23.7.1808, 15.9.1808.
[124] Diary, 3.4.1809. For this reason, Jean Cateline was exempted from militia service.
[125] Diary, 10.7.1808, 1.2.1811.
[126] Diary, 19.10.1808, 20.10.1808, 1.1.1809, 5.1.1809, 9.1.1809.

in the kitchen of the 'upper' house, and he resumed work after breakfast as if nothing had happened.[127]

Early in 1810, Jean's illness flared up with unprecedented severity. Beginning in February with 'pain in all his bones and joints',[128] it culminated in complete collapse in March:

> *Sunday 4 March 1810*: Jean was up almost all day yesterday, but in pain. Around eight in the evening, he & Jean Guilbert, who were in the kitchen with the girls, went outside for a moment, & as they were returning, Jean collapsed just outside the back door. We thought for about an hour that he might be dying. Nico Breton & Eleazar came & carried him into the parlour, where Jean Guilbert & I stayed up with him all night. He remained quiet but very weak.

For the next three nights, Jean lay in the parlour, with Mollet sleeping fully dressed on the floor beside him.[129] Feeling slightly better, Jean returned to his own room on the fourth day, and tentatively began working again some ten days later.[130] The same pattern then resumed as previously, but in accentuated form: spells of illness, intermittent drunkenness, bad-tempered departures, swift returns, acceptance back.[131]

In the autumn of 1811, Jean Cateline's illness entered another acute phase, and he was unable to work from October to the following January.[132] So ill was he during this period that Mollet recorded he needed 'assistance to dress himself, as also to lift food & drink to his mouth'.[133] Mollet's patience throughout this saga was remarkable. As well as foregoing his unruly farm servant's work, he had fed him, kept him warm, purchased medicines for him, and even kept a vigil by his bedside. Jean showed no sign of a long-term cure, however, and Mollet recorded further bouts of illness in April and May 1812.[134] Sadly, we have no detail on how the saga reached its conclusion, as this volume of the diary ended two months later, and the next volume is missing. All that is known comes from the Castel parish burial register: Jean Cateline died on 4 October 1812, aged twenty-six.

---

[127] Diary, 26.10.1809.
[128] Diary, 27.2.1810.
[129] Diary, 8.3.1810. 'Without undue discomfort,' Mollet noted.
[130] Diary, 13.3.1810.
[131] Diary, 26.11.1810, 1.2.1811, 2.2.1811, 4.2.1811, 8.2.1811.
[132] Diary, 14.1.1812.
[133] Diary, 29.11.1810.
[134] Diary, 4.4.1812, 22.5.1812.

By this time, Charles Mollet was also involved with Jean Cateline's elder brother Pierre. Pierre Cateline (1783–1824) had worked briefly for Mollet as a day labourer in the late 1790s.[135] He had then served an apprenticeship as a plasterer and roof-tiler, and in due course became a journeyman under master tradesman James Le Page.[136] Pierre's later involvement with Mollet began in January 1809 when, aged twenty-five, he came to see Mollet during a period of under-employment, and asked him if he might labour for him for a few weeks (his brother Jean was by now Mollet's farm servant).[137] Mollet assented, and Pierre worked for him until May, when he resumed his usual employment as a plasterer.[138] Thereafter, Charles Mollet began using James Le Page's firm for plastering jobs in both town and country.[139] In November 1810, James Le Page died and Pierre stepped into his shoes as a master tradesman, employing his own journeymen and apprentices.[140] Mollet continued to use his services, and, as their dealings multiplied, regularly invited him to dine, sup and take tea at his home.[141]

At the end of 1812, Pierre Cateline purchased a house in Vauvert, on the outskirts of town.[142] This was a stone's throw from Charles Mollet's own town properties and made him doubly useful to Mollet. By 1815, Pierre had become Mollet's *de facto* agent in St Peter Port, liaising with his tenants in la Profonde Rue, recruiting new tenants, receiving rents on his behalf, and generally supervising his properties.[143] For Pierre, this arrangement was also beneficial, as, in return for his services, he had free use of part of the stable and garden at la Profonde Rue, and a regular supply of work from Mollet, who continued to employ him for all his maintenance needs.[144]

As well as becoming practically reliant on Cateline, Mollet, by now in his mid-seventies, became increasingly personally dependent on him. With many friends having pre-deceased him, Mollet was less socially active than

---

[135] Diary, Notes relating to 1796 and 1797, 3.9.1798.
[136] Diary, 3.6.1807.
[137] Diary, 5.1.1809.
[138] Diary, 20.5.1809.
[139] Diary, 28.5.1810, 11.7.1810.
[140] Diary, 10.11.1810, 12.3.1811, 5.9.1811, 21.6.1812.
[141] Diary, 17.2.11, 10.5.1812, 27.5.1812, 24.5.1812, 7.6.1812, 5.7.1812.
[142] 5.12.1812, Contrats pour Lire, Greffe.
[143] In the past, Bonamy Dobrée, Mollet's nephew by marriage, had performed this role for him, but – for reasons unknown – Dobrée disappeared from Mollet's journal completely after 1808.
[144] Diary, 16.5.1817.

previously. Pierre stepped into the gap and became one of Mollet's most frequent visitors. By 1817, he was calling on Charles Mollet several times a week, and was even admitted to private suppers in Mollet's room.[145] Moreover, if he ever failed to come when expected, Mollet noted his absence in his diary.[146]

Mollet's association with Pierre Cateline eventually drew him deeply (some might say inappropriately) into the tradesman's private affairs. One matter in which Mollet became notably embroiled concerned Pierre's relations with his wife Margueritte (*née* Rougier). By 1817, after more than ten years of marriage and the birth of several children, the couple were not getting on. Mollet's first allusion to the Catelines' marital problems came in June of that year, when Mrs Cateline let it be known that she objected to the large amount of time her husband was spending at Mollet's house. 'I have long been aware of this,' Mollet wrote,

> [so] I decided to raise the matter with him today. He told me with some pain & repugnance that his wife had treated him badly for some time, & had treated him particularly badly after the last time he was here (5 June), even though he had returned home before nine.[147]

Pierre's claims may sound slightly odd (and facts outlined below will cast doubt on them), but Mollet seems to have believed his story without question. Pierre's visits became more frequent still, and he continually reinforced the picture he had painted of his wife's ill-conduct: 'gives him endless trouble'; 'ill-treats him more than I was aware'; 'continues to make his life difficult'.[148]

In the spring of 1818, Pierre applied for a judicial separation from his wife. Knowing that Charles Mollet was well-respected, he enlisted him as a witness in support of his case, and Mollet attended Court on the day of the hearing in order to give testimony in his favour. In the event, Mollet did not have to take the stand, as Pierre was persuaded to negotiate a settlement with his wife before any evidence was taken.[149] As eventually approved, the settlement allowed Pierre to keep custody of his children (with twice-weekly

---

[145] Diary, 5.2.1817, 2.3.1817.
[146] Diary, 16.10.1817, 23.11.1817.
[147] Diary, 22.6.1817.
[148] Diary, 5.9.1817, 15.10.1817, 22.2.1818.
[149] Diary, 14.3.1818.

visits to their mother), and obliged him to pay her 4s 6d a week in maintenance.[150]

Following this event, there were only another four months until Mollet's diaries fell silent. Pierre Cateline was however a constant presence in them till the last page. Charles Mollet's final mention of the plasterer came just two days before the end, when he recorded that Cateline had dined at his home.[151]

Whether Pierre Cateline was taking advantage of the elderly Mollet will never be known. There is a slight hint that he might have been creaming off some of the income from la Profonde Rue in an entry from 1818 where Mollet recorded receipt of rent from a new tenant short of the amount he was sure had been agreed.[152] More substantially, a newspaper report of a Court case which took place two years after Mollet's death suggests that Pierre was perhaps not the innocent party he had sought to appear to Mollet. In January 1821, Pierre's estranged wife was found guilty of bigamy, having remarried while only separated.[153] Several of the couple's former neighbours (a Mrs Shale, Mrs Maindonal, Mrs Perry and Mrs Le Noury) testified in her defence that it was Cateline who had been violent towards her – locking her in the house, threatening to throw her out of the window, etc. Her defence advocate, Charles De Jersey, went so far as to say that Pierre had treated her with *la dernière cruauté*.[154] Whatever the truth of the matter, Pierre Cateline did not make old bones. He died in March 1824, aged only forty-one.[155]

What was it about all these young men? Mollet's relationships with them seem to have existed on a different plane from his ordinary social relationships. Were they his surrogate sons, or were they something more? If we had access to the excisions from his journal, or a key to his codes, we might have a better idea. As it is, we have only unanswered questions. It would be remiss in a historian not to raise such questions, but equally, no historian should draw conclusions without clear evidence. Readers will make up their own minds.

---

[150] Diary, 20.3.1818. On judicial separation in the nineteenth century, see R.-M. Crossan, *A Women's History of Guernsey, 1850s–1950s* (Benderloch, 2018), pp. 96–9.
[151] Diary, 30.7.1818.
[152] Diary, 25.6.1818.
[153] Divorce was not possible in Guernsey until the twentieth century.
[154] *L'Indépendance*, 27.1.1821.
[155] Pierre may have had the same condition as his brother. Mollet occasionally recorded spells of illness suffered by the young plasterer, in one instance referring to it as 'acute rheumatism' (Diary, 4.4.1812). The surname Cateline is now extinct in Guernsey.

Conclusion

The last few years of Charles Mollet's diaries were peppered with intimations of mortality. Every month or two saw the deaths of people he had known for decades. Even his pets were reaching the end of their spans. 'She is old & deaf', Mollet wrote of his dog Sappho in June 1818, 'so she will probably not live much longer.'[1] The same was equally true of the dog's owner, who was undoubtedly beginning to feel his age. The account Mollet wrote of his introduction to Lieutenant-Governor Henry Bayly in 1818 could not have been more different from his earlier enthusiastic encounters with incoming Lieutenant-Governors:

> *Wednesday 22 April 1818*: I breakfasted at Mary's, where Monsieur Marie & Eleazar joined me at 10 o'clock. We looked over Mary's garden together, then went to Candie & made a tour of the garden there with Peter. Just as we were leaving Candie, the Governor (General Bayley), to whom I had never spoken, arrived at the house. He had come on purpose to meet me, so I was obliged to stay & make his acquaintance. I went to his home with Peter, Sophy, &c., to see the preparations for a party he is giving tomorrow to celebrate the Prince Regent's birthday. I returned here at 2 o'clock feeling very tired & went straight to bed.[2]

Within less than a year of this unlooked-for introduction, Charles Mollet had departed this life. He had continued his journal till nigh on the end, but the events of his final six months remain enigmatic, as nothing is left of his last c.200 entries save the stumps of cut-out pages.[3]

Whatever Mollet's closing reflections, we know from contemporary newspapers and church records that he died on 28 February 1819, and on 9 March was buried in the Castel churchyard. Sadly, his precise resting-place is unknown, as inscriptions on the expensive (but soft) stone used for elite monuments have weathered away, and there is no contemporary cemetery plan. In an ironic twist of fate, the humble headstone of his servants Abraham and Elizabeth Machon – plain but robust – still bears its inscription for all to see.

---

[1] Diary, 24.6.1818.
[2] Major-General Bayly (1769–1846) had succeeded Sir John Doyle as Lieutenant-Governor in 1816.
[3] Introduction, p. 2.

On the whole, Charles Mollet had had a comfortable and, some would say, unexciting life. Certainly, his diary contains nothing like the drama to be found in the diaries of Napoleonic veterans or privateers. Nevertheless, the journal is rich in information rarely to be found elsewhere, not least its close detail on eighteenth-century farming practices, on everyday domesticity, and on local families great and humble. On a wider scale, too, the journal reflects all the changing conditions Guernsey experienced over its author's seventy-six years: war and invasion threat; religious change; language change; economic boom and bust; the beginnings of significant immigration and emigration – in sum, it embodies a vast fund of information, of which the present volume has barely scratched the surface.

Charles Mollet died without issue, so his property passed, as per Guernsey law, to his collateral male heirs (surviving nephews or great-nephews). They put Mollet's farm up for auction, and in May 1820 it was purchased for 21,000 *livres tournois* (c.£1,500 stg) by the retired Irish army officer Colonel Ambrose Lane.[4] Colonel Lane, who began the process of extending and modifying the house, lived there with his wife and family until 1844.[5] From this point onwards, the property passed through many disparate hands to the present day.

Charles Mollet himself was probably all but forgotten within a century of his death. The diaries, handed down through ever more distant generations, were doubtless equally forgotten. They might even have disappeared into oblivion had not the ageing Marjorie Barnes, in the absence of surviving descendants of her own, thought to donate them to a public repository in 1951. The diaries have now been at the Priaulx Library for more than seventy years. Even so, they have not to date received the attention they deserve. This is partly owing to their fragility, but chiefly to the language in which they are penned. Hopefully, the full translation of all six volumes, on which the present book is based, will both remedy that problem and help preserve the precious originals – for sheer age now imparts to the diaries a greater historical value than ever.

I will, however, end this book on a personal note. From my own perspective, the core significance of Charles Mollet's diaries lies more in the realm of the human than the historical. In his 1,500 pages, Mollet has left something of his essence as a person and, even at three centuries' distance, I

---

[4] 31.5.1820, Contrats pour Lire, Greffe.
[5] 19.10.1844, Contrats pour Lire, Greffe.

(and I hope others) can find much in it with which to identify. Given our essential transience as human beings, it is vaguely comforting that the diaries' survival has enabled at least one eighteenth-century Guernseyman, in some sense, to live on.

Appendix 1
Marjorie Barnes' ancestry

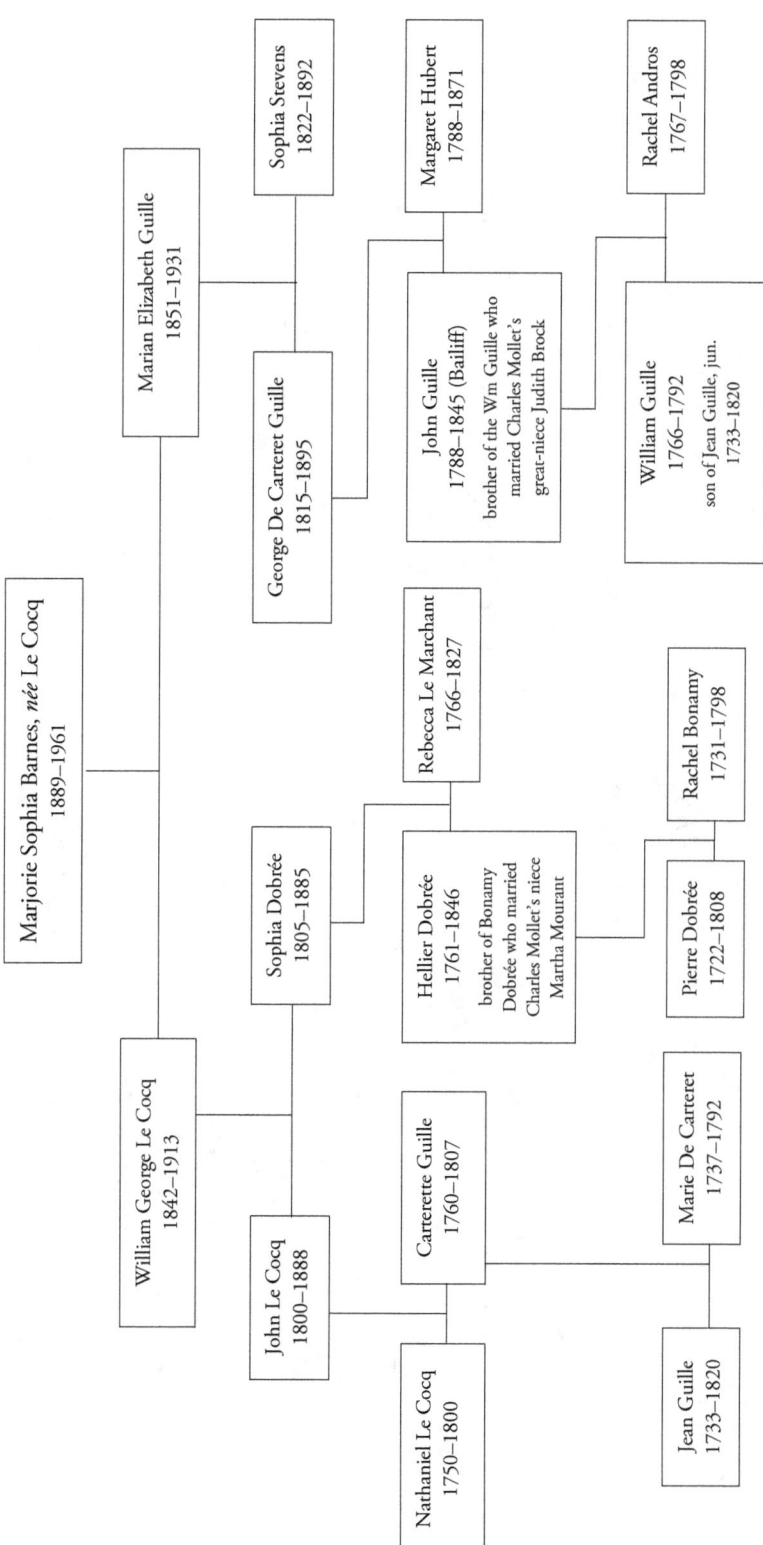

Appendix 2
Mollet family tree, ascending

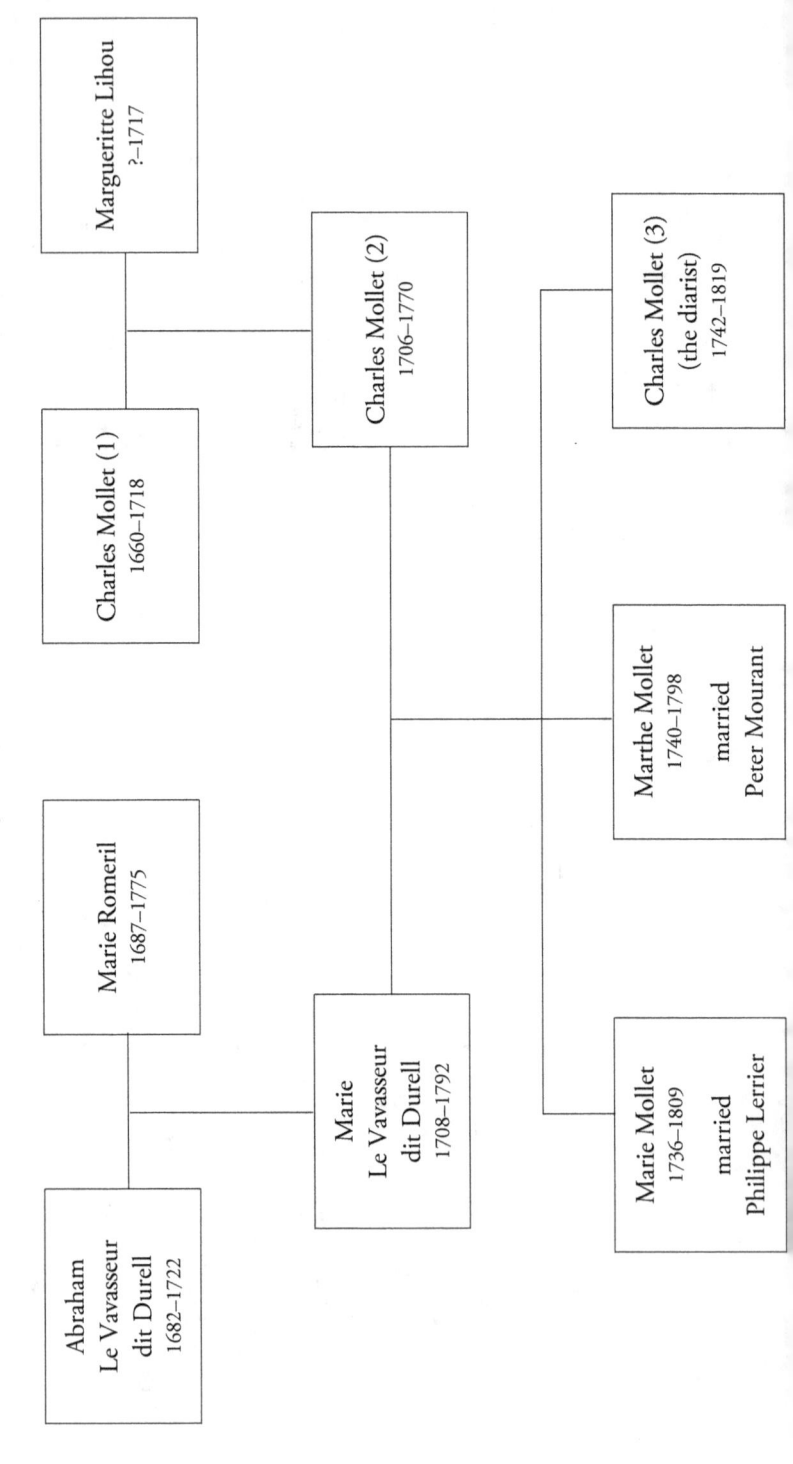

Appendix 3
Mollet family tree, descending

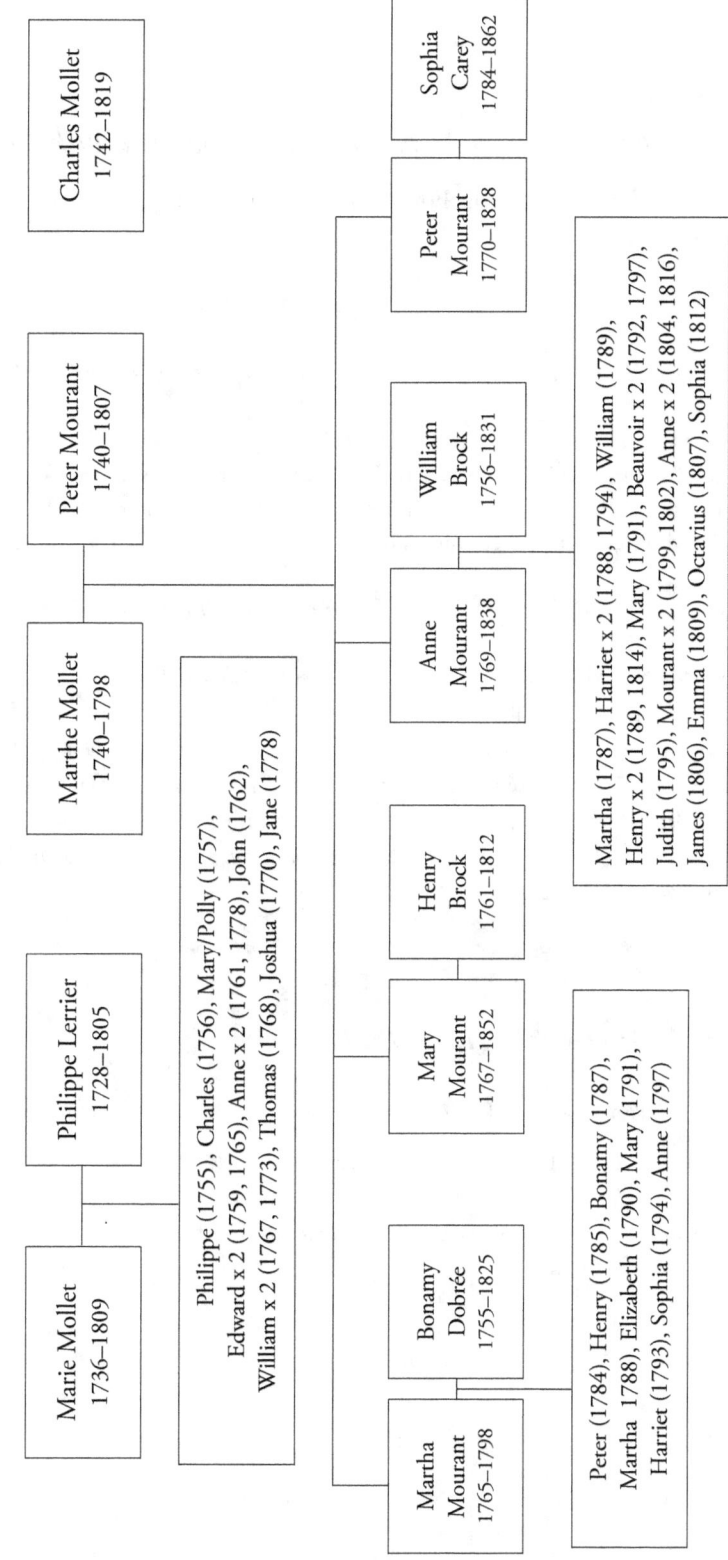

Appendix 4

Composition of principal families associated with Mollet

These outlines are based on Edith Carey's handwritten genealogies held at the Priaulx Library.

Brock

William Brock (1725–1768) married Judith De Beauvoir (1730–1776)

William was a brother of John Brock (1730–1777), father of the large family which included Bailiff Daniel De Lisle Brock, Major-General Sir Isaac Brock, John Savery Brock, Irving Brock and Mary Brock (wife of Thomas Potenger). This made the Brocks who married Mollet's nieces first cousins of the more famous Brocks.

Children of William Brock and Judith De Beauvoir:

Mary Brock (1752–1800) wife of *Jean Carey of 'Choisi'*, for whom see below
Martha Brock (1753–?)
William Brock (1756–1831) husband of Mollet's niece *Anne Mourant*
Judith Brock (1758–1816) wife of *Dr Jean [De] Sau[s]marez*, for whom see below
Henry Brock (1761–1812) husband of Mollet's niece *Mary Mourant*
Harriet Brock (1763–1858) wife of *Sir Thomas Saumarez*, for whom see below
James Brock (1767–1805)

Carey

Jean Carey of 'Choisi' (1748–1821) married Mary Brock (1752–1800)

Jean Carey and Mary Brock had twelve children, including:

Rev. Thomas Carey (1772–1849), Rector of St Saviour, husband of Mary Maingy
Captain William Carey (1776–1808)
Mary Carey (1779–1864), wife of *Rev. Thomas Brock* (1777–1850),
    Rector of St Peter

Dobrée (of 'Bellevue')

Nicolas Dobrée (1732–1800) married (1) Susanne Le Pelley
(2) Elizabeth Gilchrist

Children of Nicolas Dobrée and Susanne Le Pelley:

Elizabeth Dobrée (1753–1826) wife of *Rudolf Utermarck*
Daniel Dobrée (1754–1814), Captain, RN
Rev. Nicolas Dobrée (1755–1843), Castel Rector
Peter Dobrée (1756–1843)
Charles Dobrée (1757–1780)
Susanna Dobrée (1759–1843), wife of *John Siegfried Fischer*
Augustus Dobrée (1760–1845)
Mary Dobrée (1762–1791), wife of *William Piercy*

Children of Nicolas Dobrée and Elizabeth Gilchrist:

Thomas Godfrey Dobrée (1770–1851), husband of *Mary Waugh*
Harry Dobrée (1771–1851)

Dobrée (of 'Beauregard')

Pierre Dobrée (1722–1808) married Rachel Bonamy (1731–1798)

Children of Pierre Dobrée and Rachel Bonamy:

Mary Dobrée (1754–1825)
Bonamy Dobrée (1755–1825), husband of Mollet's niece *Martha Mourant*
Elisha Dobrée (1756–1844), diarist
Samuel Dobrée (1759–1827), banker in London
Peter Dobrée (1760–1843)
Hellier Dobrée (1761–1847)
Henry Dobrée (1762–1766)
Rachel Dobrée (1764–1842), wife of *Philip Bainbrigge*
John Dobrée (1766–1812)
Elizabeth Dobrée (1777–1845), wife of *Philip Melvill*

De Havilland

Generation 1
Jean De Havilland (1706–1770) married Marie Dobrée (1712–1763)

Jean De Havilland and Marie Dobrée had eight children, including:

Catherine De Havilland (1731–1810), wife of Thomas Dobrée
Mary De Havilland (1732–1820), wife of Thomas Smith, mother of
  George Smith
John De Havilland (1734–1810), husband of Mary Dobrée
James De Havilland (1739–1783), husband of Anne Bonamy
Martin De Havilland (1746–1806), HM Prévôt 1777–1806
Peter De Havilland (1747–1821), Bailiff 1810–1821

Generation 2
Peter De Havilland (1747–1821) married   (1) Carterette Fiott
(2) Emilia Tupper

Peter De Havilland and Carterette Fiott had seven children, including:

Carterette De Havilland (1772–1844), wife of *George Smith*, mother of
  Sophia Smith and *Mary Harriet Smith*
Catherine De Havilland (1773–1860), wife of HM Procureur
  Thomas De Sausmarez (for whom see below)
Thomas Fiott De Havilland (1775–1866), Jurat 1846–1856, husband of
  Elizabeth De Sausmarez (daughter of HM Procureur
  Thomas De Sausmarez, for whom see below)
Anne De Havilland (1778–1847)
Charles De Havilland (1786–1844), military officer, husband of
  Martha Saumarez (daughter of Dr Richard Saumarez, for whom see below)
Mary De Havilland (1789–1854)

Peter De Havilland and Emilia Tupper had no children

De Sausmarez/Saumarez

Dr Matthew De Sausmarez (1719–78) married   (1) *Susanne Dumaresq*
                                            (2) *Carterette Le Marchant*

Matthew De Sausmarez and Susanne Dumaresq had only one child:

Susanne De Sausmarez (1743–1830), mother of Rev. Thomas Brock

Children of Matthew De Sausmarez and Carterette Le Marchant:

Anne [De] Sau[s]marez (1752–1846)
Dr Jean [De] Sau[s]marez (1755–1832), husband of *Judith Brock*
Admiral Sir James Saumarez (1757–1832)
General Sir Thomas Saumarez (1760–1845), husband of *Harriet Brock*
Charlotte [De] Sau[s]marez (1763–1860), wife of *Rev. Nicolas Dobrée*
Dr Richard Saumarez (1764–1835)

It is thought that Thomas and James changed their surname from 'De Sausmarez' to 'Saumarez' in order to make it appear less French to the British forces in which they served. Richard, an English-based surgeon, followed his brothers' example, and – by analogy – the name change was sometimes extended to their Guernsey-based siblings.

Dr Matthew De Sausmarez was a brother of HM Procureur Jean De Sausmarez (1706-74), the father of Mollet's friend Thomas De Sausmarez, who became HM Procureur in 1793. Matthew's children were thus all first cousins of HM Procureur Thomas De Sausmarez (1756–1837).

Thomas De Sausmarez (1756–1837) married   (1) *Martha Dobrée*
                                                (2) *Catherine De Havilland*

Thomas De Sausmarez and Martha Dobrée had eleven children, including:

Elizabeth De Sausmarez (1782–1818), wife of *Thomas Fiott De Havilland*
John De Sausmarez (1790–1870), HM Comptroller 1830–1845, Jurat 1847–1870

Thomas De Sausmarez and Catherine De Havilland had seventeen children, including:

Catherine De Sausmarez (1797–1851)
Durell De Sausmarez (1800–1859)
Anne De Sausmarez (1801–1872)
Rose De Sausmarez (1802–1841)
James De Sausmarez (1806–1846)

Guille

Generation 1
Jean Guille, sen. (1711–1778) married Elizabeth Andros (1708–1788)

Jean Guille, sen. and Elizabeth Andros had ten children, including:

Jean Guille, jun. (1733–1820)
Thomas Guille (1737–1796)
Nicolas Guille (1742–1807), merchant based in Barcelona, father of *Caroline Guille* (1777–1801)
Charles Guille (1743–?)
Dr Richard Guille (1745–1818)
Rachel Guille (1751–1803), who died unmarried

Generation 2
Jean Guille, jun. (1733–1820) married Marie De Carteret (1737–1792)

Jean Guille, jun. and Marie De Carteret had four children:

Carterette Guille (1760–1807)
Esther Guille (1762–1839)
William Guille (1766–1792)
George Guille (1768–1792)

Generation 3
Carterette Guille (1760–1807) married *Nathaniel Le Cocq* (1750–1800) and had five children

Esther Guille (1762–1839) married *Jean Carey Metivier* (1758–1796) and had six children, including the poet and lexicographer *George Metivier* (1790-1881) and the Jurat *William Metivier* (1791–1883)

William Guille (1766–1792) married *Rachel Andros* (1766–1798) and had three children, including *John Guille* (1788–1845) who became Bailiff in 1843, and *Rev. William Guille* (1792–1869) who married Mollet's great-niece *Judith Brock* and became Dean of Guernsey in 1862

Appendix 5

Frequently mentioned employees of Mollet's

Etienne Lihou (1742–1832)
Son of Thomas Lihou and Judith Breton; husband of Marie Le Page
Day labourer for the entire span of the diaries

Pierre Gavet (1752–1818)
Son of Etienne Gavet and Marthe Cohu; husband of Marie Nicolle (and later Judith Tostevin)
Farm servant 1775–1787

Eleazar Ingrouille (1766–1832)
Son of Paul Ingrouille and Anne Ingrouille; husband of Elizabeth Robert
Day labourer from the early 1780s onwards (latterly only occasionally)

Abraham Machon (1770–1835)
Son of Abraham Machon, sen. and Elizabeth Ingrouille; brother of Pierre Machon and Daniel Machon; husband of Elizabeth Le Ray
Farm servant 1789–1790, 1792 onwards

Elizabeth (Lisabo) Le Ray (1775–1850)
Daughter of Nicolas Le Ray and Marie Le Page; wife of Abraham Machon
Domestic servant from 1793 onwards

Daniel Ferbrache (1782–1851)
Son of Jean Ferbrache and Rachel Nicolle; husband of Judith Trachy
Farm servant 1798–1805

Pierre Cateline (1783–1824)
Son of Jean Cateline, sen. and Thomasse Gallienne; brother of Jean Cateline and James Cateline
Day labourer 1796–1798, January–May 1809

Jean Cateline (1786–1812)
Son of Jean Cateline, sen. and Thomasse Gallienne; brother of Pierre Cateline and James Cateline
Farm servant 1806–1812

Appendix 6

Relatedness of Mollet's employees
(employees' names are capitalised)

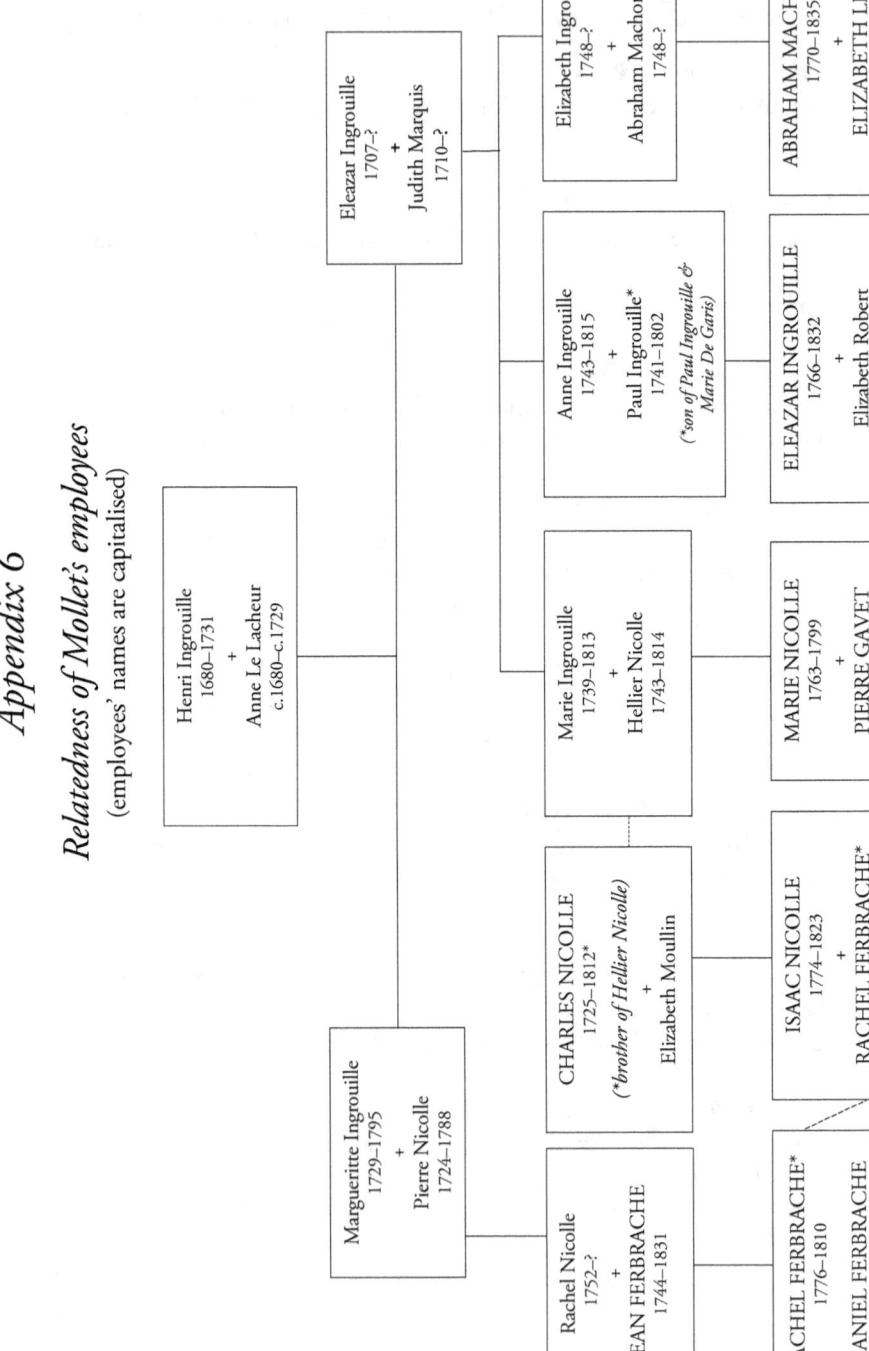

Appendix 7

Mollet's symbols and codes

A. 20 May 1773

B. 19 August 1773

C. 5 May 1776

D. 28 June 1776

E. 9 June 1777

F. 21 October 1778

G. 18 and 19 May 1780

H. 1 September 1780

240 *Charles Mollet and his World*

I. 8 December 1780

J. 27 December 1780

K. 11 February 1785

L. 14 November 1794

M. 27 April 1796

N. 7 September 1799

O. 20 April 1802

P. 30 March 1803

Q. 10 February 1804

R. 21 February 1811

Mollet's symbols and codes 241

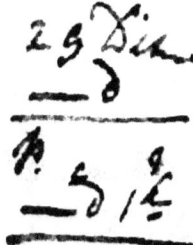

S. 29 March 1812

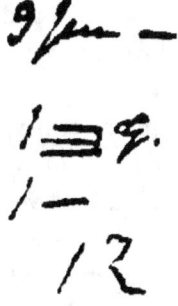

T. 9 November 1815

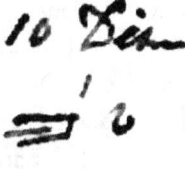

U. 10 March 1816

V. 9 June 1816

W. 18 July 1817

X. 26 July 1817

Y. 10 April 1818

Z. 9 June 1818

Appendix 8

Mollet's language

The linguistic situation in Guernsey towards the mid-point of Charles Mollet's life was neatly summed up by F.B. Tupper: 'The language of all classes in their own families was, with few exceptions, either French or Guernsey French, chiefly the latter; but the upper classes could speak English.'[1] Like many of his peers, Charles Mollet was effectively trilingual, speaking *guernésiais* with his servants in the kitchen and farmyard; English with Lieutenant-Governors and British army officers; and French with Huguenot ministers and *émigrés*. With his older Guernsey peers – who were generally not native speakers of English – Mollet probably spoke *guernésiais* or French. This would, for instance, have been the case with Peter De Havilland, whose efforts to master English have been documented elsewhere.[2] With peers of a younger generation, however, Mollet might well have spoken English. Many people of Mollet's class twenty or thirty years his junior had been educated in England, or had other links with that country. It is telling in this respect that, whereas Mollet used French-style diminutives for peers of his own generation (Manon for Marie, Janneton for Jeanne, Gotton for Marguerite), he used English forms for a younger generation (Polly, Jenny, Peggy).[3]

There is, however, a wealth of subtler linguistic evidence embedded within the language of Mollet's journal itself. As noted in Chapter 1, *guernésiais* had no written form, so Mollet wrote the journal in French (or an approximation thereto). His daily entries, hurriedly written, abound with inconsistent spellings, grammatical infelicities, clumsy sentence construction, and tangled paragraphs.[4] In this raw, unpolished state, however, they provide many clues as to Charles Mollet's everyday linguistic practice, and thus to the linguistic state of Guernsey two or three hundred years ago.

---

[1] F.B. Tupper, *The History of Guernsey and its Bailiwick* (Guernsey, 1854), p. 367. Tupper was born in 1795 but was writing about the 1770s.
[2] R. Hocart, *Peter de Havilland: Bailiff of Guernsey, A History of his Life, 1747–1821* (Guernsey, 1997), p. 26.
[3] He even referred to his great-nephew Beauvoir Brock as 'Beaver' (Diary, 30.4.1806).
[4] Examples of Mollet's letters survive which show that, when it was necessary to write formally in French (or English), he was quite capable of writing without major lexical or grammatical errors. This is particularly apparent in letters to Admiral Philippe D'Auvergne preserved in the National Archives (see Bibliography for references).

As it happens, a small number of diary entries (forming no more than 1 per cent of the total) are in English, which usefully allows us to gauge Mollet's proficiency in that language. These entries were written during Mollet's sojourns in England in 1771 and 1789. There is no explanation as to why Mollet wrote them in English, but perhaps it was to give himself extra practice in the language he was having to use every day. The following examples are fairly typical of the rest. Mollet's difficulty with past tenses in particular suggests that his English was not that of a native speaker:

> *Friday 8 May 1789*: left Lulworth. Gone to Upton Mills & through Osmington to Weymouth, where arriv'd for dinner at Mr Spicer's. Then gone to Checkrel & Portland. Rode to see the light house. Mr Henry Pitt & his youngest brother in law Mr [......] Allen have sup'd with me at Mr Chiles, where I stay the night.
>
> *Saturday 9 May 1789*: Mr Allen has breakfasted with me & we have rode around the Island together. Return'd to Weymouth about two o clock. Gone to Checkrel in the evening.

Mollet's journal also indicates that he was not a native speaker of Parisian French. Interspersed with the standard French in which he sought to couch his entries are large numbers of *guernésiais* words. The following is a small sample of some of the stock *guernésiais* terms (many of them to do with farming and the land) which Mollet habitually used in his diaries:

belle – n. farmyard[5]
charrière – n. cart-track[6]
dauvelle – n. dowel[7]
ébléter – v. to crush clods[8]
écaplir – v. to de-bark and square off the trunks of felled trees[9]
écoques – n. the green tops of root vegetables[10]
épader – v. to trim hedge-bottoms[11]

---

[5] M. De Garis, *Dictiounnaire Angllais-Guernesiais* (1967; Chichester, 1982 edn) – *belle, besle* or *bêle*.
[6] De Garis – *tchérière*.
[7] De Garis – *dovell*.
[8] De Garis – *ébiettaïr*; F. Le Maistre, *Dictionnaire Jersiais–Français* (Jersey, 1966) – *ébliêter*.
[9] Le Maistre – *ècaplyi*.
[10] De Garis, *écocques*.
[11] De Garis – *épâdaïr*.

esne – n. cutting (as in plant)[12]
forsière – n. headland (as in a ploughed field)[13]
fossé – n. earthbank[14]
fouillière – n. litter (as of piglets)[15]
lief – n. roof frame[16]
ozaune – n. pane of glass[17]
patate – n. potato[18]
plais – n. scalded pig carcase[19]
quesce – n. cow parsley, hogweed[20]
roia – n. batten, rafter[21]
taille – n. task[22]
varet – n. freshly ploughed unsown ground.[23]

Mollet also used many grammatical and syntactic forms characteristic of *guernésiais* but not of standard French. Here are a few examples:

the use of *ès* instead of *aux* for *à* + *les*, e.g., *faire un tour ès Moullins* [24]

the use of *avoir* instead of *être* as auxiliary in the perfect tense of verbs of motion, e.g., *je n'ai point sorti* [25]

the placing of adjectives of colour before rather than after the noun, e.g., *la rouge vache, la noire jument* [26]

---

[12] De Garis – *êne*.
[13] H. Moisy, *Dictionnaire de Patois Normand* (Caen, 1887) – *forière*. Note that, although I have spelled this word with a grave accent, Mollet did not generally use grave accents himself.
[14] De Garis – *fossaïe*.
[15] De Garis – *foullière*.
[16] Le Maistre – *lief*.
[17] De Garis – *ozaune*.
[18] De Garis – *patate*.
[19] G. Metivier, *Dictionnaire Franco-Normand ou Recueil des Mots particuliers au Dialecte de Guernesey* (London, 1870) – *plâie*.
[20] De Garis – *tchiesse*.
[21] De Garis – *rouâs*.
[22] De Garis – *taïle*.
[23] Moisy – *varet, voret*.
[24] Diary, 16.1.1771.
[25] Diary, 15.12.1776.
[26] Diary, 4.1.1816, 17.2.1816.

the use of the verb *aider* with an indirect rather than a direct object, e.g., *Lisabo a aidé à Nanon*[27]

the use of a gender peculiar to *guernésiais* in preference to that used in French for the same noun, e.g., **une** *orme* (an elm), **une** *pouce* (an inch).[28]

Finally, when Mollet spelled out numbers such as 70, he tended to use the local base-ten forms rather than the standard French forms (in this case *septante* rather than *soixante-dix*).[29]

Mollet doubtless used all these words and constructions quite unconsciously, as *guernésiais* was the language in which his thoughts were formulated. Nevertheless, there was another – paradoxical – side to his writing, since, even at this early date, his journal also shows evidence of English intrusions. Some of these were words for new things obtained from England for which *guernésiais* had not coined a term: *un frame de hot bed*; *le blowing stove*; *des shutters*; *des prints*; *le Bath stove*; *un spencer*; *du blacking à souliers*.[30] Others are terms for old things in a new context: *des blankets*; *des shrubs*; *un mourner*; *un hat band*; *un carpet*.[31] Still others are calques: *le papier de nouvelles*; *le dresseur*.[32]

Grammatical/phraseological calques on English (perhaps a more insidious form of intrusion) are also in evidence in Mollet's journal. For instance:

the rendering of *fruit* in the collective singular where it would be so in English, but not in French: *il a cueilli du fruit* instead of *il a cueilli des fruits* ('he picked some fruit')[33]

---

[27] Diary, 5.1.1792.
[28] Diary, 13.12.1774, 19.5.1801.
[29] Diary, 5.9.1810.
[30] Diary, 7.12.1772, 1.5.1780, 22.9.1787, 27.3.1789, 25.10.1798, 3.12.1799, 21.2.1811.
[31] Diary, 5.5.1779, 6.2.1786, 31.10.1794, 28.1.1799, 11.12.1809. The blankets were military blankets for soldiers; the shrubs were ornamental ones imported from England; mourners and hatbands marked new funerary practices brought in from across the Channel; the carpet, which Mollet had ordered from England, was a novelty in a rural home.
[32] Diary, 28.1.1804, 1.7.1807.
[33] Diary, 4.8.1795.

the use of the verb *tirer* with a direct object as if it were the simple equivalent of the English verb 'to shoot': *il a tiré deux pies* ('he shot two magpies') instead of *il a tué/abattu deux pies*[34]

the use of the verb *introduire* as if it were the equivalent of the English verb 'to introduce': *je lui ai introduit à Monsieur le Fer* instead of *je l'ai présentée à Monsieur le Fer*[35]

the use of a combination of *appeler* + *à* calqued on the English 'to call at': *j'ai appelé au Presbytère* (instead of *je suis passé au Presbytère*)[36]

the use of the preposition *sur* in contexts where the English preposition 'on' is used but where *sur* would be inappropriate in French: *il a dîné sur du poisson* (instead of *il a dîné de poisson* or *mangé du poisson*)[37]

In sum, Mollet's journal presents us with a picture in two contrasting halves. On the one hand, his frequent unconscious recourse to *guernésiais* shows that this language was still firmly implanted as his native mode of expression. On the other hand, his equally frequent and unconscious adoption of English forms shows that English had already begun to colonise his brain. Mollet, of course, was not typical of country-dwellers in that he belonged to a small elite more exposed to English than the average rural parishioner. His workmen Pierre Gavet, Abraham Machon and Eleazar Ingrouille probably spoke a purer form of *guernésiais* than he did. Gavet, Machon and Ingrouille were all born between 1752 and 1770. What, however, of Pierre Nicolle, Mollet's youngest fosterling, who was born in 1805? When Charles Mollet sent Pierre to school in St Peter Port in 1816, he noted that he was doing so because, at such a school, Pierre would have 'an English schoolmaster'.[38] Mollet did this with Pierre's best interests at heart, but his stance (widely shared among rural contemporaries) also ensured that his own personal experience of linguistic disruption would be replicated.

---

[34] Diary, 15.5.1804. The French verb *tirer* cannot be used as a synonym for 'to kill' in the context of shooting. If used with an object, it requires the preposition *sur*, in the sense of 'to shoot at'.

[35] Diary, 17.1.1811. The French verb *introduire* is not used in this way. However, what is even more peculiar here is Mollet's use of the indirect object pronoun *lui*.

[36] Diary, 26.10.1798.

[37] Diary, 3.10.1810.

[38] Diary, 12.4.1816.

By the time of Pierre Nicolle's death in Victorian times, rural parishioners of all classes were in a position very similar to that encapsulated in Mollet himself.

Appendix 9

Apple and pear varieties grown by Charles Mollet

Varieties in italics appear only in the last volume of the diaries and were probably raised by Mollet himself.

Apples	Pears
Amaryllis Pippin	*Beau Machon*
Améré	Bonne Louise
Apouas	*Breton*
Aromatic Pippin	*Bretonnière*
Artichaux	Cadillac
Barbary	*Carène*
Barbary Muscat	César
Bonne d'Octobre	*Charles*
Bouet	Chaumontel
Cat's Head	*Coignassier*
Ceinture	*Courtenay*
Codling	Douce Renette
Espagnole	*Durell*
Fiellu	Gansell's Bergamot
Gillyflower	*Lerrier*
Golden Pippin	*Long Cateline*
Grand Haut	*Mouille Bouche*
Grandmère	Pépin de France
Gros Brehaut	*Petit Cateline*
Gros Cateline	*Romeril*
Gros Limon	Rousselet
Gros Sur	*Senesson*
Grouin	St Michel
Houard	*St Sauveur*
London Russet	Swan Egg
Madame Painsec	*Temple*

Martrenge
Nonpareil
Norfolk Pippin
Permain
Quarendon
Red Streak
Renette Blanche
Renette Grise
Ribstone Pippin
Sang
St Pierre
Surier
Surpitard
White Pippin
Wine

Union
Vavasseur
Vert Doucet
Virgouleuse
Worcester Black

Appendix 10

French émigrés mentioned by Mollet

An effort has been made to identify *émigrés* who socialised with Charles Mollet using online resources, lists preserved at the National Archives (Kew), and the following reference works:

D.A. Bellenger, *The French Exiled Clergy in the British Isles after 1789* (Bath, 1986)
R. de l'Estourbeillon, *Les Familles Françaises à Jersey pendant la Révolution* (Nantes, 1886)
H. Forneron, *Histoire Générale des Emigrés pendant la Révolution Française*, 2 vols (Paris, 1884)
C. Hettier, *Relations de la Normandie et de la Bretagne avec les Iles de la Manche pendant l'Emigration* (Caen, 1885)
J. Vidalenc, *Les Emigrés Français, 1789–1825* (Caen, 1963)

Where it has been impossible to identify an *émigré*, the individual's name is rendered exactly as Mollet gave it. Dates of first mention follow each individual.

1. Paul-Christophe de Robien (1731–99), Marquis de Robien of le Fœil in Brittany **9.8.89**
2. le Comte du Parc **9.4.91**
3. le Comte de Kernel **9.4.91**
4. le Chevalier de Médic **9.4.91**
5. Charles-François du Bot du Grégo, Marquis de la Roche (1741–1812) **12.9.91**
6. Louis-François-Joseph de Bourbon, Comte de la Marche (1734–1814) **4.10.91**
7. Thomas-François de Beaudrap, Seigneur de Biville **17.10.91**
8. Catherine-Vincente Barbier, Comtesse de Lescoët **26.4.92**
9. Marie-Jeanne-Aimée Poulpiquet, Comtesse de Coatlez **26.4.92**
10. Monsieur le Moine, Curé of St Agnan **26.9.92**
11. Monsieur le Moine, Curé of Hubert-Folie **26.9.92**
12. Jean-Charles Dancel (1762–1836), Curé of Valognes **17.2.93**
13. Monsieur Groult, Curé of Néhou **14.3.93**
14. Monsieur Groult (a priest, nephew of the above) **14.3.93**
15. Monsieur d'Urville (probably a member of the Dumont d'Urville family from Urville, near Caen) **16.4.93**
16. Monsieur d'Urville (another member of the same family) **16.4.93**
17. Jean-François Bourdon (born 1744), Seigneur de Verson **7.5.93**

18. Bertrand Faure (1758–95), Seigneur de Saint-Romain-de-Colbosc in Normandy **7.6.93**
19. Joseph-Jean-Baptiste du Trévou, a Royalist executed in Vannes in 1795 **12.6.93**
20. Monsieur Chapel (a priest) **17.6.93**
21. Pierre Bourget, Curé of Noyal-sur-Vilaine in Brittany **17.6.93**
22. Monsieur Vardonne **4.7.93**
23. Monsieur de St Fraquaire **4.7.93**
24. Monsieur de la Valinerie **4.7.93**
25. Monsieur de la Valinerie (son of the above) **4.7.93**
26. Monsieur le Tellier (Mons. de la Valinerie's nephew, who may have been the priest Louis-Sébastien Le Tellier, known to have died in Jersey in 1794) **4.7.93**
27. Ferdinand-Georges-Amable de la Roque, Comte de Ménillet **26.7.93**
28. Jean-Marie-René de Leuvre de Qu[i]erqueville **7.11.93**
29. René-Charles de Percy, Seigneur de Tonneville (1748–95) **2.1.94**
30. Monsieur Sauvegrain, Curé of Secqueville-en-Bessin **22.5.94**
31. Denis Jallobert de Monville (1758–1819) **19.6.94**
32. Dominique Jallobert de Monville (1767–1837) **19.6.94**
33. Monsieur du Sausé **15.7.94**
34. Monsieur de la Foidre, Curé of Moisville **27.7.94**
35. Monsieur de la Foidre, Curé of Boissy-Lamberville **27.7.94**
36. Monsieur Du Fou **25.8.94**
37. Adolphe-Charles de Mauconvenant (1743–1829) **14.9.94**
38. Bonaventure-Corentin de Mauconvenant (1767–95) **14.9.94**
39. Monsieur de Barneville **14.9.94**
40. Gilles de Carné-Trécesson (c.1759–95) **11.11.94**
41. Monsieur de Bergerac **4.12.94**
42. Armand de Chateaubriand (1768–1809) **21.2.95**
43. Monsieur de Belfonds **21.2.95**
44. Gaspard-Pierre de Morel de Than (1760–1843) **5.5.95**
45. Abbé François-Philippe Vattier (1765–1802) of Lisieux **6.5.95**
46. Monsieur de Pirey **16.5.95**
47. Jacques-Louis-Gabriel du Mesnildot (1760–1821) **16.5.95**
48. Anne de Blégier Pierre Grosse, Baronne de la Garde (1767–1836) **26.5.95**
49. Pierre-Henri de Blangy (1756–1823) **7.6.95**
50. Auguste-Pierre de Blangy (1766–1827) **7.6.95**
51. Pierre-Constantin de Blangy (1722–1800) **or** his son Bon-Henri de Blangy (1775–1827) **7.6.95**
52. René-Jean Paris, assistant parish priest of Janzé (diocese of Rennes) **22.10.95**
53. Monsieur Morvan (a priest) **22.10.95**
54. Gabriel-Charles-Marie Levieil de la Marsonnière (1775–1808) **13.11.95**
55. Monsieur de la Cour **11.12.95**

56. Félix-Barnabé Yvetot (1764–1809), parish priest of Saint-Eny (Coutances) **11.12.95**
57. Monsieur de Rouville **11.12.95**
58. Armand-Mériadec Le Gonidec de Traissan (1752–1814) **18.12.95**
59. Balthazar-Hyacinthe Le Gonidec de Traissan (1754–1817) **18.12.95**
60. Monsieur de Blanville **21.12.95**
61. Marie-Pierre-Jean Le Tellier de Vaubadon (1768–1844) **14.1.96**
62. Marc-Antoine Le Bachelier (1751–1816), Seigneur de Saon **20.1.96**
63. Jean-François de Hercé (1776–1849), nephew of Urbain-René de Hercé, Bishop of Dol **23.2.96**
64. Jean-Baptiste Le Vicomte de la Houssaye (1732–1810) **6.3.96**
65. Renaud de la Houssaye (born 1779) **6.3.96**
66. Claude-Antoine Coulon (1746–1820), former vicar-general of Nevers and royal chaplain **13.3.96**
67. Alexandre de Ricouart, Comte d'Hérouville (1761–1842) **13.3.96**
68. Mathurin-René de la Villéon (1752–1806) **18.3.96**
69. Monsieur Marie **18.3.96**
70. Monsieur de Ruvigny **23.3.96**
71. Armand-Louis-Charles de Gontaut-Biron, Marquis de Biron (1771–1851) **23.3.96**
72. le Chevalier Lamberté **3.4.96**
73. Monsieur St Jore **4.4.96**
74. Henri Delaroche-Vernay **10.4.96**
75. Monsieur de la Rosière **10.4.96**
76. Monsieur de Volée **22.4.96**
77. Monsieur du Taillas **22.4.96**
78. Monsieur Denouville **22.4.96**
79. Monsieur de la Valade **22.4.96**
80. Guy, Comte de Vossey (1766–1859) **2.5.96**
81. Paul de Nourquer du Camper (1776–1849) **2.5.96**
82. Monsieur Flambart **15.5.96**
83. Hyacinthe de Folliot de Fierville (1739–1817) **15.5.96**
84. Monsieur le Chevel **5.6.96**
85. Monsieur du Camp **11.6.96**
86. Charles de Péronne (born 1762) from Saint-Nicolas, near Granville **24.6.96**
87. Louis Harscouët de Saint-George (1755–1830) **26.6.96**
88. Monsieur Scelles (surgeon) **19.7.96**
89. Victurnien-Jean-Baptiste de Rochechouart, Duc de Mortemart (1752–1812) **31.7.96**
90. le Chevalier d'Idouville **25.8.96**
91. Jacques de Kerouartz, Vicomte de Kermellec (1761–1844) **8.1.97**
92. Monsieur de Casenave **20.2.97**

93. Pierre de Calbiac (1732–1815), Royalist army officer from the Cévennes, **or** his son Martial de Calbiac (1757–1870) **23.3.97**
94. Abbé Toussaint-François de la Motte Rouge (1755–1823), Canon of Tréguier Cathedral **15.4.98**
95. Louis-Quentin Desprez de Montpézat (born in 1747), Seigneur d'Ambreuil **3.10.98**
96. Frère François Marie (Capuchin friar whose civil name was Jean Mortier) **16.4.99**
97. Monsieur l'Huillier **26.5.99**
98. Monsieur du Plessis Pasco **3.1.00**
99. Monsieur de Filleau **26.6.00**
100. Charles de Graimberg (1774–1864) **29.11.00**
101. Monsieur Daucourt **6.8.01**
102. Jean-Marie-Bernard Bégny **15.10.01**
103. Monsieur Doucet (a priest) **15.11.01**
104. Louis-François-Antoine-Maurice de Payen de l'Hôtel, Baron de la Garde **7.10.02**
105. Félicité de la Bourdonnaye, Comtesse de Vossey (1784–1807) **23.3.04**
106. Céleste-Octavie de la Bourdonnaye (1787–1863) **23.3.04**
107. Constant de Botherel du Plessis (1776–1860) **18.9.07**
108. Charles-Auguste Brajeul (1761–1825), Rector of Saint-Quay in Brittany **18.9.07**
109. Jean-Joseph de Calonne **22.3.08**
110. Marie-Laurent-Thibéry de Nattes de Nadaillan **22.3.08**
111. Louis-Joseph-Guy Landry de Vauxlandry (1730–1813) **26.7.11**

Appendix 11
Books owned by Charles Mollet

This is a sample of Mollet's library, reconstructed from the records he made of book loans in his end-of-year notes. It is offered as an indication of his interests and tastes. The author, title and first publication date of Mollet's books are given, although he may have owned subsequent editions.

French books

Voltaire, *Œuvres Complètes* (1784–9)
Jacques-Henri Bernardin de Saint-Pierre, *Etudes de la Nature* (Paris, 1784)
Jean-François Marmontel, *Contes Moraux* (1766)
Anon., *Mémoires Secrets pour servir à l'Histoire de la République des Lettres en France depuis 1762 jusqu'à nos Jours* (1777–89)
Nicolas-Toussaint des Essarts, *Choix de Nouvelles Causes Célèbres avec les Jugemens qui les ont Décidées* (1785)
Charles Théveneau de Morande, *Le Gazetier Cuirassé ou Anecdotes Scandaleuses de la Cour de France* (1771)
Mathieu François Pidanzat de Mairobert, *Anecdotes sur la Comtesse du Barry* (1775)
Mathieu François Pidanzat de Mairobert, *L'Espion Anglais, ou Correspondance entre Milord All'Eye et Milord All'Ear* (1785)
François Lemarié and Honoré Lacombe, *Nouveau Dictionnaire d'Anecdotes, ou l'Art d'Eviter l'Ennui* (1789)
André Guillaume Contant d'Orville, *Les Nuits Anglaises, Ou Recueil de Traits Singuliers, d'Anecdotes, d'Evènements Remarquables, de Faits Extraordinaires* (1770)
Claude Emmanuel L'Huillier Chapelle and François Le Coigneux de Bachaumont, *Voyage de Messieurs Chapelle et Bachaumont* (1708)
Joseph Audra, *Histoire Générale à l'Usage des Collèges, depuis Charlemagne jusqu'à nos Jours* (1770)
Samuel Auguste Tissot, *Avis au Peuple sur sa Santé* (1761–82)
Félix Vicq-Dazyr, *Essai sur les Lieux et des Dangers des Sépultures* (1778, translated from an Italian treatise by Scipione Piattoli)
Robert Xavier Mallet, *Dissertation sur la Manière de Cultiver des Plantes Choisies* (1778)
Salomon Gessner (tr. Michel Huber), *Idylles et Poëmes Champêtres* (1762)
Jacques Delille, *L'Homme des Champs, Ou les Géorgiques Françaises* (1800)
Philippe-Sirice Bridel, *Le Conservateur Suisse, Ou Recueil Complet des Etrennes Helvétiennes* (1783–1831)
Etienne Gibert, *Observations sur les Ecrits de M. de Voltaire, principalement sur la Religion* (1788)

English books

Daniel Defoe, *Robinson Crusoe* (1719)
James Boswell, *Life of Samuel Johnson* (1791)
James Boswell, *Journal of a Tour to the Hebrides with Samuel Johnson* (1785)
Thomas Sheridan, *The Life of the Rev. Dr Jonathan Swift, Dean of St Patrick's, Dublin* (1787)
Maria Edgeworth, *An Essay on Irish Bulls* (1802)
Robert Molesworth's *Account of Denmark as it was in the Year 1692* (London, 1694)
James Lind, *An Essay on Diseases incidental to Europeans in Hot Climates, with the Method of Preventing their Fatal Consequences* (1768)
William Meyrick, *The New Family Herbal; Or Domestic Physician* (1790)
William Marshall, *On Planting and Rural Ornament* (1796)
Thomas Martyn, *The Language of Botany: Being a Dictionary of the Terms Made Use of in that Science* (1793)
Godfrey Smith, *The Laboratory: Or School of Arts, Containing a Large Collection of Valuable Secrets, Experiments, and Manual Operations in Arts and Manufactures* (1740)
James Hervey, *Theron and Aspasio: or a Series of Dialogues and Letters upon the Most Important and Interesting Subjects* (1775)
Mark Akenside, *The Pleasures of Imagination* (1744)
Joseph Addison and Richard Steele, *The Spectator* (collected edition, 1712–15)
George Saville Carey, *The Balnea, Or an Impartial Description of all the Popular Watering Places in England* (1799)
Philip Falle, *An Account of the Isle of Jersey* (1694)

Appendix 12

Spring bird arrivals

Between 1793 and 1808, Mollet noted (more or less systematically) the dates on which he first saw or heard certain migratory birds in Guernsey.

Year	Cuckoos	Swallows	Wrynecks	Turtle-doves
1793	21 April	30 April	14 April	1 May
1794	17 April	20 April		
1795	11 April	22 April		11 May
1798	10 April	1 May		10 May
1799	17 April	5 May	20 April	8 May
1800	21 April	5 May	9 April	8 May
1801	16 April	26 April	31 March	20 April
1802	18 April	26 April	5 April	
1803	5 April	7 May	18 April	7 May
1804	21 April	19 May	7 April	4 May
1805	14 April	2 May	28 April	13 May
1806	19 April		5 April	
1807	23 April	8 May	16 April	8 May
1808	18 April	2 May	11 April	9 May

Bibliography

Primary Sources

Greffe, St Peter Port, Guernsey
Amerci en Plaids
Amirauté
Contrats pour la Date
Contrats pour Lire
Contrats pour Lire et pour la Date
De Sausmarez Collection
Livres d'Amerci
Livres en Crime
Ordonnances

Island Archives, St Peter Port, Guernsey
AQ 155/1 – Castel Parish Tax Lists, 1808–28
AQ 0680/01 – Rental of William Le Marchant of L'Hyvreuse
AQ 1004/01 – St Peter Port Tax Book, 1797–1803
AQ 1017/8 – Castel Parish Register, 1764–1809
AQ 1083/01 – Castel Parish Register, 1664–1764
AQ 1083/3 – Castel Parish Register, 1748–1835
AQ 1085/33 – letter from Thomas De Sausmarez to Charles Mollet, 28.2.1817
AQ 1133/021 – copy of conveyance of a house from Charles Mollet to Abraham Machon, 1815
AQ 1314/52 – Hubert Le Cocq's answers to family history questions posed by Marian Guille, c.1900
AQ 1330/02 – Livres de Perchage du Fief des Vingt Bouvées du Villain Fief le Comte
AQ 1572/03 – diary of Elisha Dobrée, 1771–85
AQ 1572/04 – diary of Elisha Dobrée, 1786–99
AQ 1572/05 – diary of Elisha Dobrée, 1800–17
SG 23/43 – Relevé des Propriétaires du Castel, 1817

Priaulx Library, St Peter Port, Guernsey
E.F. Carey's scrapbooks and genealogies
F.C. Lukis, 'Reminiscences of former days in connection with Guernsey' (unpub. MS)
Charles Mollet's journals and papers

Jersey Archive
Book 53, series D/Y/K4 (Public Registry)

National Archives, Kew
HO 98/25 – list of French clergy sent from Guernsey to Southampton, July 1796
HO 98/28 – list of Frenchmen in Guernsey, 1805
PC 1/117A/134 – letter from Charles Mollet to Philippe D'Auvergne, 16.3.1796
PC 1/118C/9 – letter from Charles Mollet to Philippe D'Auvergne, 27.3.1797
PC 1/118C/16 – letter from Charles Mollet to Philippe D'Auvergne, 7.8.1797
PC 1/118C/94 – letter from Charles Mollet to Philippe D'Auvergne, 21.8.1797
PC 1/119A/82 – letter from Charles Mollet to Philippe D'Auvergne, 1.1.1800
PROB 11/1248/217 – will of Lieutenant-Colonel William Brown

London Metropolitan Archives
HO9/GY/B/01/015/001 – Guy's Hospital Admissions Register, 1809

Bank of England Archives, London
AC27/6731 – Stock Ledger, 1765–71

Kent History and Library Centre
U1350/C41/156 – letter recommending Rev. Etienne Gibert to Jeffery Amherst's patronage, 22.6.1782

Durham University Library
Papers of Charles, Earl Grey of Howick, GRE/A/1166/1 – letter from G. Fisher to Earl Grey, 16.8.1797

Guernsey newspapers and magazines
La Gazette de Guernesey
L'Indépendance
Le Magasin Méthodiste
Le Publiciste
The Guernsey and Jersey Magazine

Secondary Sources

Pre-1920 publications

Anon., *Almanach Journalier à l'Usage de l'Ile de Guernesey pour l'Année 1797* (Guernsey, 1797)

Anon., *Guide to the Island of Guernsey* (Guernsey, 1826)

Anon., *Portrait and Biographical Record of Guernsey County, Ohio* (Chicago, 1895)

Bellamy, T., *Guernsey Pictorial Directory and Stranger's Guide* (Guernsey, 1843)

Benoît, D., *Les Frères Gibert: Deux Pasteurs du Désert et du Refuge* (Toulouse, 1889)

Berry, W., *History of the Island of Guernsey* (London, 1815)

Boruwlaski, J., *Memoirs of the Celebrated Dwarf, Joseph Boruwlaski, A Polish Gentleman* (Birmingham, 1792)

Carey, E.F., (ed.), *Guernsey Folk Lore from MSS by the late Sir Edgar MacCulloch* (London, 1903)

Clarke, L.L., *Redstone's Guernsey & Jersey Guide* (1841; Guernsey, 1843 edn)

Clarke, L.L., *The Island of Alderney* (Guernsey, 1851)

De Guerin, T.W.M., 'The English garrison of Guernsey from early times', *Transactions of the Guernsey Society of Natural Science and Local Research*, 5 (1905), pp. 66–81

de l'Estourbeillon, R.M.J., *Les Familles Françaises à Jersey pendant le Révolution* (Nantes, 1886)

Dicey, T., *An Historical Account of Guernsey* (London, 1751)

Duncan, J., *The History of Guernsey* (London, 1841)

Forneron, H., *Histoire Générale des Emigrés pendant la Révolution Française*, 2 vols (Paris, 1884)

Hettier, C., *Relations de la Normandie et de la Bretagne avec les Iles de la Manche pendant l'Emigration* (Caen, 1885)

Inglis, H.D., *The Channel Islands*, 2 vols (London, 1834), 2

Jacob, J., *Annals of Some of the British Norman Isles Constituting the Bailiwick of Guernsey* (Paris, 1830)

Lee, G.E., (ed.), *Actes des Etats de l'Ile de Guernesey, 1651–1780* (Guernsey, 1907)

Lee, G.E., (ed.), *Actes des Etats de l'Ile de Guernesey, 1780–1815* (Guernsey, 1910)

Marquand, E.D., 'The Guernsey dialect and its plant names', *Transactions of the Guernsey Society of Natural Science and Local Research*, 5 (1905), pp. 31–47

Marquand, E.D., 'The Guernsey dialect names of birds, fishes, insects, &c.', *Transactions of the Guernsey Society of Natural Science and Local Research*, 8 (1905), pp. 512–31

Marshall, J., *An Analysis and Compendium of All the Returns made to Parliament Relating to the Increase of Population* (London, 1835)

Metivier, G., *Dictionnaire Franco-Normand ou Recueil des Mots particuliers au Dialecte de Guernesey* (London, 1870)

Moisy, H., *Dictionnaire de Patois Normand* (Caen, 1887)
Quayle, T., *A General View of the Agriculture and Present State of the Islands on the Coast of Normandy* (London, 1815)
Robertson, T., *General Outline of the Report upon the Size of Farms* (Edinburgh, 1796)
Tourtel, R.H., 'Words peculiar to our insular dialect not found in any glossary,' *Transactions of the Guernsey Society of Natural Science and Local Research*, 7 (1916), pp. 300–15
Tourtel, R.H., 'List of words, phrases, &c., peculiar to our insular dialect', *Transactions of the Guernsey Society of Natural Science and Local Research*, 8 (1918), pp. 102–9
Tupper, F.B., *The History of Guernsey and its Bailiwick* (Guernsey, 1854 and 1876 edns)
Warburton, J., *A Treatise on the History, Laws and Customs of the Island of Guernsey* (Guernsey, 1822)

Post-1920 publications

Allez, J.C., *Guernsey Farming in the 1920s* (Guernsey, 1998)
Balleine, G.R., *The Tragedy of Philippe D'Auvergne* (Chichester, 1973)
Bellenger, D.A., *The French Exiled Clergy in the British Isles after 1789* (Bath, 1986)
Bertucci, L., 'Therapeutic attractions: early applications of electricity to the art of healing', in Whitaker, H., Smith, C.U.M. & Finger, S. (eds), *Brain, Mind and Medicine: Neuroscience in the Eighteenth Century* (New York, 2007)
Bramall, G., 'The architects and builders of Guernsey', *The Review of the Guernsey Society*, Winter 1993/4, pp. 82–5
Bromley, J.S., 'A new vocation: privateering in the wars of 1689–97 and 1702–13', in Jamieson, A.G. (ed.), *A People of the Sea: The Maritime History of the Channel Islands* (London, 1986)
Carey, E.F., 'Peter Le Mesurier, Governor of Alderney, 1793–1803', *Transactions of la Société Guernesiaise*, 10 (1926), pp. 45–61
Carey, E.F. (ed.), 'A trip to Guernsey in 1798 by W.T. Money', *Transactions of la Société Guernesiaise*, 11 (1931), pp. 236–51
Clapp, S., 'Catholic priests exiled in Guernsey after escaping la terreur of the French Revolution', *The Review of the Guernsey Society* (Spring 2015), pp. 20–3
Crossan, R.-M., *Poverty and Welfare in Guernsey, 1560-2015* (Woodbridge, 2015)
Crossan, R.-M., *Criminal Justice in Guernsey, 1680–1929* (Benderloch, 2021)
Cunnington, W.& P., *Handbook of English Costume in the Eighteenth Century* (London, 1957)
Day, A., 'A Russian army on Guernsey and Jersey', *The Review of the Guernsey Society* (Summer 1997), pp. 40–5
De Garis, M., *Dictiounnaire Angllais-Guernesiais* (1967; Chichester, 1982 edn)

De Sausmarez, C.H., 'Lazare Carnot's plan for the invasion of the Channel Islands, 1794', *Transactions of la Société Guernesiaise*, 19 (1974), pp. 416–34

Everard, J.A. & Holt, J.C., *Jersey 1204 The Forging of an Island Community* (London, 2004)

Ewen, A.H. & De Carteret, A.R., 'The Guernsey lily', *Transactions of la Société Guernesiaise*, 19 (1973), pp. 269–86

Fagan, B., *The Little Ice Age* (New York, 2000)

Fawcett, T., *Bath Commercialis'd: Shops, Trades and Market at the 18th-Century Spa* (Bath, 2002)

Fussell, G.E., *The History of the Farmer's Tools: British Farm Implements, Tools and Machinery AD 1500–1900* (1952; London, 1981 edn)

Girard, P.J., 'The windmill of Les Hougues, Castel', *Transactions of la Société Guernesiaise*, 25 (1955), pp. 399–401

Girard, P.J., 'Country life and some insular enterprises of the late 19th century', *Transactions of la Société Guernesiaise*, 19 (1972), pp. 88–105

Girard, P.J., 'Cider making in the Channel Islands', *The Review of the Guernsey Society* (Summer 1979), pp. 34–6

Hocart, R., 'The building of the New Town', *Transactions of la Société Guernesiaise*, 23 (1992), pp. 342–77

Hocart, R., *Peter de Havilland: Bailiff of Guernsey, A History of his Life, 1747–1821* (Guernsey, 1997)

Hocart, R., 'Jean Guille and the management of the St. George estate, 1714–1721', *Transactions of la Société Guernesiaise*, 26 (2007), pp. 252–75

Hocart, R., *Guernsey's Countryside: An Introduction to the History of the Rural Landscape* (Guernsey, 2010)

Hocart, R., 'Monsieur de St. George: Jean Guille (1712–78)', *Transactions of la Société Guernesiaise*, 26 (2010), pp. 670–98

Hocart, R., *The Country People of Guernsey and their Agriculture, 1640–1840* (Guernsey, 2016)

Hocart, R., *Guernsey in the Reign of Charles II* (Guernsey, 2020)

Hubbell, A., 'How Wordsworth invented picnicking', *Romanticism*, 12 (2006), pp. 44–51

Jamieson, A.G. (ed.), *A People of the Sea: The Maritime History of the Channel Islands* (London, 1986)

Jamieson, A.G., 'The Channel Islands and smuggling, 1680–1850', in Jamieson, A.G. (ed.), *A People of the Sea: The Maritime History of the Channel Islands* (London, 1986)

Jamieson, A.G., 'The return to privateering: Channel Island privateers, 1739–83', in Jamieson, A.G. (ed.), *A People of the Sea: The Maritime History of the Channel Islands* (London, 1986)

Johns, J.R., *The Smugglers' Banker: The Story of Zephaniah Job of Polperro* (1997; Clifton-upon-Teme, 2008 edn)

Lefebvre, G., *Cherbourg à la Fin de l'Ancien Régime et au Début de la Révolution* (Caen, 1965)
Le Maistre, F., *Dictionnaire Jersiais–Français* (Jersey, 1966)
Le Mesurier, H., 'The Le Mesuriers who lived at les Beauchamps' [sic], *The Quarterly Review of the Guernsey Society* (Spring 1959), pp. 11–14
Loudon, I., *Death in Childbirth: An International Study of Maternal Care and Maternal Mortality, 1800-1950*, (Oxford, 1992)
Loveridge, J., *The Constitution and Law of Guernsey* (1975; Guernsey, 1997 edn)
Marshall-Fraser, W., 'A history of banking in the Channel Islands and a record of bank-note issues', *Transactions of la Société Guernesiaise*, 14 (1949), pp. 378–443
McCormack, J., *Channel Island Houses* (Guernsey, 2015)
McCormack, J., *Channel Island Churches* (Chichester, 1986)
McCormack, J., 'Guernsey pigs', *The Review of the Guernsey Society* (Summer 1994), pp. 40–3
Mills, R.J.W., ' "L'île des bannis": Jersey, Britain and the French emigration, 1789–1815', *European Review of History*, 28 (2021), pp. 99–123
Moore, R.D., *Methodism in the Channel Islands* (London, 1952)
Morley, G., *Smuggling in Hampshire & Dorset, 1700–1850* (1983; Newbury, 1990 edn)
Neeson, J.M., 'Gathering the "humid harvest of the deep": the mid-summer cut vraic harvest in nineteenth-century Guernsey', *Transactions of la Société Guernesiaise*, 26 (2008), pp. 521–38
Ogier, D.M., *Reformation and Society in Guernsey* (Woodbridge, 1996)
Ogier, D.M., *The Government and Law of Guernsey* (2005; Guernsey, 2012 edn)
Ozanne, C., 'Adventures of a Channel Islander in France in the 18th century', *Transactions of la Société Guernesiaise*, 3 (1928), pp. 275–83
Parks, E., *The Royal Guernsey Militia: A Short History and List of Officers* (Guernsey, 1992)
Platt, R., *Smuggling in the British Isles: A History* (2007; Stroud, 2011 edn)
Priaulx, T.F., 'Cider-making, an old-time Guernsey industry', *Transactions of la Société Guernesiaise*, 15 (1953), pp. 286–92
Priaulx, T.F., 'Some 18th century legal tangles and family squabbles involving le Groignet estate', *Transactions of la Société Guernesiaise*, 15 (1954), pp. 401–3
Priaulx, T.F., 'Guernsey's roads', *The Review of the Guernsey Society* (Winter 1974), pp. 83–5
Priaulx, T.F., 'Our hedges', *The Review of the Guernsey Society* (Summer 1977), pp. 46–8
Priaulx, 'Friquets and Largisses', *The Review of the Guernsey Society* (Winter 1977), p. 84
Shayer, D., 'What path did the Crescent follow? Sir James Saumarez's escape, June 8th 1794', *Transactions of la Société Guernesiaise*, 24 (1997), pp. 290–9

Stevens Cox, G., *St Peter Port, 1680–1830: The History of an International Entrepôt* (Woodbridge, 1999)
Stevens Cox, G., *The Guernsey Merchants and their World* (Guernsey, 2009)
Stevens Cox, G., *Social Life in Georgian Guernsey* (Guernsey, 2014)
Trotter, J.M.Y, 'Early Guernsey postal history', *Transactions of la Société Guernesiaise*, 15 (1950), pp. 28–43
Turk, M.G., *The Quiet Adventurers in Canada* (Detroit, 1979)
Turk, M.G., *The Quiet Adventurers in North America* (Detroit, 1983)
Vidalenc, J., *Les Emigrés Français, 1789–1825* (Caen, 1963)
Warren, J.P., 'Extracts from the diary of Elisha Dobrée', *Transactions of la Société Guernesiaise*, 10 (1929), pp. 493–551
Warren, J.P., 'Extracts from the diary of Elisha Dobrée, continued', *Transactions of la Société Guernesiaise*, 11 (1930), pp. 106–23
Whitaker, H., Smith, C.U.M. & Finger, S. (eds), *Brain, Mind and Medicine: Neuroscience in the Eighteenth Century* (New York, 2007)
Zionkowski, L. & Klekar, C., (eds), *The Culture of the Gift in Eighteenth-century England* (New York, 2009)

Index

A
accidents
    sustained by Mollet, 18
    sustained by Mollet's mother, 203–4
accounts (Mollet's), 26, 79
acorns, 76
advertisements (offering Mollet's property for sale), 101
agricultural equipment, 52–3
agriculture (as practised in Guernsey), 32–4, 61–2, 67
aide-de-camp (Mollet's service as Lieutenant-Governor's), 99, 133, 206
alarms (of invasion), 129–30, 131, 134–5, 137
Alderney
    general, xxi, 92
    Mollet's residence in, 92–9
allegations (concerning Mollet), 126
almonds, 94
America (North), 29, 32, 197–8, 206, 218
    see also Guernsey County (Ohio); Prince Edward Island; Virginia
Amherst, Field Marshal Sir Jeffery (Governor of Guernsey, 1770–94), 100, 166 n. 59, 206
Andros, Charles, jun. of les Piques (Mollet's godfather), 45–46
Andros, Charles, sen. of les Piques, 46
Andros, James of les Piques (Mollet's godfather), 45–46
Andros, Rachel of les Piques (Mollet's godmother), 45–46
Anglicanism (in Guernsey), 35, 165
apples
    for cider-making, 72–3, 248–9
    for eating, 72, 248–9
Arbuthnot (privateer), 83
Arbuthnot, Vice-Admiral Mariot, 130
area (of Guernsey and comparable islands), 27
Arfvidson & Son (of Gothenburg, merchants), 90
arrests (of Mollet, while in France), 133
artichokes, 74, 145, 178
asafoetida, 55

asparagus, 74, 145
Assembly Rooms, 31, 164
auction
    of Mollet's belongings post-death, 52, 140, 141, 144, 147
    of Mollet's farm post-death, 226

B
Bailiff, HM (functions of), 39
ball (formal), 164
banks (local, failure of), 101
barbers, 147
barley, 57, 60, 62, 68–9, 120, 144
Barlow family, 160
Barnes, Marjorie Sophia, *née* Le Cocq (donor of Mollet's journals), 25, 226, 229
barometer, 140
barracks, 134, 171
basket-makers, 60–1
Bath (Mollet's visit to), 186–7, 195
Bath Stove, 140
Bayly, Major-General Henry (Lieutenant-Governor of Guernsey, 1816–21), 225
beans
    broad, 74, 145
    French, 74, 145
bedrooms (in Mollet's house), 93 n. 77, 140, 141, 212, 214
beech mast, 76
beer, 72 n. 161, 146
bees, 52, 62
Bell family, 160
Berry, Elizabeth (wife of Rev. Etienne Gibert), 208–8
Bethel Chapel, 84, 166, 193 n. 83
Billets d'Etat, 119
birds
    crops damaged by, 57
    spring arrivals of, 256
Bishop & De Jersey (local bankers), 101 n. 113
Blanchard, Jean-Pierre-François (French balloonist and showman), 109, 177–8
Blondel, Thomas (farm labourer; farm servant), 211
blowing stove, 140
books (Mollet's) *see* library (Mollet's)
bornements, 120
Boruwlaski, Jósef (Polish musician and entertainer), 109, 177

Bowden family, 160
Bowls, Thomas (grocer), 91, 174
bracken, 52, 77, 143, 197
brandy, 29, 94, 95, 146, 198
Braye du Valle, 27 n. 2, 151
bread, 68, 69, 77, 144
breakfasts, 146–7, 162
Breton, Nicolas (farmer), 61
Bristol (Mollet's visits to), 186–7
broccoli, 71
Brock & Le Mesurier (of London, banking agents), 101
Brock, Anne/Nancy (Mollet's niece; wife of William Brock) *see* Mourant, Anne
Brock, Daniel De Lisle (Bailiff, 1821–42), 48, 167, 187, 232
Brock, Harriet (sister of Henry and William Brock, sen.; wife of General Sir Thomas Saumarez), 167, 232, 235
Brock, Henry (husband of Mary Mourant; brother of William Brock, sen.; Jurat, 1802–12), 48, 157, 159, 166, 167, 175, 187, 231, 232
Brock, John Savery (brother of Daniel De Lisle Brock), 106, 167, 232
Brock, Judith (Mollet's great-niece; daughter of William Brock, sen.; wife of Rev. William Guille), 25, 229
Brock, Judith (sister of Henry and William Brock, sen.; wife of Dr Jean [De] Sau[s]marez), 167, 232, 235
Brock, Major-General Sir Isaac (brother of Daniel De Lisle Brock), 48, 232
Brock, Mary (Mollet's niece; wife of Henry Brock) *see* Mourant, Mary
Brock, Mary (sister of Daniel De Lisle Brock; wife of Thomas Potenger), 167–8, 232
Brock, Thomas (Anglican clergyman; son-in-law of Jean Carey of 'Choisi'), 166, 178, 194, 232
Brock, William, jun. (doctor; son of Anne Mourant and William Brock, sen.; diarist's nephew), 157, 183, 218, 231
Brock, William, sen. (husband of Anne Mourant; brother of Jurat Henry Brock), 48, 157, 166, 167, 175, 231, 232
Brown, Lieutenant-Colonel William (Lieutenant-Governor of Guernsey, 1784–93), 92, 99, 163, 164, 195–6, 206–7
Bruce, Mary (Duchess of Richmond), 108, 164–5
Brunswick Regiment (sojourn of in Guernsey), 172–3
Burnett & Durand (of Montpellier, merchants), 94–5
Burton, Brigadier-General Napier Christie (Lieutenant-Governor of Upper Canada), 164
butchers, 64–5, 67
butter, 64, 143, 144

C

cabbages, 71, 198
Caen, 48, 157, 188
cakes, 145
camellias, 78
'Candie' (house belonging to Mollet's brother-in-law Peter Mourant), 47, 99, 110, 142, 157, 158, 159
candles, 141
Carey, Jean (of 'Choisi'; Jurat, 1772–6), 104, 120 n. 11, 162, 232
Carey, Mary (wife of Major-General John Gaspard Le Marchant; sister of Sophia Carey), 157
Carey, Sophia (wife of Peter Mourant, jun.), 48, 157–8, 231
Carey, Thomas (Anglican clergyman; son of Jean Carey of 'Choisi'), 166, 194, 232
carnations, 164
carpenters, 52, 60
carpet, 140
Carré, Jean (Mollet's Guernsey business partner), 90–1
carriages (closed), 153
carrots, 74
Cartault, Rachel (diarist's paternal aunt) *see* Mollet, Rachel
carting (performed by Mollet's men for new road), 152
carts, 52, 114
Castel Club, 160–2
Castel parish
    area and location, 27, 33, 36
    churchwardens, 49, 117, 118 n. 3, 119
    Douzaine, 44, 118–19, 120, 121, 127
    meetings, 119
Castle Cornet, 123
Cateline, Jean (farm labourer; farm servant), 219–21, 237
Cateline, Margueritte (wife of Pierre Cateline) *see* Rougier, Margueritte
Cateline, Pierre (brother of Jean Cateline; farm labourer; plasterer; building contractor), 222–4, 237
Catholicism, Roman
    general, 35, 36
    Mollet's attitude to, 195
cattle
    doctors, 66
    exports, 65
    husbandry, 63–6

cauliflowers, 71
census (agricultural, of Guernsey, 1817), 33, 215, 217
census (of St Peter Port, 1791), 99
cereals, 67–9
chaises/gigs, 150
champart, 67
Channel Islands (relationship with English Crown), 37, 38
Château des Marais, 114, 206
Chaumière, La (country residence of Robert Porret Le Marchant), 100 n. 109
Chefs de Famille, 38, 39
Chepmell, William (merchant; nephew of Philippe Lerrier), 48, 95, 186
Cherbourg
    Mollet's visits to, 132–3, 187–8
    mutiny at, 132–3
cherries, 72 n. 158
chestnuts, 76
Chevauchée de St Michel, 214
chickens, 57, 62, 144
chicory, 74
Chief Pleas, 40
children
    deaths of, 181
    natural, of Lieutenant-Governor William Brown, 195–6
    paid to gather cider apples, 72
chocolate, 94
Christian family (tenants of Mollet's), 89
chrysanthemums, 74, 78
churchwardens, 49, 117, 118 n. 3, 119
cider
    home production and consumption, 60, 72–3, 145
    sales, 73
Clarke, Louisa Lane (writer and folklorist), 85
clay pit, 52
clergymen (Mollet's association with), 165–7, 169–70
clock, 140
clothing (worn by Mollet and his servants), 147–8, 210
clover, 57, 65, 68, 69, 75
club *see* Castel Club
coal, 141
cockerel (Mollet attacked by), 184–5
cod (dried), 144
coffee, 145–6

coffee-houses, 175–6
cold frames, 54, 74, 77
Colomez, Jean (Alderney-based surgeon), 95
compost, 78
Comptroller, HM (functions of), 39
Condamine family, 159–60
conger eels, 144
conjurors (visits of to Guernsey), 178
Constable, parochial
    general, 39, 117
    Mollet's service as, 117–27
coopers, 29, 60, 61, 76, 94, 186 n. 38
co-planting (of flowers and vegetables), 74
correspondence (Mollet's), 26, 100, 198
Coulon, Claude-Antoine (*émigré* priest), 169, 195, 252
court *see* Royal Court
Coutart family, 159–60
cowpats (for firing), 142
crabpots, 76
crafts (rural, in Guernsey), 33–4
cream, 145
Crescent (naval ship commanded by Sir James Saumarez), 134–5, 167
cress, 74, 125
Cuba, 218
cuckoos, 256
cucumbers, 74
culture (traditional, of Guernsey), 34, 173–4, 214
curds, 145
currency (used in Guernsey), xiii

D

dahlias, 26, 78
dairy, 52, 64, 216, 217
Dalrymple, Lieutenant-General Sir Hew (Lieutenant-Governor of Guernsey, 1796-1802), 108, 128, 135–6, 163
D'Auvergne, Philippe (British naval officer; Prince/Duc de Bouillon), 26 n. 8, 136
Davy, Joseph (grocer), 91, 174
deafness (Mollet's), 194
deaths, perinatal (of mothers), 168, 182–3, 199
debts (Mollet's collection of from smugglers), 96–7
deer, 191

De Havilland, Peter (Bailiff, 1810–21), 83, 162, 186, 193, 234, 242
Déhuzet, le (original name of Mollet's farm), 44–5, 49
Delaroche-Vernay, Henri (*émigré*, tenant of Mollet's), 86, 168, 252
de Peyster, Lieutenant-Colonel Arent (British military officer), 164
de Rullecourt, Baron Philippe (French military officer), 131, 132
De Sausmarez *see also* Saumarez
[De] Sau[s]marez, Dr Jean, 87, 167, 235
De Sausmarez, Thomas (HM Comptroller, 1777–93; HM Procureur, 1793–1830), 105, 162, 235
deserters (naval and military), 125
De Ste Croix, Marie (diarist's paternal aunt) *see* Mollet, Marie
De Ste Croix, Marie (diarist's god-daughter), 147 n. 59
des Vallées, Michel-Louis Lamy (French merchant and politician), 188
de Vauxlandry, Louis-Joseph-Guy Landry (*émigré*), 171, 253
de Vossey, Guy (French Royalist naval officer, *émigré*), 178, 252
diaries (eighteenth-century local), 23
diet (of Mollet's household), 144–5
dinner, 146–7
distilling (Mollet's venture into), 91–2
Dobrée family of 'Beauregard', 166–7, 233
Dobrée family of 'Bellevue', 166–7, 233
Dobrée, Bonamy (husband of Mollet's niece Martha Mourant; son of Pierre Dobrée of 'Beauregard'), 25, 48, 90, 95, 157, 166, 175, 178, 187, 222 n. 143, 229, 231, 233
Dobrée, Elisha (local diarist; son of Pierre Dobrée of 'Beauregard'), 23, 56 n. 46, 115, 167, 187, 193 n. 79, 233
Dobrée, Harry (son of Nicolas Dobrée of 'Bellevue'; merchant; Jurat, 1836–57), 173, 233
Dobrée, Martha (Mollet's niece; wife of Bonamy Dobrée) *see* Mourant, Martha
Dobrée, Nicolas (Anglican clergyman; son of Nicolas Dobrée of 'Bellevue'), 194, 233
Dobrée, Pierre (merchant, of 'Beauregard'), 90, 229, 233
dogs, 57, 62, 191–2, 225
Domaillerie, la,
    general, 51, 84–5, 111
    'legend' concerning, 85
domestic servants *see* servants (domestic)
Douzaines, parochial (functions of), 39, 44
Doyle, Lieutenant-General Sir John (Lieutenant-Governor of Guernsey, 1803–16), 136, 151, 172–3
droughts, 57
drunkenness, 175, 219–20

Duchess of Kingston (privateer), 83–4
Duchy of Normandy, 37
ducks, 62
duel (Mollet's, with Peter Le Mesurier of Alderney), 98–9
Du Four, Nicolas (cattle doctor), 66
Duquemin, Jean (cattle doctor), 66
Dutch Brigade (British fighting unit), 172
Dutch oven, 144

E
earthbanks, 51–2
eau de menthe (Mollet's distillation of), 91
eau de noyau (Mollet's distillation of), 91
Ebelling family (Mollet's tenants), 88
écu see currency
eggs, 57, 62
elections
    of Jurats, 40, 119–20
    parochial, 38–9, 117, 127
electrification (for health), 183
emigrants (known to Mollet), 197–8
emigration, 32, 197–8
émigrés (from the French Revolution), 36, 136, 146, 168–70, 250–3
enclosure (of land in Guernsey), 33 n. 26,
England (Mollet's sojourns in), 96–7, 186–7
English (language), 34–5, 242, 243, 245–6
Englishmen (employed by Mollet), 58, 59, 152, 189
epidemic, 183
Eturs, les (Mollet's fields at), 51, 151–2, 153
exchange (of horticultural goods among Mollet's friends), 78
excisions (from Mollet's journal) 24–5, 225

F
fair (livestock), 65 n. 107
farm labourers (employed by Mollet), 58–9, 60
farm servants (employed by Mollet), 58, 59, 86–7, 189, 210–12, 237, 238
farmhouse (Mollet's), 52, 139–40
farming *see* agriculture
farmstead (Mollet's), 52
fascines, 137

Ferbrache, Daniel (farm labourer; farm servant; sailor; fisherman; smallholder), 142, 200, 210–11, 217–20, 237, 238
Ferbrache, Judith (wife of Daniel Ferbrache) *see* Trachy, Judith
Fermain (private clubhouse at), 175
ferrets, 189
fields (names of Mollet's), 51
firearms, 122, 128
fires (domestic), 141–2
firing (materials used for), 141–2
fish (consumed by Mollet's household), 144, 145
fishing, 34
flour, 69, 144, 145 n. 47, 213
flowers (grown by Mollet), 77–8
food
    preparation of, 143–4
    supplied to Mollet's workers, 58, 59, 60, 149
forenames (traditional Guernsey), 36 n. 38
Fort George, 134
fortifications, 38, 130 n. 75
fosterlings (Mollet's), 199–200
France (Mollet's sojourns in), 48–9, 132–3, 187–8
French (language), 24, 34, 242, 243
French Revolution, 36, 132–3, 188
French Revolutionary and Napoleonic Wars, 29 n. 10, 133–4, 168–73
Frenchmen (employed by Mollet), 58, 59
Frère François Marie (Capuchin friar and herbalist; *émigré*), 91, 170, 174, 191 n. 67, 195, 253
frosts, 56
fuchsias, 78
fund-raising (for destitute *émigrés*), 170
funerals (attended by Mollet), 180, 207
furniture (Mollet's), 140
furze, 52, 77
furze oven, 144

G

galettes (type of bread roll), 145 n. 47
garrison (British, of Guernsey), 30, 38, 123–4, 134 n. 92,
Gavet, Marie (wife of Pierre Gavet) *see* Nicolle, Marie
Gavet, Pierre (farm servant; smallholder), 86, 93, 186, 212–14, 237, 238, 246
geese, 62

Gibert, Elizabeth (wife of Etienne Gibert) *see* Berry, Elizabeth
Gibert, Etienne (Anglican clergyman), 107, 165–6, 195, 207–8
gift-giving, 178–9
gin, 94, 95, 146, 198
gleaning (of fields after harvest), 62 n. 84, 69
god-daughter (Mollet's) *see* De Ste Croix, Marie
god-parents (Mollet's), 45–6
Goodwin, Matthew (States' architect and surveyor), 151, 152–3
gooseberries, 74
gorban (peat), 142
gorse *see* furze
gout, 159, 183
government stocks *see* securities (government)
Governors of Guernsey (general), 38
grafting (of fruit trees), 73, 76, 215
grain (parochial imports of in time of dearth), 119, 121
Grand Moulin du Roi (King's Mill), 43–4, 214
gravel pit, 52
great-nieces and -nephews (Mollet's), 25, 35, 36, 48, 156, 157, 218, 226, 231
great-great-nieces and -nephews (Mollet's), 156
Green, Major-General Sir William (military engineer), 164
greenhouse, 77, 138, 220
Greffier, HM (general), 39
Grey, Lieutenant-General Charles (1st Earl Grey; Governor of Guernsey, 1797–1807), 100
Groignet, le (farm neighbouring Mollet's), …xvii
Grut, Thomas (Anglican clergyman), 208
guernésiais (language), 24, 34–5, 243–5
Guernsey County (Ohio), 32, 198
Guernsey lilies, 78–9, 179
guests (Mollet's entertainment of), 145, 147, 154, 155, 163
Guille, Caroline (daughter of Nicolas Guille of Barcelona), 161–2
Guille, Jean, jun. (1733–1820; Seigneur of St George; Jurat, 1778–82), 105, 160, 161, 181–2, 229, 236
Guille, Jean, sen. (1712–78; Seigneur of St George; Jurat, 1752–78), 121, 191, 236
Guille, John (grandson of Jean Guille, jun.; Seigneur of St George; Bailiff, 1843–5), 25, 229, 236
Guille, Judith (Mollet's great-niece; wife of Rev. William Guille) *see* Brock, Judith
Guille, Nicolas (Barcelona-based merchant; son of Jean Guille, sen.), 160, 236
Guille, Rev. William (grandson of Jean Guille, jun.; Dean of Guernsey, 1862–9) 25, 194, 234
Guille, Richard (surgeon; son of Jean Guille, sen.), 160, 236

gunpowder, 122
Guy's Hospital (Daniel Ferbrache's stay at), 218

H

Hampton Court (Mollet's visit to), 186
harvests
    general, 56, 62, 69, 75
    poor, 32, 57, 69, 119, 121
hats (Mollet's sales of), 89–90
haws, 76
hay, 75
Haye du Puits, Le Marchant family of, 161, 162
heatwave, 55–6
Heaume, Anne/Nanon (domestic servant), 211
hemp, 76
hens *see* chickens
herbs (culinary, grown by Mollet), 74
Hero (privateer), 83
herrings, 144
hoes, 53 n. 17
Holland, 78, 94, 95
honorifics (used in Guernsey), 36
horse-racing, 176
horses, 62–3, 149, 184, 197
Hospital
    Country, 32 n. 24, 68, 118, 120, 124
    Town, 32 n. 24, 201
hotbeds, 74, 78
Houguette, la, Ozanne family of, 161
housework (performed by Mollet's female servants), 143–4, 149–9
Huguenots, 30, 165, 242
Hunter (privateer), 83
hunting, 191–92

I

illness
    suffered by Jean Cateline, 220–1
    suffered by Mollet, 183–5, 215
illuminations (celebratory), 95
immigration (to Guernsey), 30, 32 n. 25
inbreeding (of local population), 36–7

India, 56, 65, 209
Ingrouille, Eleazar (farm labourer; farmer), 73, 93, 212, 214–15, 217 n. 102, 237, 238, 246
Ingrouille, Henry (brother of Eleazar Ingrouille; emigrant to North America), 197
Ingrouille, Paul (miller; father of Eleazar Ingrouille), 214, 238
inheritance law (local), 44, 120, 226
innkeepers' tax (to fund soldiers' lodgings), 123–4
insurance (of Mollet's farmhouse), 139
Irving, Lieutenant-Colonel Paulus Aemilius (Lieutenant-Governor of Guernsey, 1770–83), 122, 128–9, 151, 163
Isle of Man, 27
Isle of Wight, 27
Ivy Castle *see* Château des Marais

J
jam, 145
Jean, Philippe (Jersey-born miniaturist; husband of Mollet's god-daughter), 147 n. 59
Jersey
    French attacks on, 129, 131
    general, 27, 37, 38, 164, 170 n. 81, 171, 172, 189
    Mollet's relatives in, 45, 47, 84, 131, 141, 155, 156, 158, 178
    Mollet's sojourns in, 48, 150, 164, 164, 183, 185–6, 188
Jurats (general), 39 *see also under* elections

K
kale, 68, 71, 198
Keeper (Mollet's dog), 62
Kennedy family (Mollet's tenants), 88–9
King George III of England, 97–8, 192
King John of England, 37
King Louis XVI of France, 116, 133, 187–8
kitchen (Mollet's), 113, 140, 141, 144, 210
Kite (privateer), 83

L
laburnums, 78
lamb, 145
lamps, 141
landholdings (nature and size of in Guernsey), 33, 37
Lane, Colonel Ambrose (purchaser of Mollet's farm after his death), 226
language shift, 34–5, 242–7

laundry (washing of), 148–9
Le Cheminant family (Mollet's cousins), 44, 156
Le Cheminant, Daniel (publican, Mollet's cousin), 118, 156 n. 5
Le Cheminant, James (carpenter, Mollet's cousin), 156
Le Cheminant, Rebecca (diarist's paternal aunt) *see* Mollet, Rebecca
Lefebvre, Nicolas (HM Prévôt, 1806–51), 162
legislation (local), 40, 89, 124, 127, 128 n. 65
Le Lacheur, Thomasse (diarist's paternal great-grandmother), 44
Le Marchant, Hirzel (son of Bailiff William Le Marchant; HM Procureur, 1774–93), 98, 161
Le Marchant, James & James (of Rotterdam, merchants), 95
Le Marchant, Josias (of la Haye du Puits; Jurat, 1802–31), 161, 205
Le Marchant, Judith (wife of Josias Le Marchant) *see* Ozanne, Judith
Le Marchant, Major-General John Gaspard, 157
Le Marchant, Marie (wife of Robert Porret Le Marchant) *see* Ozanne, Marie
Le Marchant, Mary (wife of Major-General John Gaspard Le Marchant) *see* Carey, Mary
Le Marchant, Robert Porret (son of Bailiff William Le Marchant; Bailiff, 1800–1810), 100
Le Marchant, William (Bailiff, 1771–1800), 87, 193
Le Mesurier, Abraham (of les Beaucamps, merchant), 161
Le Mesurier, Jean (Alderney Governor, 1744–93), 92
Le Mesurier, Peter (Alderney Governor, 1793–1803), 92, 93, 94, 98, 107, 186
lemon essence, 145 n. 47
Lennox, Charles (3rd Duke of Richmond), 164
Le Page, Anne/Nanon (domestic servant), 196
Le Page, Elizée (militia bandmaster; emigrant to North America), 198
Le Page, James (master plasterer and roofer), 183, 222
Le Patourel, Barry (ship-builder), 75
Le Pelley family (Mollet's neighbours), 61 n. 78, 173–4
Le Ray, Elizabeth/Lisabo (domestic servant; wife of Abraham Machon), 86–7, 91, 101, 141, 142, 198–9, 216–17, 225, 237, 238
Lerrier, Marie (diarist's sister; wife of Philippe Lerrier) *see* Mollet, Marie
Lerrier, Mary/Polly (diarist's niece; daughter of Philippe Lerrier, sen.), 158, 159, 231
Lerrier, Philippe, jun. (doctor; diarist's nephew), 132 n. 83, 229
Lerrier, Philippe, sen. (merchant and ship-owner; diarist's brother-in-law), 47, 48, 158, 186, 230, 231
letters (Mollet's) *see* correspondence
lettuce, 74, 145
Le Vavasseur dit Durell, Abraham (diarist's maternal grandfather), 45, 230
Le Vavasseur dit Durell, Jean (diarist's maternal uncle), 84

Le Vavasseur dit Durell, Marie (diarist's mother; wife of Charles Mollet, sen.), 45, 49, 131–2, 142, 158, 203–4, 230
Liberty (pleasure yacht), 187, 193
Liberty Club, 193
libraries (circulating), 190
library (Mollet's), 190–1, 254–5
licence trade, 32, 173
Lieutenant-Governors
    general, 38
    Mollet's association with, 162–4
Lihou, Etienne (farm labourer; gardener; smallholder), 59, 73, 237
Lihou, Margueritte (diarist's paternal grandmother), 44, 230
lilacs, 78
lime (as fertiliser), 55
lime-pit, 52, 69
limpets, 62
livestock fair *see* fair (livestock)
livre de perchage, 46 n. 11
livre tournois see currency
loans (of cash, made by Mollet), 82–3
London (Mollet's visit to), 186
longue veille (Christmas celebration), 173–4
lucerne, 65, 75
lye (used in laundering clothes), 149 n. 70

M

MacCulloch, Allaire, Bonamy & Co. (local bankers), 101 n. 113
Machon, Abraham (farm servant; smallholder), 86–7, 101, 143, 152, 192, 215–17, 225, 237, 238, 246
Machon, Daniel (brother of Abraham Machon; emigrant to North America), 197
Machon, Elizabeth (daughter of Abraham Machon and Elizabeth Le Ray; subsequently wife of Thomas Sarre), 217
Machon, Elizabeth (wife of Abraham Machon) *see* Le Ray, Elizabeth
Machon, Pierre (brother of Abraham Machon; farm labourer; farm servant; shoemaker; sailor), 211
mackerel, 144
magnolias, 78
mail packet service from Weymouth, 190
manure, 53–4
Marett, Thomas (Mollet's Alderney business partner), 93, 97, 98, 99
maritime trade, 28–30

Index 279

market (produce sales at), 61–2, 63, 64, 67, 70, 74
market-place (new), 31
Marquand, Isaac (nephew of Elizabeth Machon; fosterling of Mollet's), 199–200
McCrea family, 160
mealtimes, 146–7
medicine, 191, 221
melons, 74, 145
merveilles (type of cake), 145 n. 47
Methodists, 35–6, 195
Metivier, George (poet and lexicographer), 155 n. 1
Migault, André (Anglican clergyman), 165, 193
militia, 38, 40, 122–3, 128, 211
mills (also millers and milling), 43–4, 69, 214
Mollet family history, 43–5, 230
Mollet, Charles (diarist's father), 44–5, 46–7, 49, 230
Mollet, Charles (diarist's grandfather), 43–4, 230
Mollet, Marie (diarist's aunt; wife of Nicolas De Ste Croix), 45
Mollet, Marie (diarist's sister; wife of Philippe Lerrier), 45, 47, 131, 182, 185 n. 32),
  186, 204, 230, 231
Mollet, Marthe (diarist's sister; wife of Peter Mourant), 45, 47, 156, 158, 182,
  204, 230, 231
Mollet, Pierre (diarist's great-grandfather), 43
Mollet, Rachel (diarist's aunt; wife of Thomas Cartault), 45
Mollet, Rebecca (diarist's aunt), 44, 156
Mollet, Thomas (diarist's uncle), 44–5
Mont d'Aval (Mollet's fields at), 51
Mont Saint-Michel (Mollet's visit to), 188
Moravians (religious sect), 195, 208
Mortier, Jean *see* Frère François Marie
Mount Tambora (1815 eruption of), 56
Mourant, Anne/Nancy (diarist's niece; wife of William Brock), 48, 157, 182, 231
Mourant, Edward (Anglican clergyman), 165–6, 195, 208–10
Mourant, Martha/Patty (Mollet's niece; wife of Bonamy Dobrée), 25–6, 47, 48,
  90, 157, 158, 182, 231
Mourant, Marthe (diarist's sister; wife of Peter Mourant, sen.) *see* Mollet, Marthe
Mourant, Mary (diarist's niece; wife of Jurat Henry Brock), 26, 48, 157, 159,
  205, 231
Mourant, Peter, jun. (diarist's nephew; husband of Sophia Carey), 48, 156–7,
  159, 188, 231
Mourant, Peter, sen. (merchant and ship-owner; diarist's brother-in-law), 47, 92,
  95, 96, 146 n. 51, 158–9, 187, 230, 231
Mourant, Sophia (wife of Peter Mourant, jun.) *see* Carey, Sophia

Mouriaux House (Mollet's Alderney home), 93, 95, 116
mutual assistance (among farmers), 61
myrtles, 78

N
narcissi, 78
neutrality (Guernsey's, in time of war) 28
Newell family (Mollet's tenants), 88–9
newspapers (Mollet's consumption of), 190
Nicolle, Marie (domestic servant; wife of Pierre Gavet), 86, 212, 213, 238
Nicolle, Pierre (Mollet's fosterling), 200, 246–7
Nine Years War 28
Nonconformity (religious), 35, 195
Nova Scotia, 198

O
oats, 66, 68–9
offal, 65, 144
Ollivier, Michelle (diarist's paternal great-grandmother), 43
onions, 74
orchards, 57, 61, 72, 74, 84, 86, 139
Ordinance of 5.10.1778 (regulating Constables' tenure), 127
ormers, 192
osier, 76
oxen, 61, 63, 65, 70, 114, 215, 216
Ozanne, Jacques (Mollet's tenant; husband of Marie Cohu), 199
Ozanne, Judith (daughter of Jurat Jean Ozanne; wife of Josias Le Marchant), 161, 205
Ozanne, Marie (daughter of Jurat Jean Ozanne; wife of Robert Porret Le Marchant), 101–1, 161, 205
Ozanne, Richard (of les Mourains), 172 n. 96
Ozanne, Susanne/Suzon (daughter of Jacques Ozanne; Mollet's fosterling; domestic servant), 143, 199

P
'Paradis' (Mary Brock's new house in the Grange, St Peter Port), 159
parishes of Guernsey
    French and English names of, xiii
    functions of, 38–9
    sizes of, 27
parlour (Mollet's), 140, 141, 145

parsnips
    general, 69–70
    ploughing in preparation for, 70
    use of in pig husbandry, 66–7
peacocks (and peahens), 62, 178
pears, 72, 248–9
peas, 71
peat see *gorban*
pews (belonging to Mollet), 84, 193, 217
philanthropy (Mollet's), 196–201
Phoenix Insurance Co., 139
picnics, 177, 215
piece-workers (employed by Mollet), 59–60
pigeons, 52, 62
pigs, 66–7
pigsties, 52, 54 n. 21
plays (theatrical, seen by Mollet), 176–7
ploughs, 52
plums, 72 n. 158
policing (Constables' duties in respect of), 124–6
Ponchez, le (farm neighbouring Mollet's), xvii, 51
ponds, 52
population
    of Guernsey, 27–8, 158 n. 25
    of St Peter Port, 28
pork (salt), 66, 67, 144
potatoes, 69, 70–71, 85, 125, 144, 176, 197, 198
Potenger, Mary (wife of Thomas Potenger) see Brock, Mary
Potenger, Richard (son of Thomas Potenger and Mary Brock), 168
Potenger, Thomas (of les Vauxbelets, Anglican clergyman without cure), 168, 183, 232
poultices, 184
poultry, 62, 69, 145
poverty (in Guernsey's countryside), 196
Préel, le (Mollet's property at), 85–6, 87
pregnancies (of Mollet's relatives), 182
pregnancy outside wedlock, 195–6
Presbyterianism (in Guernsey), 35
preserves (made by Mollet's household), 145
press-house (for cider-making), 52
priests (*émigré* Roman Catholic), 169–70
Prince Edward Island, 32, 197–8

Prince William Henry (later King William IV of England), 212
prisoners-of-war (French), 170–1
privateering, 28–9, 32, 129
privateers (Mollet's investments in), 83–4
privy (Mollet's), 52, 54 n. 21
Privy Council, 38
Procureur des Pauvres (parochial), 118 n. 5, 119
Procureur, HM (functions of), 39
Profonde Rue, la (Mollet's property at), 84, 87–9, 222, 224
prosecution (of Mollet, for shooting dog), 191–2
purchases (Mollet's, of real property), 51, 84–6

Q
Quakers, 35, 195
quarter (local measure of volume), 47 n. 12
Quiberon peninsula (French Royalist attack on), 169

R
rabbits, 57, 191
Radford, James (farm servant lost at sea), 189, 210
raspberries, 74, 145
rats, 57
Receiver, HM
    duties of, 38 n. 42, 67 n. 125
    Mollet's application for appointment as, 100
redcurrants, 74
Reformation (Protestant), 35
religion (of Guernsey), 35–6, 195
religious practice (Mollet's), 193–4
Renouf, Joseph (Town Hospital schoolmaster; father of Sir Peter Le Page Renouf), 190
rentes, 46 n. 10, 81–2, 216
Revolution, French *see* French Revolution
rheumatism, 183, 191, 220, 224 n. 155
rhododendrons, 78
rice, 69
Richmond, Duchess of *see* Bruce, Mary
Richmond, Duke of *see* Lennox, Charles
roads
    condition of, 150
    Constables' duties in respect of, 120–21
    new, 137, 150–3

Roche family, 159–60
Roche, Anne (daughter of HM Sergeant Jean Roche), 160
Romeril, Marie (diarist's maternal grandmother; wife of Abraham Le Vavasseur dit Durell), 45, 156 n. 2, 230
rose water (Mollet's distillation of), 91
roses, 91, 164
rotation (of crops), 68–9
Rougier, Margueritte (wife of Pierre Cateline), 223–4
Royal Court, 39–40, 121
Roze & Reboul (of Toulon, merchants), 95
rum, 29, 94, 95, 146, 198
Russian soldiers (sojourn of in Guernsey), 171–2

S
salting bench, 67
samphire, 192
sand
    as soil improver, 55
    as floor covering, 140
sarcloir (weeder), 53
sardines, 145
Saumarez *see also* De Sausmarez
Saumarez, Admiral Sir James, 66, 134–5, 167, 235
Saumarez, General Sir Thomas (brother of Admiral Sir James Saumarez), 167, 178, 235
Saumarez, Lady Harriet (wife of General Sir Thomas Saumarez) *see* Brock, Harriet
scarlet fever, 183
schools, 199–200, 246
Scott, Colonel Hercules (of the 103rd Regiment), 136–7, 152
scythes, 53, 69
sea-bathing, 192
sea journeys (hazards of), 188–9
seamstress, 148
sea-stocks (given by Mollet to emigrants), 198
sea water (as fertiliser), 55
seaweed
    as fertiliser, 54–5
    permitted times for gathering and cutting, 54, 211
securities (government), 47
sedan chair, 150
Sencière, la (Mollet's fields at), 51, 52

separation (judicial), 223–4
servants (domestic), 142–4, 148–9
sharecropping, 90
shaving, 147, 197
shield-budding *see* grafting
ship-owners, 28–9, 30, 31–2
shipwrecks, 188
shore-gathering, 192
shrubs (ornamental, grown by Mollet), 77–8
sick people (bedside vigils and visits), 198–9, 214, 221
Skinner, George (Lieutenant-Governor William Brown' son), 196
Skinner, Mary (servant of Lieutenant-Governor William Brown; mother of his children), 196
Skinner, Richard (Lieutenant-Governor William Brown' son), 196
slugs, 62
Small, Major-General John (Lieutenant-Governor of Guernsey, 1793–6), 135, 163 n. 44
smuggling (and smugglers), 29, 31, 92, 93, 96–7
snow, 56
social structure
    of Guernsey's countryside, 34, 36
    of St Peter Port, 30, 36
soldiers (British)
    criminal activities of, 125–6
    employed by Mollet, 59, 152
soldiers (German) *see* Brunswick Regiment
soldiers (Russian) *see* Russian soldiers
Solier, Pierre (Anglican Minister of Alderney), 95
spades, 53
Spain, 29, 94, 95, 160, 218
spar gads (used in thatching), 75 n. 183
spirits
    general, 29, 146
    Mollet's imports and sales of in Alderney, 94–5
St George, Guille family of, 121, 160, 161–2, 181–2, 236
St Peter Port
    area and location, xiii n. 1, xx, 28
    as an entrepôt, 29, 30, 31
    growth of, 27, 31
    property in owned by Mollet, 84, 87–9
    ratepayers of, 30
stackyard, 52, 69

staddle stones, 52
States of Guernsey, 40, 119–20
still (alembic), 91, 92
stillbirths (suffered by Mollet's sister), 182
stonemasons, 60, 61
storms, 56–7
stoves, 140
stramonium (herbal remedy), 191 n. 67
strawberries, 74, 145, 178
strokes (paralytic), 158, 204
Studdart family (Mollet's tenants), 88
subscriptions
    to charitable causes, 170, 196–7
    to circulating libraries, 190
sugar, 92
summer of 1816 (weather disruptions), 56–7
surnames (Guernsey), xiii, 36
swallows, 256
Swift (privateer), 83
symbols and codes (Mollet's use of), 25, 203, 224, 239–41

T

tailors, 148
Tartar (privateer), 83
taverns
    Constables' duties in respect of, 124
    in the Castel parish, 174–5
    laws regulating, 124
taxation (local), 30, 38, 46–7, 49, 118, 123–4
tea, 29, 145
tearooms, 175
tenants (Mollet's), 86–9, 168
tethering (of cattle), 65
thatched roof (Mollet's difficulty over in St Peter Port), 89
thatchers, 60, 61
theatre (local), 31, 176–7
thefts (rural), 125–6
Thom, Alexander (ship-builder), 75
threshing, 53, 59, 69, 71
timber and iron (Mollet's imports and sales of), 90–1
tithe (Mollet as collector of), 67–8

titles *see* honorifics
tobacco, 29, 146
Torteval (parish), 27, 43, 165, 166
torve, 142
tourelle (staircase), 140, 204
towers (loophole), 130
Trachy, Judith (wife of Daniel Ferbrache), 219
Trade and Navigation (Acts of), 29 n. 13
tradesmen and craftsmen (employed by Mollet), 60–61
travels (Mollet's), 185–9
Treaty of Amiens, 133 n. 90, 171
trees (non-fruiting)
    Mollet's cultivation of, 76
    Mollet's sales of, 73, 75–6
tripe, 65, 144
tuberculosis, 181–2, 199, 200
tulips, 78
turkeys, 62
turnips, 68, 69, 70, 125
turtle-doves, 256
Tuzets, les (Mollet's fields at), 51, 151, 152
twine, 76

U

'upper' house (owned by Mollet), 86–7, 101, 143 n. 32, 200, 212, 216, 217
umbrellas, 150

V

Vague & Bonelli (of Valencia, merchants), 95
Vallat, Isaac (Anglican clergyman), 165
Vaudin, Laurence (ship-builder), 75
veal, 64, 145
vegetables (grown by Mollet for table use), 74
vetch, 75
Viel, Mrs (Mollet's landlady in Bath), 186
vinegar, 145
Virginia, 29, 198, 218
Volage (Mollet's dog), 62
Voltaire (French writer), 191, 193, 207 n. 22, 254
volumes (number of in Mollet's journal), 24
Vulture (privateer), 83

W

wages
> children's, paid by Mollet, 72
> female, paid by Mollet, 143, 148, 149
> male, paid by Mollet, 58–9, 60, 61, 72

walking (as mode of travel), 149–50
War of American Independence, 29 n. 10, 121–2, 129–30, 132 n. 84
warehouses/houses in St Peter Port owned by Mollet, 84, 87–9, 99, 222, 224
wars (eighteenth-century), 29 n. 10, 30
washerwomen, 148–9
wasps, 57–8
watch-duty, 130, 136
Waugh, Captain (later Major) John, 99, 164
weasels, 57
weather, 55–6
West Indies, 29, 95, 206
wheat, 46 n. 10, 47 n. 12, 68–9
Whigs, 98 n. 95
wigs, 147
Williams, Thomas, jun. (son of Alderney Greffier), 96, 208–9
Williams, Thomas, sen. (Alderney Greffier), 96, 98
windows
> Mollet's, smashed in Alderney, 97–8
> of Mollet's farmhouse, 140

wine
> general, 29, 146
> Mollet's imports and sales of in Alderney, 94–5

winnowing, 53, 69
workhouse *see* Hospital
wrynecks (birds), 256

Y

'year without a summer' (1816) *see* summer of 1816

www.ingramcontent.com/pod-product-compliance
Lightning Source LLC
Chambersburg PA
CBHW070642120526
44590CB00013BA/829